DANIEL O'CONNELL AND THE ANTI-SLAVERY MOVEMENT:
'THE SADDEST PEOPLE THE SUN SEES'

DANIEL O'CONNELL AND THE ANTI-SLAVERY MOVEMENT: 'THE SADDEST PEOPLE THE SUN SEES'

BY

Christine Kinealy

Routledge
Taylor & Francis Group

LONDON AND NEW YORK

First published 2011 by Pickering & Chatto (Publishers) Limited

Published 2016 by Routledge
2 Park Square, Milton Park, Abingdon, Oxfordshire OX14 4RN
711 Third Avenue, New York, NY 10017, USA

First issued in paperback 2015

Routledge is an imprint of the Taylor & Francis Group, an informa business

BRITISH LIBRARY CATALOGUING IN PUBLICATION DATA

Kinealy, Christine.
Daniel O'Connell and the anti-slavery movement: 'the saddest people the sun sees'.
1. O'Connell, Daniel, 1775–1847. 2. Antislavery movements – United States – History – 19th century. 3. Abolitionists – Ireland – Biography.
I. Title
326.8'0973-dc22

ISBN-13: 978-1-138-66328-2 (pbk)
ISBN-13: 978-1-8519-6633-2 (hbk)

Typeset by Pickering & Chatto (Publishers) Limited

CONTENTS

For my beloved nephew, Matthew Chapman, 1982–2010

ACKNOWLEDGEMENTS

The origins of this book lie in a chance meeting in Washington in 1997. I was there to lecture on the Irish famine and a senator who had been in the audience afterwards approached me to talk about Daniel O'Connell – the champion of black slaves. It was not an aspect of O'Connell's career of which I had any knowledge, but my interest was aroused. As I delved more into the topic, I came to realize that O'Connell, the wizard who delivered Catholic Emancipation and the pragmatist who failed to bring about a repeal of the Act of Union, played a massive, but largely unacknowledged, part in the abolition movement on both sides of the Atlantic.

The completion of this project would not have been possible without the input of many people. I would like to pay special tribute to the librarians and archivists of the British Library in London, the American-Irish Historical Society, the New York Public Library, the Royal Irish Academy, the National Library of Ireland, Boston Public Library and the Merseyside Maritime Museum. In particular, I would like to thank Alan Delozier, archivist at Seton Hall University, and Bruce Lancaster, Kathleen Juliano and Madeline Nitti-Bontempo of Drew University Library. A very special thanks is due to Stephen Butler, my Research Assistant in the United States, who assisted me in locating a number of obscure newspaper and journal articles. Being able to share my passion for the topic also made the research even more exciting than it otherwise would have been.

The text has been read and commented on by a number of people. I am especially grateful to Francine Sagar, Susan Bailey, Jodi Church and Barry Quest, each of whom has brought their diverse expertise to bear on earlier drafts. I have benefited from the input of Dr William Rogers, who has shared his considerable knowledge of Irish-America with me. I would also like to thank my editor at Pickering and Chatto, Mark Pollard, for encouraging me to complete the project, and for patiently dealing with my many, seemingly trivial, queries. Of course, any remaining faults, mistakes or omissions are my sole responsibility.

Finally, I would like to pay tribute to my children, Siobhán and Ciarán, who have graciously shared their mother with Daniel O'Connell for a number of years. Their support, input and joyous presence has been invaluable.

Of course, this book will not be the last word on O'Connell and slavery, but it seeks to contribute to viewing the Liberator outside the confines of Irish politics, and recognizing him as a politician who championed human rights throughout the world. And it is in this latter role, I believe, that O'Connell's true greatness lies.

INTRODUCTION: BLACK, WHITE AND GREEN.

> I am for speedy, immediate abolition. I care not what caste, creed, or colour, slavery
> may assume. I am for its total, its instant abolition. Whether it be personal or politi-
> cal, mental or corporal, intellectual or spiritual, I am for its immediate abolition. I
> enter into no compromise with slavery; I am for justice in the name of humanity and
> according to this law of the living God.[1]

This uncompromising statement was made in 1832 by Daniel O'Connell, argu-
ably one of the most important European politicians of the nineteenth century.
Despite his relatively humble Irish origins and the disadvantages associated
with being a Catholic, during his lifetime he acquired a legendary status and
an international influence that few politicians enjoy. His reputation inspired his
followers throughout the world, while it dismayed his adversaries. O'Connell's
autocratic style of leadership proved to be both controversial and divisive. However, his life-long commitment to constitutional tactics inspired politicians who
came after him – from William Gladstone to Mary Robinson – who believed his
philosophy provided valuable lessons for later generations of Irish nationalists.
Yet O'Connell's interests and his impact spread far beyond Ireland and the Irish
community.

O'Connell's concern with humanitarian issues arose, in part, from his
Enlightenment education and its ideals of liberty and progress. Throughout his
long political career O'Connell was involved in many reform issues. He spoke
in defence of 'the Tolpuddle Martyrs', Poles under Tsarist rule, emancipation
for British Jews, separation of church and state for France and Spain and even
the Papal States, the condition of peasants in India, and the abolition of Negro
slavery'.[2] Additionally, O'Connell was concerned with the treatment of Maoris
in New Zealand and of Aborigines in Australia. He was also opposed to prize-
fighting boxing, flogging and the death penalty.[3] According to one of his early
biographers, Margaret Cusack:

> O'Connell's philanthropy was neither sectarian nor national: all men were his broth-
> ers, and he pleaded alike for all. His liberality was seen again and again in his defence

of the consciences of Dissenters, whose religious liberty he would guard with a sacredness which they had not always extended to others.[4]

However, of all the progressive causes which he became involved with, it was anti-slavery, the leading humanitarian issue of the day, that most emotionally engaged O'Connell and about which he admitted he was 'most ardent'.[5] By playing a central role in this movement, he became the hero of American abolitionists. They, in turn, were in no doubt about the value of having somebody with the power and presence of O'Connell as their advocate. As early as 1839, John Greenleaf Whittier, a Quaker poet and dedicated abolitionist, wrote:

> One million of ransomed slaves in the British dependencies will teach their children to repeat the name of O'Connell with that of Wilberforce and Clarkson. And when the stain and caste of slavery shall have passed from their own country, he will be regarded as our friend and benefactor, whose faithful rebukes and warnings and eloquent appeals to our pride of character borne to us across the Atlantic, touched the guilty sensitiveness of our national conscience, and through shame prepared the way for repentance.[6]

Whittier described O'Connell's support of abolition in terms of his wider quest for social justice, writing 'American slavery but shares in his common denunciation of all tyranny: its victims but partake of his common pity for the oppressed and persecuted and the downtrodden'.[7] This sentiment was shared by the Glasgow Emancipation Society which, upon the occasion of making him an Honorary Member, described O'Connell as 'a friend of humanity, but especially, on this occasion, as the friend of the Slave'.[8] Clearly, O'Connell's involvement in anti-slavery issues consolidated his international fame and demonstrated that his politics transcended simply Irish, Catholic or national concerns. Nonetheless, this aspect of O'Connell's remarkable career remains little known today.

O'Connell's role as a leading champion of abolition has not been extensively explored by his biographers. The multiple books about O'Connell, and even the eight volumes of his edited letters, give little idea of his pivotal role within various anti-slavery movements.[9] By the same token, historians of abolition have paid scant attention to the contributions of either Ireland or of O'Connell in anti-slavery.[10] Yet, for over twenty years, O'Connell showed himself to be a devoted and unwavering champion of the slave – whether in the West Indies, India or the United States. According to the historian Maurice Bric, 'O'Connell's involvement in the anti-slavery movement sheds some small light on the paradoxes of a career that made him a radical and a conservative, a nationalist and an internationalist, and a champion of equality in a deferential society'.[11] The chapters that follow explore this important, but overlooked, aspect of O'Connell's political life, and the impact of his participation in Ireland, Britain and the United States.

O'Connell brought an overtly Catholic dimension to the anti-slavery struggle. Until he became involved, the movement had been associated with Quakers and Protestant evangelicals, who were able to draw on their international church connections, and their family and business contacts. This was the case not only in Ireland, but also in Britain and America. In the latter, the attempts to reach out to Irish supporters through O'Connell brought the anti-slavery movement 'to reach beyond the traditional bitter hostility of Protestants toward the papacy and "Jesuitism" and ... constitute an important phase in the history of egalitarian thought in America'.[12] O'Connell also brought an overtly Irish dimension to a struggle that had been associated with Britain, but more specifically, England, leading David Walker, a freed black American, to declare in 1830, 'The English are the best friends the coloured people have upon earth'.[13] In the subsequent decades, O'Connell and his compatriots were to prove repeatedly their commitment to freeing the slave from his or her bondage.

Anti-slavery had widespread support in Ireland and it brought the people, and notably Irish Catholics, into mainstream transatlantic politics. In addition to O'Connell, prominent Irish abolitionists included James Haughton, Richard Robert Madden,[14] Richard Davis Webb, Mary Ann McCracken, Richard Allen, Thomas Spring Rice, and the second Marquis of Sligo. However, O'Connell clearly outshone his compatriots, and was frequently likened to William Wilberforce in terms of his importance to the movement. In a cause that attracted some of the most remarkable men and women of the period, O'Connell was conspicuous – a fact recognized by many of his contemporaries.[15]

The Act of Union of 1800, by bringing Irish politicians into the Parliament in Westminster, changed not only British, but international politics. An early indication of this was the slave issue. O'Connell was to claim on a number of occasions that the cause of anti-slavery had benefitted from the Act of Union as Irish MPs had played a key role in the 1807 and 1833 acts, abolishing the slave trade and slavery respectively in the West Indies. He portrayed Irish people as lovers of liberty, who enjoyed a special affinity with oppressed peoples elsewhere. O'Connell also frequently suggested that Ireland's anti-slavery traditions dated back to the time of St Patrick.[16]

Was Irish support for abolition informed by their own experiences as a colonized people? The rise of the anti-slavery movement was taking place when the political relationship between Ireland and Britain was undergoing a number of changes. For centuries, British conduct in Ireland had been based on the premise that the Irish were racially inferior. This was evident as early as 1366 when the Statutes of Kilkenny enshrined in legislation that the Irish were inferior to their Norman invaders. Thus the Anglo-Norman settlers were forbidden from mixing with, or behaving like, the native Irish. The creation of an area known as the 'Pale' – an area controlled by the English King – provided the physical embodiment of this racial segregation, with the Irish being both spatially and ideologically regarded as being 'beyond the Pale'.

The condition of the Irish – especially the Catholic Irish – in the eighteenth and early nineteenth centuries led to comparisons between their poverty and oppression to that of slaves.[17] Although many of the repressive penal laws, mostly aimed at Catholics, had been removed in the late eighteenth century, Catholics could still not be Members of Parliament. This only changed in 1829 following a campaign spearheaded by O'Connell. In 1800, the Act of Union had united the parliaments of Britain and Ireland. Regardless of the changed political context, Irish people were clearly not regarded as equal partners within the Union, but continued to be viewed through the prism of colonialism and racism.[18]

The racial stereotyping that had been a feature of Britain's relationship with Ireland, both before and after the Act of Union, has been compared by some historians as having parallels with the attitudes towards, and treatment of, black slaves. Richard Ned Lebow believed that depicting the Irish as 'black' and therefore inferior to the 'white' British, was an important tool in the continuing subjugation of Ireland. These attitudes reached their zenith in the nineteenth century, after the union with Britain had taken place.[19] The psychiatrist Denis Jackson supported the view that the Irish were viewed by the British as black, 'not in the sense of physical pigmentation, but in the original pejorative sense of the Anglo-Saxon word for being dull and lacking in intelligence'.[20] The English writer, Charles Kingsley, confirmed this. When visiting Ireland in 1860, he was disturbed by what he saw, compelling him to write to his wife, 'I am haunted by the human chimpanzees I saw along that hundred miles of horrible country ... to see white chimpanzees is dreadful; if they were black, one would not feel it so much, but their skins, except where tanned by exposure, are as white as ours'.[21]

Centuries of being dispossessed of their land had left Irish Catholics impoverished and dependent on a single crop, the potato. The comparison between Irish Catholics and plantations slaves was opposed by some contemporaries, who felt it diminished the awfulness of slavery.[22] However, the poverty of the Irish shocked even the escaped slave Frederick Douglass, who visited the country at the end of 1845. Years after his visit, he remained disturbed by the condition of the Irish he had seen. In a lecture he gave in Ohio in 1854 he stated: 'I say, with no wish to wound the feelings of any Irishman, that these people lacked only a black skin and woolly hair, to complete their likeness to a plantation negro ... the Irishman, ignorant and degraded, compares in form and feature with the negro'.[23]

In 1843, at the height of the repeal agitation, O'Connell published *A Memoir on Ireland: Native and Saxon*. In it, he outlined his view that British involvement in Ireland had been defined by its view of the Irish as racially inferior. Furthermore, British racism had allowed the extermination of the Irish throughout the long centuries of colonial engagement.[24] O'Connell died in May 1847, at the height of a tragedy remembered as 'the Great Hunger', during the course of which over one million people died.[25] Many Irish people believed that the Famine could have been avoided if Ireland had been properly governed.[26] Some militant nationalists even regarded the British government as culpable of deliberate genocide, suggesting that plantation slaves were better treated than free Irish Catholics.[27] O'Connell, while frequently using the rhetoric of having been born a slave, had not agreed with this assessment, pointing out:

> The [Irish] peasant has the heath to recline upon; he has the mountain with its lively stream, and he returns to his humble hut, as to some genial clime, and he indulges his paternal and filial affections, amidst his family, not the less concentrated for being poor.[28]

In 1833, the British government abolished slavery in the West Indies. The Slavery Abolition Act was viewed as a considerable victory for the British anti-slavery movement. It not only ended slavery in the British West Indies, it served to inspire abolitionists throughout the world, especially in the United States. Rejoicing in the United Kingdom was short-lived, as the apprenticeship system, which replaced slavery, was just as oppressive and proved to be simply another form of bondage. O'Connell was one of the leaders of the campaign to end apprenticeship, which finally happened in 1838.

Victory in 1833 and again in 1838 allowed the attention of British and Irish abolitionists to turn to America. For many radicals and liberals in Europe, America presented a paradox – how could a country conceived in a struggle for liberty enslave so many people? How could slavery be justified in an increasingly liberal and democratic world? Furthermore, how could it be tolerated in the United States, the cradle of modern democracy? For some, religion and the redemptive role of slavery in exposing the enslaved to Christianity provided an answer. In this way, slavery could be viewed as an escape from life in Africa. The evidence that cruelty towards slaves was increasing in the early decades of the nineteenth century, combined with the lack of any religious instruction, made such righteous arguments difficult to justify.[29] Unlike other leading contemporary abolitionists, O'Connell never visited the United States, India, or the West Indies, although he campaigned for abolition in each place.[30] Following the abolition of slavery in the British colonies in 1833, his attention became increasingly focused on the American slave-holding states, thus taking his abolition arguments into the geographical heartland of slavery. External pressure was regarding as essential to the ending of slavery in the United States. As one Boston abolitionist explained 'Irish, Scotch and English interference is to slavery what a Spanish fly is to a fever.'[31] However, it took a further thirty years and a violent civil war to bring about the ending of slavery there.

For American abolitionists, both black and white, O'Connell's contribution was unsurpassed. As early as December 1832, 'Negroes of the Abyssinian Baptist Church' honoured O'Connell by reading a speech he had made in London earlier in the year. They also adopted a number of valedictory resolutions, including one to this 'uncompromising advocate of universal emancipation, and the friends of the oppressed Africans and their descendants'.[32] The black American abolitionist, Charles Lenox Remond, after meeting O'Connell in London in 1840, felt reinvigorated by the contact on the grounds that 'For thirteen years I have thought of myself as an abolitionist, but I had been in a measure mistaken, until I listened to the scorching rebukes of the fearless O'Connell'.[33] In 1842, the most famous American abolitionist, William Lloyd Garrison, reprinted extracts of O'Connell's speeches of the previous ten years in his paper, the *Liberator*, explaining that, 'They will seethe like lightening, and smite their thunderbolts. No man, in the wide world, has spoken so strongly against the soul-drivers of this land as O'Connell'.[34]

Abolitionists in the United States believed that O'Connell was ideally placed to woo Irish immigrants to the cause of anti-slavery. While O'Connell's condemnation of slavery was unequivocal, the extent to which Irish settlers in America were complicit in slavery was less clear. Large-scale emigration from Ireland, even before the Great Famine, had taken large numbers of Irish men and women overseas. Before 1845, approximately 1,500,000 Irish people had settled in America, a large portion of whom were Protestant.[35] Increasingly, those who fled were poor and Catholic and their arrival fuelled the anti-immigrant views of the nativist, Know-Nothing Party. Consequently, many Irish-Americans supported the Democratic Party, who tended to be more sympathetic to immigrants – but who were vociferous opponents of abolition.[36] As a result of this allegiance, Irish immigrants found themselves by default opposed to abolition. Regardless of the vulnerability of their situation, O'Connell repeatedly asked the Irish in America to make a stand against slavery. By doing so, he was, in effect, asking them to criticize the Constitution of their adopted home and to promote disunion in the country. Irish-Americans, led by their churchmen, rejected O'Connell's request, and overwhelmingly refused to support abolition.

Did this refusal mean that they opposed abolition, or were they simply keen to appear as good Americans? This point was made by the *Boston Pilot* in June 1842, which postulated that the fact that many Irish in American did not support the abolitionists, did not mean that they supported slavery.[37] Significantly, O'Connell misunderstood the role of the Catholic Church in America. Whilst his campaigns to win Catholic Emancipation and repeal had relied on the support and administrative network provided by the Irish Catholic Church, the American Catholic Church in the 1840s was antagonistic to abolition and did not support O'Connell in pursuing this aim. Crucially, O'Connell's involvement in American abolition raised other spectres that were unresolved and problematic: where did Irish immigrants fit into their new host society; what was their relationship with black people in America, free or otherwise; what was the role of the Catholic Church in this struggle? If slaves were freed, would they take low-paid employment from unskilled Irish immigrants? Ultimately, O'Connell's interventions with Irish-Americans demonstrated the limitations of his political vision and his lack of understanding of the lives of his fellow countrymen after they had left their homeland. This point was made by John Collins, a leading abolitionist in Massachusetts. He believed that O'Connell's vitriolic denunciations hurt both Irish-Americans and the abolitionist cause. While other abolitionists were extolling the virtue of O'Connell's interventions, he claimed that O'Connell 'has done them much mischief by his contempt frequently expressed of slave-holders. The Irish were suffering much in consequence of his course'.[38] However, Collins, in separate communication, also written in 1842, admitted:

> Nine tenths of the Irish are, at heart, thorough-going abolitionists. Yet it is very easy for these orators and editors who are capable of making 'the worse appear the better case', to make them believe that patriotism, religion and philanthropy demands their non-interference with slavery.[39]

As Collins made clear, supporting abolition in America was vastly different from supporting it in Ireland, and O'Connell's demands placed Irish immigrants in a fraught situation, that was not fully appreciated by many abolitionists or by later critics. If O'Connell had made the same appeals fifteen years later, the response may have been different.

The historian Theodore Allen has suggested that, 'Irish history provided a case of racial oppression without reference to alleged skin colour'.[40] For Allen, Ireland provided a mirror image of American racial oppression and white supremacy. When transplanted to America, however, he believed that 'Irish haters of racial oppression' were transformed into white supremacists.[41] A few years later, a similar theory was developed by Noel Ignatiev, who argued that in America, the Irish 'became white'. For him, 'the truth is not, as some historians would have it, that slavery made it possible to extend to the Irish the privileges of citizenship, by providing them another group to stand on, but the reverse, that assimilation of the Irish into the white race made it possible to maintain slavery'.[42] More recently, Peter O'Neill has argued that 'colour and religion became wedges that divided two peoples who otherwise might have become formidable allies against a common oppression'.[43] He suggested that 'Any chance of lasting solidarity between Black and Green was lost in the exclusionary "melting pot" of America then under construction'.[44] Ironically, while many poor Irish emigrants viewed emigration to America as a liberating journey, to escape from the tyranny of British rule, for black Africans the journey was the opposite, and signified their passage into slavery.

Clearly, whilst anti-slavery enjoyed extensive support within Ireland, the relationship between slavery and the Irish in America was more ambivalent. The debate coincided with the large influx of Irish immigrants, which was to increase as a consequence of the Great Famine. Immigration helped to reinvigorate the anti-immigrant feeling, one manifestation of which was the spread of the anti-Catholic, Know-Nothing Party. Just as Irish-Americans were searching for an identity, so too were native-born Americans. O'Connell, who had never visited the United States, was not forced to confront these tensions first-hand. However, for those Irish who resided there, especially newly-arrived immigrants, to attack the institution of slavery was disloyal and marked them out as being 'un-American'. The abolitionist William Cooper Nell summed up their response thus, 'The opposition of Irishmen in America to the coloured man is not so much a Hibernianism as an Americanism'.[45] Irish historian Bill Rolston added further complexity to the debate by suggesting that Irish racism, in fact, had its roots in Ireland and had been evident during the visits of various black abolitionists. Thus racism and anti-racism had co-existed in Ireland in the years prior to the mid-nineteenth mass emigration.[46] His contention suggests that voyaging across the Atlantic was not the only reason for Irish-American resistance to abolition.

Irish immigrants who opposed abolition had a number of powerful champions, both in Ireland and in the United States. Many who supported repeal were uncomfortable with O'Connell's high profile statements on slavery. John Mitchel, renowned for his militant nationalism and social radicalism on Irish issues, when he arrived in the United States in 1853 made clear his support for slavery. The Irish-born Bishop (later Archbishop) John Hughes of New York was also opposed to O'Connell's interventions. Simply, he believed abolitionism to be unconstitutional.[47] Moreover, like many others, he disliked the perceived extremity of American abolitionists and their support for women's suffrage and labour rights. If some Irish-Americans were ambiguous in their attitude to slavery, they were unambiguous in their dislike of abolitionists. Did O'Connell's interventions on slavery achieve anything? Despite his growing influence in the transatlantic movement, O'Connell remained a divisive figure. Many attacks were made on his personal and political integrity, one suggesting that his involvement in abolition was calculating and cynical, his motive being to wield more influence in the British Parliament.[48] However, O'Connell's involvement in anti-slavery divided his supporters in Ireland and served to undermine support for the cause of repeal amongst Irish-Americans. Championing abolition lost support for the repeal movement in the United States and it lost support for O'Connell in Ireland. According to the historian Douglas Riach, 'O'Connell's abolitionism had little lasting influence on a country in which so many saw

America as a haven for the immigrant, a beacon of republican liberty, a potential ally against England, and a munificent provider of relief and aid'.[49] This view was not shared by O'Connell's fellow abolitionists, in Britain, Ireland or America. American abolitionists believed that British and Irish public opinion would play a crucial part in ending slavery and they regarded O'Connell their most important champion, who had overtaken Thomas Buxton and William Wilberforce in significance.[50] On the eve of the American Civil War, O'Connell's speeches were being reprinted, as an important weapon in the battle for hearts and minds that preceded the actual conflict.[51] His words now found a much more receptive audience amongst Irish-Americans. Finally, O'Connell's participation in the movement highlighted both the Irish and the Catholic involvement in the leading humanitarian issue of the nineteenth century. In essence, O'Connell was motivated by his life-long quest for justice and human rights, and he brought to this task the same energy and passion that he had brought to achieving Catholic Emancipation and a repeal of the Act of Union. In 1829, as O'Connell was beginning to win recognition within the anti-slavery movement, he informed a meeting of the Cork Anti-Slavery Society that:

> In the estimate of my pretensions and abilities, I shall say I bring zeal and perseverance to the cause ... I cannot be temperate upon it. I must be intemperate; it is for liberty or slavery, therefore I have but one choice and must be intemperate for liberty.[52]

Until his death 1847, he remained true to this principle. In a career in which he sometimes chose pragmatism over principle, O'Connell's stance on abolition was consistent and frequently unpopular. His unwavering commitment to the cause of abolition, and to human rights generally, marked him out as one of the truly great statesmen of the nineteenth century.

In 1823, Daniel O'Connell had helped to found the Catholic Association for the purpose of trying to win the right for Catholics to sit in the British Parliament. Within a short time, he had built a disciplined, mass political movement that had no equivalent in Europe. The success of this movement brought O'Connell to the attention of the British government. His refusal to use physical force to achieve his ends made him an unusual nationalist leader, while his knowledge of the law made him an adversary to be feared by the authorities. Shortly after founding the Catholic Association, O'Connell met James Cropper, a leading British anti-slavery campaigner, who was visiting Ireland. O'Connell was immediately won over to the cause. His involvement gave a Catholic dimension to what had traditionally been a movement associated with various nonconformist denominations, even in Ireland. Chapter 1 examines O'Connell's early involvement with the British and Irish abolition movements and his determination to agitate for two diverse political ends.

The granting of Catholic Emancipation in 1829 enhanced O'Connell's political reputation not only in Ireland, but throughout the rest of Europe and in the United States. Although he declared that his main purpose was now to bring about a repeal of the Act of Union, he played an active part in all of the main political debates of the day, especially those concerning the abolition of slavery in the British Empire. His impassioned speeches brought him further publicity and mixed attention. It also brought him to the notice of American abolitionists, notably the outspoken William Lloyd Garrison, who regularly reprinted in his newspaper, the *Liberator*. Chapter 2 outlines O'Connell's growing reputation in both Britain and North America as a champion of anti-slavery. In 1835, O'Connell entered into an alliance with the British Whig Party and as a consequence, repeal was put on the political back-burner. During this period, he consolidated his reputation as a leading figure in the campaign against slavery. His interventions against slavery meant that he was becoming the leading international figure in the abolition movement. As Chapter 3 demonstrates, his uncompromising statements were causing concern in the United States and even led to him being publically condemned in the American Senate.

The year 1840 was a momentous one for Daniel O'Connell as he revived the repeal movement with the avowed purpose of overturning the Act of Union of 1800. In the same year, he spoke at the first International World Anti-Slavery Convention in London. Although Thomas Clarkson, the acknowledged leader of British anti-slavery, was the President, O'Connell was the star, captivating delegates from around the world. Chapter 4 explores O'Connell's rise to become the leading figure in transatlantic anti-slavery. An outcome of the London Convention was that O'Connell promised to organize an address from the people of Ireland to the Irish in America, appealing to them to support abolition. Absorbed with his repeal activities, the Irish Address was actually penned by fellow Irishmen Richard Webb and James Haughton. They clearly had underestimated the antagonism that the appeal would engender. Chapter 5 looks at the growing divide between anti-slavery sentiment between the Irish in Ireland and the Irish in America. O'Connell had declared 1843 to be the year in which the Act of Union would be repealed. This did not prove to be the case. The year was notable, however, for O'Connell making some of his most excoriating attacks on American slaveholders, culminating in the 'Cincinnati Letter'. As Chapter 6 shows, O'Connell's virulent denunciation of slavery polarized opinion amongst his fellow repealers, while alienating Irish-American opinion. Yet, he continued to campaign on behalf of the slave despite advanced years, and failing health.

O'Connell died in May 1847, but his influence continued. Throughout the 1850s, the slave question increasingly dominated American political discourse, yet successive administrations failed to stop the descent into civil war. During this decade, the speeches of O'Connell were frequently reprinted and his arguments were used to bolster the abolitionist cause. As a consequence, his writings became one of the most powerful tools in the propaganda war that preceded the Civil War. Chapter 7 looks at the ways in which O'Connell's writings on slavery were used to inform and influence a new generation of Irish-American immigrants. Chapter 8 is concerned with the memory and legacy of O'Connell, in relation to the slave question. It concludes that his contribution was remarkable and that 'Ireland's greatest contribution to the anti-slavery movement in the nineteenth century was Daniel O'Connell'.[53]

1 'THE COLOUR OF SERVITUDE'

The late eighteenth century was a period of intense economic, social and political change. Improvement in communications allowed for the transfer of people and ideas on an unprecedented level. This development gave rise to some paradoxes: as enlightenment ideas spread and were consolidated by the revolutions in America and France, so too did the enslavement of people, most notably through the transatlantic slave trade. This situation was responsible for one of the most popular and international humanitarian movements of the period: anti-slavery. Britain, which had used slavery to consolidate the success of its empire, was also the centre of successive anti-slavery movements. Nor was Ireland immune from the changing political climate, embracing both political radicalism and anti-slavery ideals. Britain had been involved in the slave trade since the sixteenth century and by the eighteenth century had become the dominant European country involved in the 'middle passage', that is, the harrowing journey from Africa to the West Indies. By the 1780s, as the revolutionary tide spread across the Atlantic, British radicals increasingly likened their own situation to that of slaves. In this way, according to the historian J. R. Oldfield, 'slavery began to take on a more immediate significance, related to the political condition of thousands of native-born Britons'.[1]

The early slavery movements were led by nonconformist groups in Britain and Ireland. The Anglican Church hierarchy had a more ambivalent attitude, viewing abolition as interfering with the rights of property and, more calculating, fearing it would affect their tithe income.[2] The Society of Friends (Quakers) had been amongst the first to campaign against slavery, although their involvement tended to be sporadic and uncoordinated. In the final two decades of the eighteenth century, these efforts became more organized. In May 1787, the Committee for the Abolition of the Slave Trade was founded in London, which provided the movement with a central organization to coordinate the work of local activists. Nine of its twelve founding members were Quakers.[3] Its members included William Wilberforce, Thomas Clarkson and Granville Sharp, who each proved to be indefatigable in collecting information relating to the slave trade.[4] Clarkson, in particular, gave himself the task of bringing the condition of slaves before the British public by collecting evidence from Bristol and Liverpool about conditions in which the slave trade was carried out.[5] In 1787, Josiah Wedgwood was invited to join the Committee, and he brought to it 'an innovative genius that was perfectly attuned to the demands and rigours of eighteenth-century business'.[6] He was also responsible for designing the seal of the London Committee – depicting a black slave kneeling, encircled by the question 'Am I not a man and a brother?'[7] This iconic image was replicated in many ways, becoming a fashion accessory in addition to a political slogan. The Committee was successful in other ways, notably through coordinating a network of local and regional committees the London office creating a sophisticated lobbying machine that 'played an indispensable part in the mobilisation of public opinion against the slave trade'.[8] National petitions were organized in 1788 and 1792.[9] The latter petition contained an estimated 400,000 signatures and marked the culmination of five years of intense activity. The House of Commons bowed to this popular pressure, passing a bill to end the slave trade, but it was blocked by the Lords.[10]

Maintaining parliamentary support for the campaign was hindered by the fact that Quakers, like Catholics, had been forbidden from sitting in parliament by various Test Acts, which had required MPs to swear oaths of allegiance and supremacy before taking their seats. Clarkson persuaded Wilberforce, an MP and a recent convert to evangelicalism, to use his parliamentary position to promote anti-slavery. This marked the start of a fifty-year-long collaboration. Because of the evangelical leanings of many of the early supporters of abolition, the group around Wilberforce were referred to as the 'Saints'. The new movement appeared to be making an impact. In 1788, the government appointed a committee of the Privy Council to inquire into the trade. After 1793, war with France put anti-slavery on the political back-burner for a number of years.

Although Daniel O'Connell frequently claimed that Ireland had no historic involvement with slavery, Irish merchants had been involved with the Royal Africa Company since the seventeenth century. At this stage, slavery was viewed in a positive light: a way of saving enslaved Africans from death and exposing them to Christianity.[11] By virtue of its geographic location, and due to its position within the British Empire, Ireland inevitably played a part in the Black Atlantic economy. As the slave economies expanded in the eighteenth century, so too did Ireland's involvement. A number of Anglo-Irish gentry served as Colonial Governors, justices and officials in the West Indies, while the long voyage to the West Indies provided employment for Irish seamen.[12] A number of Irish firms, especially wine and rum merchants, traded in the West Indies. Irishmen also owned plantations and slaves, and they proved to be no more humanitarian or Christian than their British counterparts. Irish involvement was most evident on the sugar island of Montserrat, where Irish settlers were the most numerous white group, and Irish presence was evident across the economic spectrum.[13] While Ireland had not been directly involved in the eighteenth-century trafficking of slaves, by the eighteenth century, the main ports of Cork, Limerick and Belfast were benefiting from imports and exports to the slave colonies – although the British Parliament had decreed that all 'plantation goods' had to be imported to Ireland via British ports. This only changed in the more liberal atmosphere of 1779.[14] However, throughout the eighteenth century, consumer demand for cotton, tobacco, indigo and sugar all increased in Ireland. Demand for sugar, which underpinned much of the slave trade, grew particularly rapidly: in a space of only forty years, sugar imports to the city of Cork grew fivefold. The duties that the Irish government earned from these commodities helped to fund a number of prestigious building projects in the country, such as the Bank of Ireland in Dublin.[15] Thus slavery became woven in the fabric of Irish society and provided it with a number of architectural showpieces. Belfast also benefited from trade with the slave colonies. In 1786, Waddell Cunningham, reputedly the richest man in Belfast and the founding president of the local Chamber of Commerce, attempted, with Dr Haliday, to establish a slave-trading company in Belfast.[16] Both men already owned sugar estates on the island of Dominica. A few years earlier, Cunningham had given evidence before a parliamentary committee on the slave trade during which he claimed that black slaves were better off than many of the British poor.[17] Due to the strength of local opposition, Cunningham and Haliday abandoned the idea.[18]

Ireland's involvement in anti-slavery had a long pedigree. In the late eighteenth century, as revolutionary and radical ideas were spreading throughout the transatlantic world, anti-slavery sentiment was also growing. In an age when liberty and equality were being proclaimed on the streets, Irish radicals asked how could slavery continue to be justified. Very quickly, the rhetoric of abolitionism 'manifested itself in Ireland' and moral outrage was followed by practical actions.[19] Two interesting features of the early anti-slavery movement were its international appeal and the involvement of women. In Ireland, both were evident. Women, excluded from parliamentary politics, excelled at the organizational skills needed at the grass roots level of the campaign. In addition to raising funds and organizing local committees, they were in the forefront of the movement to stop using sugar grown by slaves in the West Indies. The early anti-slavery movement in Ireland attracted middle-class women such as Mary Ann McCracken and Maria Edgeworth. The latter used literary outlets as a way to prick the conscience of her fellow women, and men.[20] In a similar fashion, but less well known, the Quaker Mary Birkett wrote 'Poem on the African Slave Trade' in which she appealed to Hibernian women to use their influence to bring an end to the trade.[21]

By the late eighteenth century there were dozens of black people in Ireland. They occupied a diverse range of occupations, although the majority were domestic servants who had been sold into service and received no wages. For the historian W. A. Hart, their presence meant that 'there is no disguising the existence of slavery in Ireland at this time'.[22] It was, however, substantially different from the type of servitude that existed across the Atlantic. Moreover, there was little evidence of overt racism towards Negroes in the country.[23] A female servant in the home of O'Connell's uncle, 'Hunting Cap', was of black descent, she eventually becoming his housekeeper.[24] Early interest in the slave question was evident from the fact that a slave testimony – *The Interesting Narrative of the Life of Olaudah Equiano or Gustavus Vassa, the African* – became a bestseller in Ireland in the 1790s, as it had in Britain. Equiano, a freed slave, spent eight months touring around Ireland in 1791–92, and found the people, especially those in Belfast, warm and welcoming. His arrival in Ireland coincided with the founding of a republican association, the United Irishmen, who were a non-sectarian nationalist group. In Belfast, Equiano was the guest of the local supporters of the United Irishmen.[25] In addition to wanting an independent Irish republic, they supported an immediate abolition of slavery – a radical concept at the time.[26]

Equiano's views were supported by the Irish scholar James Mullalla. In 1792 Mullalla published a strongly worded polemic calling for an end to the slave trade. He stated that 'He who supports the system of slavery is the enemy of the whole human race. He divides it into two societies of legal assassins; the oppressors and the oppressed'.[27] He praised 'the humanity of Hibernia's fair daughters' for abstaining from using sugar, but thought it was an unnecessary sacrifice because 'Sovereigns of the earth, you alone can bring about this revolution!'[28] Mullalla concluded his pamphlet with reference to the condition of Ireland, 'which for many years has exhibited a melancholy picture of oppression and slavery'.[29] He condemned Irish Protestants who refused Catholics equal rights, which he regarded as 'disgraceful, unwise and absurd'.[30] The Irish-born politician Edmund Burke also spoke out against slavery. He had been Whig MP for Bristol from 1774–80. Towards the end of this time, he penned the *Sketch of the Negro Code*, which advocated reform of, followed by the abolition of, slavery. In 1789, he supported William Wilberforce's call for an end to the slave trade, but he afterwards pulled away from the cause so as not to offend his party.[31]

External political changes at the end of the eighteenth century contributed to a liberalization in the treatment of Catholics and other non-conformist denominations in Ireland. A series of 'Relief Acts' removed various restrictions that had been imposed a century earlier. The 1791 Act permitted Roman Catholics to practise law, to openly observe their religion, and to open their own schools. In 1793, Catholics regained the right to vote. Gradually all economic, political and social restrictions on Catholics were removed, with the exception of allowing

Catholics to sit in parliament. For some, the concessions were not enough. At the end of the eighteenth century, against the backdrop of constitutional and violent attempts to win independence, anti-slavery took root in Ireland.

A violent, republican uprising in 1798 changed the political landscape of both Ireland and Britain through the passing of the Act of Union which created the United Kingdom of Great Britain and Ireland. It also created a single unitary parliament, based in London. The 1800 Act of Union changed the dynamic of politics in Westminster by creating seats for an additional 100 Irish MPs. Some continuity was ensured by the fact that only Protestants could sit in parliament, although Catholics had acquired influence in the voting process as a result of the 1793 Catholic Relief Act. The British Prime Minister, William Pitt, had promised that Catholic Emancipation would follow the Act of Union – a promise he was unable to fulfil. Following the Act of Union, therefore, an ongoing grievance of Catholics and liberal Protestants was the refusal to allow Catholics to sit in the Westminster Parliament.

Daniel O'Connell, a Catholic born in 1775, was one of the first beneficiaries of the Relief Act that allowed Catholics to practise law. He was later to use his superb knowledge of the law to campaign for the granting of Catholic Emancipation. Although born in Country Kerry, O'Connell was educated in France, his time there coinciding with the commencement of the 1789 Revolution. In 1796, he commenced law studies in Dublin's King's Inns and was called to the Irish bar two years later. As a young barrister in the early years of the nineteenth century, he gained a reputation for working hard and sleeping little. Within a few years of qualifying, he was recognized as one of the leading barristers in Ireland and was able to live in Merrion Square, a fashionable district in Dublin.[32] O'Connell had been born at the height of the American struggle for independence, and was living in France at the onset of the French Revolution. He was present in Dublin in 1798, during the violent republican rising in his own country. These formative experiences helped to shape O'Connell's political outlook and consolidate his abhorrence of using violence for political ends. The 1798 rising confirmed his commitment to change through constitutional and legal means. Moreover, O'Connell's early years had coincided with a period of government in Ireland, know as Grattan's Parliament. Through peaceful means, after 1782 the so-called 'Protestant Patriots' of Ireland had won more autonomy for the parliament in Dublin. This period of self-rule came to an abrupt end with the Act of Union of 1800 and the consequent abolition of the Irish parliament. Yet these years of increased political independence had coincided with relative economic prosperity, and it was looked upon by O'Connell as a golden age within Ireland's political development, despite the fact that only Protestants had been allowed to sit in Grattan's Parliament. Emulating the Protestant Patriots, O'Connell wanted to bring about political change by peaceful, constitutional means, but to create a parliament that was representative of all denominations in Ireland.

Regardless of his own success, O'Connell believed that Catholics in Ireland remained second-class citizens, and without Catholic Emancipation their fates would remain at the whim of successive British governments. In 1809, O'Connell helped to draw up the constitution of a reconstituted Catholic Committee. The purpose of the committee was to bring about Catholic Emancipation. To appease their opponents, the more moderate members of the association suggested that Emancipation should be accompanied by a government veto on the appointment of Catholic bishops. O'Connell and some of the younger members totally rejected this concession, thus injecting a more militant focus into the debate. In 1814, in a speech before the Catholic Board, he said, 'I did imagine we had ceased to be white-washed Negroes and had thrown off for them all traces of the colour of servitude'.[33] O'Connell's fiery rhetoric was always tempered by his pragmatic approach to achieving his ends. In 1823, he helped to establish a new Catholic Association, with the aim of winning Catholic Emancipation by peaceful means. A number of similar organizations had been founded previously, but with little success. O'Connell had participated in the earlier associations and proved that he was a skilled orator who could excoriate his opponents. When speaking in Limerick in 1812 he had castigated a number of members of the then government for impeding Catholic Emancipation, describing them as 'bigots'. He made a pointed criticism of 'the place-procuring, prayer-mumbling Wilberforce.[34] This was a reference to William Wilberforce, an evangelical MP renowned for his work in ending the slave trade. The new Catholic Association differed from earlier ones in that O'Connell opened it up to mass membership and created an efficient party machine to control it. These changes proved to be pivotal in transforming what had been a small, ineffective, middle-class association into a disciplined, centralized mass movement. Initially progress was slow. Throughout the long campaign, O'Connell framed his demand for emancipation in terms of people's rights. When the 1825 Emancipation Bill failed to pass in parliament, he made a long, emotive speech in which he challenged the statement made by the Lord Chancellor saying 'if you emancipate the Catholics you must equally give liberty of conscience to all classes of Dissenters'. O'Connell responded:

> That is exactly what we say ... we do not come before parliament making a comparison of theological doctrines; we revere our own; we are not indifferent to them; we know their awful importance; but we say liberty of conscience is a sacred right.[35]

The struggle to win Irish independence and Catholic Emancipation took place at the same time that evangelicals and liberals throughout the United Kingdom were questioning the existence of the slave trade and of slavery.

Post-Union Ireland

The Act of Union had brought 100 MPs into the imperial parliament. William Wilberforce, the leading parliamentary campaigner against slavery viewed the arrival of Irish MPs in Westminster in 1801 as a positive thing and delayed passing a further abolition bill, hoping to garner their support.[36] Although the Irish politicians in Westminster generally voted along the traditional divisions of Whig and Tory, they did cross party lines on the issue of slavery. In 1804, thirty-four Irish MPs voted en bloc to support a motion to end the slave trade. They argued that it was a question of humanity.[37] However, in the two further readings of the bill, the initial unity dissipated and the bill was defeated. Wilberforce noted in his diary that 'The Irish members absent, or even turned against us', and from this point he realized that he could not rely on Irish parliamentary support in his quest to end the slave trade.[38]

In February 1806, Lord Grenville became Prime Minister. He and his Foreign Secretary were opponents of the slave trade and collaborated with Wilberforce to bring it to an end. In that year, the Foreign Slave Trade Bill became law. It prohibited British subjects from transporting slaves to the territories of a non-British state. The act came into force on 1 January 1807. [39] This legislation paved the way for the introduction of a measure relating to the British Empire, although the outcome was by no means certain. It fell to Grenville to guide the more controversial measure through Parliament and to persuade the House of Lords to support an ending to the trade. He made an impassioned speech arguing that the trade was 'contrary to the principles of justice, humanity and sound policy'. Regardless of the continued opposition of vested groups, 'An Act for the Abolition of the Slave Trade' was passed finally on 25 March 1807. It was carried in the House of Lords by 41 votes to 20, and in the House of Commons by 114 to 15. It was to become law on 1 May and from that date:

> The *African* Slave Trade, and all manner of dealing and trading in the Purchase, Sale, Barter, or Transfer of Slaves, or of Persons intended to be sold, transferred, used, or dealt with as Slaves, practised or carried on, in, at, to or from any Part of the Coast or Countries of *Africa*, shall be, and the same is hereby utterly abolished, prohibited, and declared to be unlawful.[40]

The legislation did not abolish slavery, but only prohibited British ships from being involved in the slave trade. British captains who were caught continuing the trade were fined £100 for every slave found on board. Trafficking did continue though: the trade of African slaves to Brazil and Cuba continued until the 1860s. The British campaign overshadowed the fact that on 2 March 1807, the American Congress had passed an act to 'prohibit the importation of slaves into any port or place within the jurisdiction of the United States … from any foreign kingdom, place, or country'. The Congress gave all slave traders nine months to close down their operations in the United States.[41] At the same time, America refused to allow a right of search on any of its vessels, by any other country. This proved frustrating to the British government as America remained adamant that she would not sign a mutual treaty with any other country.[42] Overall, the 1807 Act had given Britain a new leadership role in the Atlantic slave trade. In this capacity, during the Vienna peace negotiations of 1814 and 1815, Lord Castlereagh persuaded the other 'great powers' to sign a declaration against the slave trade. It proved to be non-binding and in the following decades thousands of slaves were shipped from Africa to Cuba and Brazil.[43] While Britain 'prided herself on giving a moral leadership in raising the profile of the Atlantic slave trade as incompatible with Christianity and civilisation, other countries viewed her efforts differently ... Her claim to be the foremost anti-slavery activist was viewed as a means of establishing an exclusive control in Africa, so that it might become as much a part of her empire as India.[44]

By the 1820s, there was general disillusionment with the outcome of the 1807 Act. Wilberforce wrote to Thomas Fowell Buxton, a Quaker brewer and philanthropist, suggesting that together they should start a crusade for the gradual abolition of slavery. Buxton had been a Member of Parliament since 1818 and had gained a reputation as a social reformer. In 1822, encouraged by Wilberforce, it was decided to form local anti-slavery societies. William Wilberforce, Thomas Clarkson, Thomas Buxton, James Cropper, Zachary Macauley and William Allen were amongst the founders of the Society for the Mitigation and Gradual Abolition of Slavery – usually referred to as the Anti-Slavery Society. The first meeting of the Anti-Slavery Society was held in London in January 1823.[45] In the same year, Wilberforce published *An Appeal to the Religion, Justice and Humanity of the Inhabitants of the British Empire in Behalf of the Negro Slaves in the West Indies*.[46] In it, he argued that:

> The long continuance of this system, like that of its parent the Slave Trade, can only be accounted for by the generally prevailing ignorance of its real nature, and of its great and numerous evils.[47]

A review of this, and other anti-slavery pamphlets, published in 1824, pointed out that, 'Of no philanthropic undertaking have the promoters had to encounter a more decided opposition than has been experienced by friends of the Negro Manumission.[48] Undaunted, the work of the abolitionists continued. Quakers remained active and founded a number of groups both in London and in the provinces.[49] The movement suffered a loss when, in 1825, Wilberforce retired from the House of Commons. He had first been elected in 1780. The parliamentary anti-slavery campaign was now to be led by Buxton. In 1825 also, Zachary Macauley founded the *Anti-Slavery Reporter*, which facilitated the dissemination of anti-slavery information and helped to promote national coordination.

The monthly paper also gave coverage to the activities of sister societies in Ireland.

In 1823, the same year that the Catholic Association was founded in Ireland, Buxton submitted to the House of Commons a resolution concerning the lawfulness of slavery. It was the first time that the question of ultimate emancipation was raised; although this issue still remained controversial and divided the leadership.[50] These activities, both inside and outside of parliament, marked the start of a renewed interest in this issue.[51] The main focus of these societies was the 'sugar colonies' of Barbados, British Guiana, the British Leeward, Jamaica, Mauritius, Trinidad, Tobago and the Windward Islands. Sugar underpinned much of the slave trade, and provided a connection between the West Indies and the metropole: 'Grown in the farthest reaches of the British Empire, sugar was eaten in the intimacy of British homes; it linked colonial sites of production of the raw materials with the domestic sites of consumption'.[52] Abolitionists pointed out that the commercial success of the sugar economies was based not solely on slave labour, but the fact that they had a protected market within the United Kingdom. This contrasted with the East Indies who employed free labour and had to pay high custom duties.[53] The renewed agitation did have a demonstrable outcome. A series of resolutions proposed by George Canning for the amelioration of colonial slavery, including a number of reforms to be implemented by colonial governors, was passed in the House of Commons in 1823. A number of abolitionists were disappointed with the measure, believing it achieved little but to remove anti-slavery from the parliamentary agenda for a number of years.[54] The revival of interest in anti-slavery was evident in the King's Speech at the opening of Parliament in February 1824. Not everbody was pleased with the renewed interest in this issue. O'Connell's wife, Mary, thought that anti-slavery was taking precedence over Irish issues, writing to her husband that 'He [the King]seems much more interested for the liberty of the West Indies slaves than for those of that part of his United Kingdom called Ireland'.[55]

In Ireland, as in Britain, opposition to slavery revived in the 1820s. In October 1824, James Cropper, a wealthy Quaker merchant from Liverpool and a leading abolitionist, visited Ireland. While there, he stayed with members of the Society of Friends who were in the forefront of the Irish campaign against slavery. Cropper was at the time chairman of the Liverpool Auxiliary Hibernian Society, which circulated scriptures and established schools in Ireland.[56] In Ireland, he was shocked by the poor conditions in which the peasantry lived.[57] Cropper was notorious for using economic arguments to suggest that slavery should be ended, if only on the grounds that slavery could not survive in a free and expanding economy. Using his knowledge of the business world, he contended that slavery was economically wasteful and that it inevitably reduced the value of land.[58] Although he pointed out his views directly to Wilberforce, the latter had shown little interest in the economic aspects of slavery.[59] Cropper persisted and founded the Liverpool Society for the Amelioration and Gradual Abolition of Slavery. This society provided a blueprint for the national society in which Cropper played a central role. Cropper also played a pivotal role in raising funds for the national organization.[60] When in Ireland, Cropper was struck by the comparison between poverty there and in the West Indies. He believed that if both countries could be developed economically, it would be to their mutual benefit. Thus, if Irish resources could be harnessed to produce textiles, these could then be exchanged for tea and sugar. In the following year, Cropper published 'The present state of Ireland, with a plan for improving the position of the people'. In it, he reasoned, 'If Irish leaders could only be made to see this connection, if the cause of Ireland could be tied to that of West Indian slavery, then monopoly and special privileges were doomed and the Irish labour and the West Indian Negro would rise together to a life of freedom and well-being'.[61] While in Ireland, Cropper helped to organize a number of anti-slavery committees and he asked for the support of Daniel O'Connell, who had attracted international attention for his work on Catholic Emancipation. O'Connell was immediately interested. As a young man, he had shown sympathy with the revolt of slaves in the French colony of St Domingo during the early stages of the French Revolution.[62] He described Cropper's plans for Ireland to the Catholic Association in Dublin and spoke of the anti-slavery campaign in favourable terms.[63] However, anti-slavery remained linked with Protestantism. In 1824, the Dublin Association for Endeavouring to Promote the Mitigation and Gradual Abolition of Slavery in the British Colonies had been formed. As in Britain, it was led by nonconformist Protestants and meetings tended to be held in Protestant halls and chapels.[64] Three years later, the Dublin Anti-Slavery Society was founded, which had close links with the London society. Clearly, anti-slavery was taking root in Ireland, but as was the case in Britain, societies tended to be local, dominated by Protestant dissenters, and favouring gradual rather than immediate abolition.

Between 1823 and 1829, Irish anti-slavery was overshadowed by the struggle to win Catholic Emancipation. O'Connell was indelibly associated with the latter campaign, but he was starting to play an active, and increasingly significant, role in the revived anti-slavery campaign. Within only a few months of meeting Cropper, O'Connell started to work with the London Anti-Slavery Society and instantly made his mark.[65] In April 1825, O'Connell attended the second annual meeting of the Society for the Amelioration and Gradual Abolition of Slavery in London. Although, at this stage, he had no official capacity, he was listed as being present alongside such seasoned campaigners as Buxton and Stephen Lushington. The Duke of Gloucester, nephew of King George III, was in the Chair.[66] Thomas Denman, an MP, referred to the presence of O'Connell in the room and alluded to 'the powerful influence he possessed over the people of Ireland and the assurance he felt of the gentleman's zeal to promote their objects'.[67] O'Connell, although a newcomer, spoke at the meeting, stating that 'he did hate despotism so much – he did detest slavery so cordially – he did abhor cruelty so strongly – that he could not refrain from raising his voice in the cause of liberty – and joining his exertions to the labour of those who would strike off from the slave his chains, and from the Briton his reproach'.[68] O'Connell's presence at the meeting even delayed him in writing to his beloved wife, Mary.[69] He confessed that he was about to write to her, but had felt 'tempted' to go to an anti-slavery meeting. Finding himself at the front, he felt 'compelled to speak, and did so for an hour'.[70] O'Connell's pleasure was palpable, he informing her, 'The Duke of Gloucester was most kind and attentive to me; in fact they set me down here as a first rate orator'.[71] At the London meeting, Wilberforce's retirement from public life was announced and the meeting paid tribute to his achievements.[72] However, the exit of anti-slavery's most seasoned advocate was matched by the appearance of another very different sort of campaigner.

The retirement of Wilberforce, the man indelibly associated with abolition, caused some alarm for the future of the campaign. His colleague, George Stephen, however, while admiring Wilberforce's humanity and kindness, also deplored his defects, the main ones being 'busy indolence' and indecision.[73] For Stephen, Wilberforce's faults were typical of a man of his 'refinement':

> He loved the small gossip of political life, and politically educated in the tone of the last century, felt, perhaps unconsciously, too much deferential regard for rank and power, irrespective, not of the morality, but of the sterling worth of the possessors.[74]

Stephen further believed that what made 1825 such a 'remarkable year' was the fact that 'Mr Denman and Mr O'Connell both made their first appearance on the anti-slavery stage, and two more able advocates could hardly have been retained'.[75] O'Connell's reputation in abolition continued to grow. In April 1827, when attending an anti-slavery meeting, he was spotted and ushered to the front to make a speech. Even at this stage, O'Connell argued not merely for emancipation, but for equality, on the grounds that 'the blacks, having become free, would in time become members of society, would fill offices of importance and finally work out their independence'.[76] O'Connell, the leader of Irish Catholics, was showing himself to be a defender of slaves throughout the world.

O'Connell's participation in anti-slavery was inevitably overshadowed by his involvement in the campaign for Catholic Emancipation. During these years, he spent much of his time between Dublin and Britain, spending little time in his beloved County Kerry where his wife remained. He continued to be committed to the use of constitutional tactics, and his experiences in London convinced him of the need for continued political agitation on the grounds that:

> We *never, never, never* got anything by conciliation ... I have the strongest and *most quiet* conviction that *temperateness, moderation* and *conciliation* are suited only to perpetuate our degradation.[77]

In 1828, O'Connell was elected to parliament in a by-election in County Clare. As a Catholic he could not take his seat. The Test Act of 1672 had prevented all non-Anglicans from holding public office, and this had been reinforced by the 1678 Test Act, which had been concerned with Roman Catholic exclusion. By the 1820s, Parliament was divided on the issue of emancipation, but the outcome of the 1828 election convinced the British government that a concession had to be made. Nonetheless, the Catholic Association continued to be harried and humiliated by the authorities. Thomas Steele, one of O'Connell's most loyal lieutenants, informed a meeting of the Catholic Association in Limerick that the treatment of Irish Catholics meant that they were '*White Slaves*', adding 'I should be glad to be informed by what other name they can be so justly described'.[78] Regardless of continuing to humiliate Irish Catholics, the Clare election galvanized the British government into steering Catholic Emancipation through Parliament.[79] The task of doing so fell upon two experienced Tory politicians, the Duke of Wellington and Robert Peel. Despite their knowledge of Irish affairs, they had been surprised by the power of the Catholic vote, leading them to believe that unless emancipation was conceded, there would be a civil war.[80] Nor was support for O'Connell's actions confined to Ireland. In January 1829, 'The Association of the Friends of Civil and Religious Liberty, and of the Friends of Ireland in New York', wrote to O'Connell assuring him that 'the eyes of enlightened nations are fixed on you and your companions'. They congratulated him on his ecumenical approach and his 'uncompromising regard for human rights'. Finally, they assured O'Connell that societies similar to theirs were being established throughout America and that 'A fund will ere long be derived from American patriotism in the United States, which will astonish your haughtiest opponents'.[81] The letter was published by the London *Times* on 2 April, just as the Catholic Relief Act was passing through Parliament.[82]

An Act granting Catholic Emancipation received Royal Assent on 13 April 1829. Its provisions applied to Catholics throughout the United Kingdom, not only in Ireland. Overall, O'Connell considered the legislation to be 'excellent', informing his wife 'I am in perfect health and spirits. I tread on air'.[83] To a friend he confided, 'It is a comfort to have struggled for this glorious object and to have assisted in achieving a bloodless revolution'.[84] Included in the Emancipation Act there was a penalty, in the form of a higher property qualification that was now required to vote in Ireland, the qualification being raised from 40 shillings (£2) to £10. The electorate was immediately reduced from 100,000 to 16,000, Catholic voters being the main losers. O'Connell regarded this part of the act as being 'bad, very bad'. [85] O'Connell attended the House of Commons on 15 May 1829. He was dismayed to hear that his election was invalid unless he took the old Oath of Supremacy, on the grounds that his election had preceded the passing of the Act. O'Connell made a personal appeal to Parliament claiming the right to take his seat without taking the oath.[86] He was unsuccessful, forcing him to face a second election in County Clare in 1829, under the new electoral regulations. O'Connell was returned, unopposed, on 30 July. It was not until 4 February 1830 that O'Connell finally took his seat in the British Parliament. His entry coincided with a reinvigorated debate about the future of Parliament itself. The granting of Catholic Emancipation had split the Tory Party and brought the Whigs into power. The reform of Parliament was a key objective of the new government, and abolitionists hope that this, in turn, would facilitate slave emancipation

After 1829, following the granting of Catholic Emancipation, O'Connell achieved heroic status amongst the international Catholic community. His victory, however, meant that he was regarded as the implacable enemy of conservative Protestants. His role in winning Catholic Emancipation consolidated his reputation as a controversial and divisive figure, but even his opponents recognized his considerable talents and his tenacity. He had mounted a popular, extra-parliamentary campaign that had been victorious, in the face of entrenched opposition. Despite his pleasure at Emancipation being granted, he privately admitted to a friend, 'How mistaken men are who suppose that the history of the world will be over as soon as we are emancipated. Oh! *That* will be the time *to commence* the struggle for popular rights'.[87]

While the campaign for Catholic Emancipation was reaching its apogee and O'Connell was attracting both international praise and opprobrium, he continued to demonstrate his commitment to the cause of anti-slavery. Throughout 1829 he spoke at a number of meetings in Ireland. A constant theme of his lectures was the hypocrisy of the United States in allowing black slavery on its soil.[88] Shortly after his re-election in July 1829, he attended a meeting in Dublin at which he called for slavery to end in the British Empire. He also addressed meetings in Cork, Dublin and London.[89] The populist tactics of the anti-slavery movement were ideally suited to O'Connell's temperament and expertise – petitions, large meetings, sustained publicity drive, a charismatic leadership, were all methods he was using to achieve Catholic Emancipation, and that he would later revive in the Repeal Association.

How would this Irishman, with no experience in parliamentary politics, cope with the rigours of life in Westminster? A frank assessment of O'Connell on the eve of winning Catholic Emancipation was offered by the aristocratic English politician and diarist, Charles Greville:

O'Connel [*sic*], although opposed by a numerous party in the Association, is all-pow-
erful in the county, and there is not one individual who has a chance of supplanting
him in the affections of the great mass of the Catholicks [*sic*]. For twenty-five years
he has been labouring to obtain that authority and consideration which he possesses
without a rival, and which is so great that they yield unlimited obedience to his individual will ... As an orator he would probably fail in the English H of C; but to a mob,
especially an Irish mob, he is perfect, exactly the style and manner which suits their
tastes and comprehension.[90]

Greville's belief that O'Connell would fail to make an impact in the House of
Commons proved to be wrong. O'Connell's abilities extended beyond merely
populist politics. After gaining Catholic Emancipation, O'Connell turned his
attention to achieving an overturn of the Act of Union of 1800. He also used his
position as an MP as a platform from which to garner publicity and support for
anti-slavery. While he had little success in his campaign for repeal, after 1829,
O'Connell proved to be an effective and charismatic champion of anti-slavery
within Westminster. Both parliamentary and popular politics were crucial to the
ending of slavery and O'Connell was a master at both. From this date, the cause
had found a new champion to rival even Clarkson, Buxton and Wilberforce.

2 'AGITATE! AGITATE! AGITATE!'

Winning Catholic Emancipation in 1829 had been a personal triumph for O'Connell. From this time onwards, his supporters referred to him as the 'Liberator'. His subsequent election to the British Parliament, and that of some of his supporters, changed the face not only of Irish, but also British, politics as they demonstrated that their interests extended beyond matters concerning Ireland. The reform of Parliament and the abolition of slavery were the two most pressing political debates, which not only engrossed Parliament, but aroused considerable public interest. O'Connell supported both and the latter brought him into contact with the leading anti-slavers of the day. His oratorical skills, his passion and intrepidness, meant that he quickly emerged as one of the movement's most influential and energetic advocates.

Following his election to the British Parliament, O'Connell dedicated himself to two issues: repeal of the Act of Union and anti-slavery. In Britain, anti-slavery brought him into contact with people who bitterly opposed his campaign for repeal, whilst in America, it brought him into contact with people who supported repeal but opposed abolition. Shortly after moving to London to take his seat, O'Connell met with anti-slavery leaders in Britain and in Westminster.[1] From the outset, O'Connell made it clear that he intended to use his place in Parliament to fight for slave emancipation. The Cork Anti-Slavery Society had requested him to submit a petition on their behalf. No other Irish MP would agree to take it. O'Connell, however, promised that he would make its delivery his first act in the House of Commons.[2] Traditionally, support for anti-slavery within the British Parliament had been centred on evangelicals, aided by those with an interest in the East Indies (India), which was also a major sugar producer and therefore a rival of the West Indies.[3] In the wake of Catholic Emancipation, Irish MPs, led by O'Connell, were increasingly important in giving their support to slavery questions in the Commons.[4]

Following Catholic Emancipation O'Connell had been forced to seek re-election to Westminster in order to comply with the new legislation, so he had not taken his seat in the House of Commons until 1830. When he did so, anti-slavery had only two dedicated champions – Thomas Fowell Buxton and Stephen

Lushington. In O'Connell, they had found a powerful advocate. It was not only anti-slavers who took note of O'Connell's presence in Westminster. According to Wendell Phillips, an American abolitionist, upon his arrival O'Connell had been approached by up to thirty members of the pro-slavery faction who offered him their unconditional support on Irish issues if he agreed not to attend any anti-slavery meetings in London.[5] O'Connell responded:

> Gentlemen, God knows that I have the most hapless constituency upon which the sun ever set, but may my right hand forget its cunning and may my tongue cleave to the roof of my mouth before, to help Ireland, I keep silent on the negro question.[6]

Throughout the whole of his seventeen-year parliamentary career, which only ended with his death in 1847, O'Connell consistently voted with the anti-slavery group.

In 1829, O'Connell had argued that immediate abolition would be dangerous on the grounds that 'though we wish for the abolition of slavery, still it should take place by degrees not instantaneously. The sudden transition from the rack to the enjoyment of liberty, may be shuddered at'.[7] Within only a few years though, he and other leading campaigners had changed their minds. In the early 1830s, there were signs that the anti-slavery campaign was becoming more militant. Initially, the movement had focused on ameliorating the condition of the slaves with a view to bringing about gradual emancipation, but increasingly, immediate and complete abolition was being demanded. This change was evident in both the United Kingdom and the United States. In general, those who led the earlier movement 'Had a religious orientation, a moderate and conciliatory tone, and ... a colonization outlook'. Many were guided by the belief that 'slavery was a sin for which God would eventually exact retribution'.[8] In the United States also, the early abolitionists:

> In their addresses to the slaveholders ... used calm and temperate language, in line with their belief that a harsher tone would seem provocative. They avoided passionate denunciations or the reciting of atrocity stories. They avowed that their plans were of a pacific nature and that any opposition to slaveholders was opposition to a brother rather than to an enemy.[9]

After 1830, abolitionists on both sides of the Atlantic were more strident and they were less constrained by religious affiliation. They no longer favoured a gradualist approach, but wanted immediate and unconditional abolition. The new breed of abolitionist was typified by O'Connell in the United Kingdom and William Lloyd Garrison and David Walker in the United States, whose approach and tactics were diametrically opposed to those of an earlier generation of campaigners. The British abolitionist George Stephen believed that a new approach was necessary if any progress was to be made, because many of the traditional supporters were:

> For the most part, of too refined an order for the rough labour required to take advantage of the political liberality just nascent among the people. They were not cut out for the rude work of meeting mobs and organizing agitation; they neither liked nor understood it, nor believed in its power.[10]

However, the new militancy and more confrontational tactics alienated not only their opponents but some of their fellow abolitionists. The unpopularity of anti-slavery was demonstrated by the fact that some of their meetings were violently broken up and the lecturers beaten in the early 1830s.[11]

In Britain, the difference in approaches led to a split in the British abolition movement, with the more militant Agency Committee being formed in 1831. It comprised of those who felt frustrated by Buxton's commitment to gradual emancipation. The Agency was dedicated to sustaining the agitation campaign on behalf of immediate emancipation. It did this through 'a regularly organized system of lecturing by agents wholly devoted to the work, followed by the establishment of auxiliary associations all over the country'.[12] Its early members included Joseph Sturge and George Stephen.[13] O'Connell always supported its demands. At this stage, some abolitionists were getting frustrated with Buxton's moderate approach and privately suggested that O'Connell should replace him as leader of abolitionists in Parliament.[14] The Agency Committee had a sub-committee for Ireland, which was represented by William Hume.[15] Despite the split, the Anti-Slavery Society and more radical Agency Committee worked together on a number of issues. In 1831, they asked voters to support only anti-slavery candidates in the imminent General Election.[16]

The new more militant approach in the movement was exemplified in the changing attitudes towards colonization. The American Colonization Society (ACS) had been founded in 1816, with the purpose of sending freed slaves back to West Africa. To this end, Liberia had been established in 1822. In 1830, Elliot Cresson travelled to Britain to try to win support for the ASC, his visit being a sign of the value placed on British public opinion. Wilberforce, Clarkson and George Thompson initially supported the ACS.[17] But some splits were becoming apparent within the American movement. Mathew Carey, an Irish-born publisher who lived in Philadelphia, was attacked in the columns of Garrison's *Liberator* for having suggested that former slaves should consider migrating to Liberia. For Garrison, this idea showed that American people were 'incapable of losing any of their animosity or prejudice toward their coloured countrymen'.[18] Garrison felt those who supported colonization were not sincere about abolition but viewed black people as inferior.[19] Freed slaves in America were also hostile to this scheme and as early as 1817 were organizing formal protests. They objected to the suggestion that they did not belong in America, viewing colonization as a new form of exile. They also 'vowed that they would never voluntarily separate themselves from their brethren in slavery'.[20] In May 1833, Garrison travelled to Britain, as the Agent of the New-England Anti-Slavery Society. The journey had been made possible by subscriptions from black supporters.[21] Garrison was criticized by anti-abolitionists in Boston for:

> his disgraceful mission to the British metropolis, whither he went to obtain pecuniary aid, and the countenance of Englishmen to wrest the American citizen's property … and also countenancing the outrageous conduct of Daniel O'Connell, who at one of his (Garrison's) meetings, called us 'a set of sheep stealers, man-murderers', and that the blackest corner in Hell's bottomless pit, ought to be, and would be, the future destination of the Americans.[22]

The article went on to recommend people on Garrison's return to go, 'armed with plenty of tar and feathers, and administer him justice at his abode at No. 9, Merchants' Hall'.[23] Garrison brought to Britain a Protest that repudiated all attempts at colonization. His aim was to persuade the leading activists, including William Wilberforce and Daniel O'Connell, to sign it.[24] Garrison's mission was successful. To show their support for the Protest, in August 1833 O'Connell and Buxton held a meeting in Exeter Hall at which O'Connell condemned those who supported colonization.[25] Following his return, Garrison promised that he would publish the main speeches from his visit, and he paid particular tribute to:

> that fearless and eloquent champion of liberty – that first of Irish patriots – Daniel O'Connell Esq., the coloured population of this country and their advocates are under heavy obligations for his masterly vindication of their cause, his terrible castigation of American slavery, and his withering satire upon the colonization 'humbug'.[26]

Despite the splits in the movement the campaign was becoming more energized. On 15 May 1830, the annual meeting of the Anti-Slavery Society was held in the *Freemason's Tavern* in London. 3,000 people attended and hundreds more could not be admitted. This level of attendance was unprecedented and led the seasoned campaigner, George Stephen, to pronounce, 'To-day the slave is free'.[27] He also admitted that the meetings only became full after they agreed to admit women – something that a number of the men had continued to resist.[28] The great warriors of the campaign were present. Wilberforce, described as 'the high priest of this philanthropic squad' was in the chair, and Clarkson, Stephen Lushington, Henry Brougham, Thomas Denman and O'Connell were listed amongst the speakers.[29] Henry Drummond made a speech attacking the barbarities of slavery, and demonstrating his admiration for O'Connell:

> Indeed he feared that 'til some black O'Connell or African Bolivar devoted his unceasing energies to the emancipation of his negro brethren, the condition of West

Indies slaves would never be that which every well wisher of the species must wish to
see him placed in (hear hear).[30]

O'Connell was one of the last to speak, only doing so after established luminar-
ies such as Buxton, Lushington and Macaulay, and other longer-term supporters
had spoken. The meeting had debated whether or not to ask Parliament to set a
date to abolish slavery in the West Indies, but had disagreed over the timetable
for emancipation.[31] O'Connell's speech was unusually cautious and conciliatory.
He suggested that 'instead of regretting that a difference had risen amongst us,
it only showed that in the variety of our zeal, we had different ways of attaining
the same object'.[32] He further warned that they could not expect to accomplish
everything in one go, 'but let them make a beginning', pointing out the danger
of setting a date for the end of slavery and then the date arriving and slavery still
existing. He therefore supported an amendment for a more gradual approach to
ensure that something could be achieved. O'Connell's speech was greeted with
shouts of 'hear hear'.[33] O'Connell's involvement in this meeting showed that he
was being taken seriously on this issue – by people within the movement. The
antagonism of some sections of the British press to him was clear, however. *Fraser's Magazine,* which reported the proceedings of the meeting favourably, noted
that O'Connell had made a speech but declined to include it in their journal on
the grounds that their readers 'do not wish to be troubled' with it.[34] O'Connell
privately responded to the continuing personal attacks by confiding to a friend,
'I only smile on the attacks made on my character. I am so familiar with every
species of calumny that, my good friend, it is really nothing but time lost to
defend me'. He went on to say, 'we have been turned into a province and now
we are made slaves by our own miserable dissensions or rather by the desertion
of those who ought to assist but actually *stab* their country'.[35] Regardless of such
public hostility, O'Connell's role as a key member of the British campaign continued. Only three days later he spoke at the annual meeting of the Anti-Slavery
Society in London. Wilberforce was in the chair.

O'Connell, together with Buxton and Lushington, was one of the three
main speakers at the annual meeting of the Anti-Slavery Society in May 1831,
held in Exeter Hall in London. At the meeting it was agreed that they wanted
the 'entire extinction of negro slavery'.[36] He was also one of the main speakers at
the 1832 annual meeting, sharing a platform with Buxton, Lushington, Lord
Suffield and Philip Crampton, the Solicitor General for Ireland and William
Allen. The purpose of meeting was to discuss, 'whether the existence of slavery
ought to be tolerated among British subjects'. In his speech, Buxton said that it
was not possible to improve the condition of slaves: slavery had to be abolished.
O'Connell seconded a motion for the abolition of slavery but, unusually, did
not speak. Crampton, a fellow Irish man, declared that, 'however divided Irish-

men might be upon other points, they were unanimous in their wish for the immediate and total abolition of negro slavery'.[37] The room was full, with many crowded outside in the Strand as they could not get in. It proved to be the largest anti-slavery meeting ever held there, indicating how much popular support had grown.[38] In the same year, Boards of Correspondence were formed in London, Edinburgh and Dublin, in an attempt to provide a more coordinated national campaign.[39]

O'Connell's arrival in Westminster coincided with a revival of anti-slavery within Parliament, mostly due to the efforts of its two champions, Buxton and Lushington. The renewed activity caused a dilemma for successive British governments that were forced to balance the competing interests of the abolitionists and of those engaged in the colonial trade. In the years between 1823 and 1831, despite seeming to make some progress within Parliament:

> Most of the governmental measures on colonial slavery, however, were to a great extend tactical devices intended to increase the illusion that ministers were pursuing an active amelioration policy and thus to prevent or reduce any pressure for more direct action.[40]

In April 1831, a motion for the abolition of slavery was introduced by Buxton into the House of Commons.[41] Buxton admitted that O'Connell's support was crucial and 'throughout [he] gave a steady and energetic support to the Anti-slavery cause'. When the debate was adjourned, he came across the house to say 'Mr Buxton, I see land'.[42] In later debates in Parliament Buxton was to rely on O'Connell's interventions and support, and he admitted that his job was harder when not supported by the Irish politician.[43] The renewed anti-slavery agitation coincided with the mounting public pressure for parliamentary reform. O'Connell had not long taken his seat in the Commons when the death of George IV in June 1830 resulted in the dissolution of Parliament and a General Election. O'Connell was re-elected and privately declared the result to be a 'triumph'.[44] The 1830 General Election was fought on the question of electoral reform, with the Whigs in favour and the Tories bitterly opposed to it. Although the latter won the election, the intransigence of the new Prime Minister – the Duke of Wellington – on the issue of reform resulted in a vote of no confidence. The Whigs came to power in 1831 and called a fresh election in order to win a strong mandate for parliamentary reform. Catholic Emancipation, therefore, had triggered a number of changes that made both the reform of Parliament and the abolition of slavery possible, and Daniel O'Connell had lost no time in championing both causes in Westminster.

Throughout 1831, the activities of the abolitionists were increasingly overshadowed by the public demand for a reform of the franchise, which became the most pressing political issue of the day. Reform was felt to be necessary as some towns with large populations had no political representation, while 'rotten boroughs' had political representation despite possessing only a small population. Moreover, the ability to vote remained limited and did not reflect the growing wealth of the industrial middle classes. In late 1831 and early 1832, anti-slavery agitation was partially suspended in order to focus on the Reform Bill, as the whole country became enthralled with the struggle to get it passed through both Houses of Parliament.[45] However, a revolt by slaves in Jamaica in December 1831 had alarmed the Whigs into appointing a Select Committee to report on measures to safely abolish slavery within the British Empire. O'Connell was a member of the committee, as was his fellow-Irishman, the Marquis of Sligo, who owned property in the West Indies. Sligo had been shocked by the evidence presented, admitting 'I then became a convert from the very evidence adduced by the West India interest itself. I entered the room a colonial advocate. I left it a decided abolitionist'.[46]

In addition to promoting anti-slavery, O'Connell supported the Reform Bill as it struggled to get passed in Parliament. The London Anti-Slavery Society also supported parliamentary reform. In April 1831, they issued an address 'To the People of Great Britain and Ireland', asking them to call meetings and to approach electors and seek their support for abolition.[47] Voters were requested to:

> Make strict enquiries of every Candidate, not only whether he is decidedly favourable to the extinction of Slavery, but whether or not he will attend the Debates in Parliament, when that question shall be discussed; herein taking special care not to be deceived by general professions of disapprobation of Slavery.[48]

In his election manifesto, O'Connell twinned parliamentary reform with the ending of slavery.[49] He spoke passionately in Parliament about the need for reform, which resulted in even his adversaries in the Whig Party cheering for him, and the usually antagonistic *Times* admitting that he had 'put the constitutional argument against the continuance of the rotten borough system with uncommon force and clearness'.[50] O'Connell himself was pleased with the response to his speech. He confided to his wife that his vanity was being 'fed by everything I hear' and that even the newspapers were treating him well.[51]

Polling in the election was held from April to June 1831. The outcome was that the Whigs gained a majority of 136 seats. O'Connell's Repeal Party emerged as the third largest. Significantly for the anti-slavery movement, the West Indian interest was reduced to only 35 seats, compared with 104 previously. Opposition to the Reform Bill continued in the House of Lords, thus it did not receive Royal Assent until June 1832.[52] The Act applied only to England and Wales, with separate legislation being passed for Scotland and Ireland. The new legislation increased the electorate and abolished 'rotten' boroughs. For

O'Connell, the impact of the reforms for Ireland was disappointing as the country still had a less favourable franchise than elsewhere in the United Kingdom. For the remainder of his parliamentary career O'Connell returned to this issue, unsuccessfully, pointing out on one occasion:

> We want equality with you, and you will not permit us to have it. You gave us a Reform Bill – it was a stingy and despicable Reform Bill ... We ought to have the same franchise which you enjoy. We were entitled to them by the Union. Why not give us an equality of civil rights?[53]

O'Connell, the champion of liberty and justice for so many people throughout the world, never felt he was able to achieve them in his own country.

The first General Election after the Reform Bill was introduced took place in December 1832. Forty repealers were returned. The extended franchise also gave a vote for the first time to the grass-roots campaigners for abolition, who were able to put pressure on their electoral representatives. This engagement was apparent in Ireland, notably in Cork, Belfast and Dublin where candidates were expected to support abolition once elected.[54] Within only a few years an important change had taken place in the anti-slavery campaign with the demand in the country being for immediate, and not gradual, abolition.[55] The reformed Parliament provided an opportunity for change and a new approach to traditional problems such as anti-slavery. Although eclipsed by the reform question, anti-slavery agitation had continued. As the struggle for parliamentary representation was reaching its climax, significant developments were taking place within Irish anti-slavery. In early May 1832 an anti-slavery petition, which had been prepared by two Quaker women, Anne Knight and Maria Tothill, and contained 187,000 signatures, was delivered to Parliament. The petition was so heavy it had to be carried into the House by four men.[56] In the same month, at a meeting of the Anti-Slavery Society in London, O'Connell had called on women to sign even more petitions. Wilberforce, however, disapproved, believing that women should confine their role to encouraging men to sign petitions.[57] On 24 May 1832, Buxton moved in the Commons for a committee to consider the best and safest way to abolish slavery in the British empire. It was a brave move and, as George Stephen observed:

> For days previously he had been assailed by all parties, and on every side. On the morning of that day he was almost torn to pieces by threats, by remonstrance, by expostulation, and, worse than all together, by advice, for even his friends dreaded the experiment.[58]

The difficulty remained as to how to persuade slaveholders, who had proved resistant to even small measures of improvement, to cooperate. Two incentives were to be offered; slaves would continue to work but for wages, and slave-owners would be paid compensation, although it was not clear if this was to be in the form of a loan or a grant. O'Connell had seen an early version of a proposal to give the plantation owners a loan of £15,000,000, to be paid for by the slaves, and responded that 'It will never, never do'.[59] The difficulties over working out the details meant that, to the disappointment of the abolitionists, the King's Speech in February 1833 made no mention of emancipation. Privately, Buxton was assured that a measure was imminent.[60] In the early months of 1833 extra pressure was put on Parliament in the form of bombarding it with petitions; by May, the House of Commons was receiving up to 500 petitions daily and the House of Lords, as many as 700.[61] Abolitionist MPs, including Buxton and O'Connell, kept up pressure within Westminster in other ways. On 19 April 1833, 339 delegates, including a number of MPs and religious ministers, met in Exeter Hall and then walked in procession to Downing Street.[62] O'Connell was part of the delegation as were members of the main Irish anti-slavery societies.[63] They had prepared an address to the Prime Minister saying that they wanted nothing short of full emancipation. Inevitably, they caused a spectacle as they paraded down the Strand and Whitehall, and their action sent a strong message to the government.[64] Only a few weeks later, a Bill for the abolition of slavery was introduced into Parliament.

It was left to the Minister for the Colonies, Lord Stanley, to bring before the House of Commons a motion for the abolition of slavery. When it was finally introduced into Parliament, in the words of George Stephen, 'Stanley produced the Bill in a speech to which he contributed the eloquence, Mr Macauley the facts, and Mr Buxton the argument'.[65] In the subsequent readings, it was O'Connell who consistently defended the rights of the slave. Inevitably, there were many disagreements regarding the details of emancipation, the only thing that achieved consensus being the opposition to colonization. And while the majority opinion in the House was that abolition should be total and immediate, even the abolitionists were less united on the other issues.

Stanley's introductory speech had raised expectations amongst abolitionists that the slaves would be treated fairly, but two contentious issues dominated the subsequent readings: how much compensation there should be and who should pay for it, and how long the duration of the 'apprenticeship' system of paid labour should be. Throughout the three readings, O'Connell spoke frequently and passionately on behalf of total emancipation, with no compensation and no apprenticeship. Initially, it was proposed that freed slaves would have to serve twelve years apprenticeship. When challenged on this point by an abolition delegation, Stanley said the government had made a promise to the West Indian Party on this matter. O'Connell, who had been one of the delegation, suggested to his colleagues that they should 'Appale [sic] to the people'. His suggestion was taken up and a mass meeting to protest against apprenticeship was held in Exeter Hall.[66] O'Connell, supported by Thomas Babington, Thomas Macauley and Lord Howick, led a heated debate against the proposed system of slave apprenticeship. Howick, who had been appointed Under-Secretary for the Colonies, resigned this position in protest against the compromises introduced during the second reading of the Bill by Stanley. O'Connell pointedly asked Stanley why he had 'declared that slavery should be abolished, but at the same time he perpetuated it under the name of apprenticeship?'[67]

Buxton feared that the uncompromising actions of his fellow abolitionists might jeopardize the whole Bill, and so he supported its second reading, although he objected to the length of apprenticeship being proposed.[70] At the second reading, apprenticeship was reduced to seven years. An initial proposal that compensation to slave-owners was to be £15,000,000 was instead made into a gift of £20,000,000.[71] Both of these proposals survived the third and final reading of the Bill.

While moderates including Buxton and Lushington were willing to accept the principle of compensation, O'Connell led a minority of seventy-seven MPs who were opposed to the proposed twenty million pound grant to slaveholders.[68] In a long, emotional speech, he challenged:

> It was proposed by this Bill to pay the planter 20,000,000*l.* sterling. Was it not an act of great justice, therefore to give the labour of the poor negro beside, thus paying twice over? ... The House had heard of the humanity of this measure, which compelled the poor defenceless negro to become an apprentice, and give his labour for the remainder of his life, thus perpetuating the slavery which this Bill, on first being introduced, professed to abolish. Were the people to be called upon to perpetuate that most repulsive and demoralizing crime, at the expense of 20,000,000*l*? ... He was anxious to control his feelings and would do so. But to those who brought forward this measure, and were ready to give it their support, he would say, if they did not, like Shylock, demand the pound of human flesh, they demanded the twelve years additional slavery from the poor negro under the pretence of friendship. Was that what the negro expected? Was that what the country so long sought for and expected? ... The country sought for the total and unconditional abolition of slavery, and with less, the country would not be satisfied.[69]

Following the passage of the 1833 Emancipation Act, the main anti-slavery societies disappeared from view. They were later subsumed into the British and Foreign Anti-Slavery Society.[72]

The introduction of apprenticeship gave rise to a new campaign for its immediate abolition, a campaign in which O'Connell played a leading role. The parliamentary debates were followed closely by abolitionists in Britain and Ireland. On 29 May, O'Connell asked the Speaker of the House to permit William Hume, the Irish representative of the Agency, to have a seat in the gallery. He pointed out that he 'solicits this favour the more anxiously as Mr

Hume represents the Irish Anti-Slavery party which is not only numerous but highly respectable'.[73] The passage of the Emancipation Bill through Parliament had been helped by the reform of Parliament in 1832, which had given more power to industrial towns, and it was in these towns that dissenters opposed to slavery had proved most effective in mobilizing support and putting pressure on their MPs. Dissenters also had proved to be most consistently opposed to apprenticeship and compensation.[74] An exception to this trend was provided by O'Connell, who had used his own popularity and personal support to persuade twenty-two Irish MPs, mainly Catholic, to vote with the minority and oppose these proposals.[75] In taking this stand, O'Connell differed from other MPs whose votes were motivated by constituency pressure or by financial considerations; rather, according to the historian Isaac Gross, the Irish leader was guided by 'altruistic sentiments on the emancipation debates and divisions'. In this way, he had more in common with Buxton and Lushington, two stalwarts of the abolitionist movement, than with many of his fellow MPs.[76] During the debates, he had proved to be the most consistent opponent of any watering down of the abolitionists' demands. Thus, within only a few years of being elected to the British House of Commons, O'Connell not only had proved his leadership qualities, he also demonstrated his commitment to a cause that brought no benefit to Ireland or to himself.

On 28 August 1833, the Slavery Abolition Bill received Royal Assent, becoming operative on 1 August 1834. Joy was tempered by sadness at the death of William Wilberforce, aged 73, on 29 July 1833, just as the bill was passing through Parliament. His name, more than that of any other individual, had become associated with the cause of anti-slavery. Nonetheless, to mark the passing of the bill, a celebratory dinner was held at the *Anchor and Crown Tavern* in London for the leading abolitionists. Members of the Society of Friends were reluctant to attend, only agreeing to do so if no toasts were made. According to George Stephen, 'O'Connell was nearly as fastidious as the Quakers for he also stipulated that no music should be allowed to interrupt the speeches'.[77] Stephen, who admitted he was partial to both music and toasts, was determined to thwart these demands, which he did effectively. At the end of the dinner, he suggested to Buxton it would appear disloyal if they did not toast the King. Buxton acceded:

> As soon as the cheers subsided, O'Connell was rising with humour on his face, all ready for an oration, but I had no mind to hear him, and giving a pre-concerted signal, the band of the Guards, hitherto concealed, struck up the national anthem ... I knew that with the first pause, O'Connell would be on his legs again, so I dispatched a note to Buxton [saying]... to omit the health of the Queen ... the Conservatives ... the ladies ... would cause offence.[78]

Following these additional toasts, a further one was called to the emancipated slaves, 'and it was received with cheers that might have been heard in the Palace Yard'. Moreover:

> The ice was now broken, and though we allowed O'Connell his speech, and excellently adapted it was to the event, toasts, healths and sentiments followed in rapid succession.[79]

This anecdote, concerning a rare moment of celebration, gives an insight into O'Connell's prominent role within the movement and how he was regarded by some of his colleagues.

Anti-Slavery Continues

While O'Connell was busy in Westminster and establishing his authority within the anti-slavery movement in Britain, anti-slavery was becoming more organized in Ireland, but in a way that was alien to O'Connell's inclusive, ecumenical approach. In 1824, the Dublin Association for Endeavouring to Promote the Mitigation and Gradual Abolition of Slavery in the British Colonies had been established. As in Britain, it was led by nonconformist Protestants. By the end of the decade, anti-slavery societies had been founded in the major towns and cities, including Dublin, Cork and Belfast. They had close contact with anti-slavery societies in Britain, especially the London Anti-Slavery Society. Zachary Macauley's *Anti-Slavery Reporter* included regular accounts of their meetings. For example, the annual meeting of the Cork association in September 1829 was reprinted in full, on the grounds that 'the transactions were so interesting that we cannot, we think, gratify our readers more than by transferring the whole account'.[80]

In 1829, the same year that Catholic Emancipation was granted, the Dublin (subsequently Hibernian) Negro's Friend Society was founded by Charles Orpen. It attracted a lot of support, especially in Cork and Dublin, but, according to Maurice Bric, 'anti-slavery was a cause rather than an organized movement in Ireland and operated there within the wider networks of reform'.[81] A feature of the early anti-slavery movement in Ireland was that it was overwhelming associated with evangelical Protestantism. This was reinforced by the fact that many anti-slavery meetings were held in Protestant halls and churches. Furthermore, anti-slavery was not only associated with Protestantism, it was frequently regarded as anti-Catholic. Two of the early members of the Negro's Friend Society were Dr Charles Orpen, a pioneer in studying deaf language, and his father-in law, Major Sirr, who was known for his anti-Catholic views. The Society was also linked with the Hibernian Bible Society, which was associated with the so-called 'second reformation', of the 1820s which had sought to covert Catholics to Protestantism.[82] The growing influence of O'Connell, therefore, begged the question, how did Irish Catholics fit into this cause?

Unlike earlier societies, the Dublin Negro's Friend Society was dedicated to the immediate ending of slavery. As its name suggested, the chief concern of the Society was with the condition of the slave, something the Dublin group had in common with a number of ladies' associations in Britain.[83] Membership was relatively expensive, £1 a year, while £20 or over ensured guardianship for life. Like some of the earlier associations, the Society allied the abolition of slavery with religion – the Protestant one.[84] The evangelical ideals of the Society were clear in its objects, namely:

> To promote the utter abolition of Negro Slavery, and also the present moral improvement of the Negro Slave, by means of the establishment of Schools, the circulation of the Sacred Scriptures, and the employment of Scripture Readers
>
> To promote the improvement of the manufacture and to encourage and facilitate the consumption of Tropical produce, not cultured or manufactured by Slave-labour, and
>
> To aid in procuring the freedom of such pious Negroes, as may be found suitable characters, to be employed as Scripture Readers, or Schoolmasters, among their brethren.[85]

In keeping with their religious beliefs, the new Society objected to the fact that slaves had to work on the Sabbath.[86]

The Negro's Friend Society criticized the 'tyrannical power' of the master, arguing that the cruel way in which a slave was treated was degrading and served to 'extinguish in him every noble or generous quality by which man is distinguished from the brutes ... even in some cases keeping him intentionally in ignorance of all true religions and morality, lest he should discover the criminality of his oppressors.[87] Again, deploying a religious prism, they argued that:

> All the evils of this unchristian system appear in their most aggravated form in the BRITISH COLONIES – under that nation, which enjoys the greatest civil, political and religious blessings of any people in the world.[88]

Like some of the earlier anti-slavery societies, the Dublin one argued that slavery could be brought down by people not using slave produce. All consumers of slave products were sustaining the system, and therefore it was the duty of everybody 'neither to buy nor sell, receive or consume the defiled produce'.[89] They recommended the purchase of sugar grown by free men in Bengal, which was cheaper than slave sugar.[90] The Society produced a number of appeals on behalf of slaves in the British colonies. They were generally emotive documents, drawing attention to the brutal aspects of the system, such as the flogging of female slaves. They also pointed out that it cost £2,000,000 each year for British forces to protect the West Indies planters. The Society called on people to petition Parliament 'for the total and speedy extinction of Negro Slavery'.[91] It added that 'real Christians' could not do otherwise.[92]

Within a year of its formation, the Dublin Society changed its name to the Hibernian Negro's Friend Society (HNFS). Continuity was ensured with Charles Orpen being named as the Director. The evangelical aspect of the Society's work remained evident, the members asserting that they would like to 'impart the consolations of Christianity to the oppressed, by circulating the Scriptures among them'.[93] Moreover, even if slavery were to be abolished and slaves given their rights, their work would continue, as slaves 'would still require all the assistance, that England could give, by means of Negro's Friend Societies, towards raising and improving his moral and religious condition'. The fact that the Anti-Slavery Society in London had no plans for long-term involvement with slaves was regarded by the Irish society as a major deficiency. They explained:

> all their plans have this disadvantage – they have a finite object of pursuit – but we an infinite. Suppose certain acts of the British Parliament passed your Society dies ... But when these societies die, ours will be entering upon the prime of life. You have England's legal dismantling of only her Colonial Slaves bondage as a final object; we have it but as the first and indispensable grade ... to raise the Negro race to that level, on which an enlarged and enlightened benevolence would wish to see.[94]

Like O'Connell, the Hibernian Negro's Friend Society suggested that Ireland had a long history of supporting anti-slavery. They reminded their colleagues in London that when Wilberforce had introduced a motion for the abolition of the slave trade in 1807 he had been supported by every Irish member. They also pointed out:

> This island was never engaged in the African Slave Trade, and probably not fifty families in the whole kingdom have any pecuniary interest in Slave properties, to blind them – it is therefore, only apathy, that we have to arouse (not interest and prejudice to contend with, as in England), and this apathy arises chiefly from ignorance on the subject. In the 11th century Ireland was involved in slavery – but it was Whites not Negroes – but it was abandoned when they realized how evil it was.[95]

As was common in British anti-slavery societies, the Hibernian Negro's Friend Society abstained from using West Indian sugar, arguing that its sale underpinned the whole system of slavery, and therefore that Irish people should only use sugar from East Indies. Furthermore, inspired by the actions of women in Birmingham, the Society established a depot for the exclusive sale of free labour produce – something that none of the Anti-Slavery Associations in England had done.[96] The spirit of militancy apparent in British and American societies was also evident in Ireland. Unlike their predecessors, both the Dublin and the

Hibernian Negro's Friend Society argued for total abolition with no compensation for the owners.[97] The HNFS believed that it was a false argument to say that education was a precondition for freedom, arguing instead for 'unprocrastinated emancipation'. Their arguments clearly found favour with William Lloyd Garrison, who reprinted some of their resolutions in his Boston newspaper.[98]

Regardless of the militancy of the reconfigured Hibernian Negro's Friend Society, on 20 July 1830, a letter from the London Anti-Slavery Society was read at their meeting, in which the former accused them of not being radical enough. This drew a long, angry response from the Irish group, who pointed out that one of their initial reasons for forming was their belief that other societies had not gone far enough. They had disapproved of their predecessor's support for the gradual abolition of slavery, wanting immediate and total abolition, something that other societies were coming around to supporting.[99] The Hibernian Negro's Friend Society argued that freed slaves should have the same rights as British-born subjects and they sought 'the religious, domestic, mental, social, agricultural and commercial improvement of the whole Negro race'.[100] The HNFS was also active in sending its agents to lecture on the abolition.[101] Although they had tried to get assistance from the English Anti-Slavery Society, 'for interesting the public mind' in Ireland, this had not been forthcoming. However, they had campaigned and managed to get some candidates to support their petitions. The HNFS had established links with the Birmingham and Calne Ladies' Anti-Slavery Association and they had worked together on educational matters. As a result of this collaboration, Captain Charles Stuart was currently touring the north and west of Ireland. One outcome was that petitions were being sent to Parliament from many parts of the country that had previously not supported the campaign. Stuart carried with him a West Indian slave whip, to demonstrate the cruelty of the system. It had proved to be so effective that the Hibernian Negro's Friend Society ordered six more whips for the same purpose. They believed that with additional support they could achieve even more positive results for abolition.[102]

The Negro's Friend Society was not the only anti-slavery society in Ireland. In 1827, an Anti-Slavery Society had been founded in Dublin. Quakers and dissenters were in the forefront of the movement, but O'Connell also gave it his support. Despite his preoccupation with Catholic Emancipation, O'Connell spoke at a meeting of the Cork branch of the Anti-Slavery Society in 1829. He was already being referred to as being an 'MP'.[103] In 1830, he was present at the annual meeting of both the Cork and Dublin Anti-Slavery Societies. O'Connell informed the Cork society that anti-slavery feeling was spreading in England and Irish people should be no less vigilant so that 'he who has liberated himself may have the pleasure of striking the chain from others'.[104] Unlike many other abolitionists, O'Connell did not confine his attacks to slavery within the British empire, but he criticized slavery everywhere. In what was to be a common feature of many of his later speeches he denounced slavery in the United States, calling the country hypocritical and describing the star-spangled banner as 'stained'.[105] The local reporter covering the meeting summed his speech up by saying:

> The nation is now awake to all of the momentousness of the issue, and we trust that Mr O'Connell will be as strenuous on the floor of parliament as on the platform at Cork in rousing any of his colleagues who may slumber at their posts.[106]

At their annual meeting, the Dublin group claimed to be disappointed with the progress that had been made, and suggested they required more men that possessed 'the love of liberty' of O'Connell.[107] O'Connell was introduced by the Reverend J McCrea, a Protestant minister and an Orangeman, who admitted that on every other issue – 'feelings, religious and political' – he had disagreed with O'Connell, but now he felt 'gratifying pleasure to share a platform with him'.[108] When O'Connell addressed the meeting he was greeted with 'long continued and enthusiastic cheering'. O'Connell made an emotive and energetic speech, asking 'how ... could it be defended that man was found degraded because he differed in colour from him who presumed to call him his slave?', he added that he was proud to say that 'amongst the various portions of the earth that had been disgraced by the abhorrent Negro slavery system, the stain had never yet rested upon Ireland'.[109] The outcome of the meeting was that, on behalf of the Irish abolitionists, O'Connell was going to present a petition to both Houses of Parliament calling for the ending of slavery. When he sat down, he was thanked with 'loud and long continued cheering'.[110] The involvement of the champion of Catholics, O'Connell, into what had been a Protestant bastion was welcomed by the meeting, one speaker describing it as 'the proud era of the union of Irish feeling, when burying in oblivion past dissensions and petty prejudices'.[111]

O'Connell also had contact with the Hibernian Negro's Friend Society in Dublin. In February 1831, they contacted him in regard to a petition from Ireland to be presented to the House of Commons in March and to:

> ... earnestly solicit the strenuous exertion of your influence and advocacy for the immediate and total abolition of a system so diametrically opposed to the dearest wishes of nearly a million of His Majesty's subjects.

They ended the letter by saying 'Relying on your friendly cooperation on this occasion'.[112] Their appeal was unnecessary as the petition was never debated, but it demonstrated that O'Connell's abilities in the movement were recognized outside of Britain. Also, within a short time and despite being largely based in London, O'Connell had emerged as the spokesperson of Irish anti-slavery, for people of all denominations.

It was not only Irish men who were becoming more active on behalf of the slaves: Irish women continued the tradition of being active in the movement. Each of the main societies had a women's auxiliary branch that proved effective in fundraising and supporting the more public activities of the men. In addition, the Hibernian Ladies' Society not only undertook the usual roles assigned to women through their activities, they showed that they were clearly following the debates in both Ireland and Britain. In 1833, they paid the *Dublin Evening Post* to include a speech made by Buxton and an address from the Anti-Slavery Society in London.[113] Their actions showed how closely events in Britain were followed and that the Irish women understood the importance of diffusing information.

Repeal

While O'Connell was proving to be a rising star in the British anti-slavery movement, his presence in Westminster was causing consternation. Within Parliament, O'Connell led the repeal group of MPs. They usually sided with the small group of British radical MPs, although O'Connell fell out with them in 1832 when they supported coercion in Ireland.[114] In general, O'Connell was regarded as a troublemaker by the two largest parties.[115] When he spoke, he was often subjected to jeering and heckling, sometimes proving so disruptive that the Speaker reluctantly intervened.[116] During one debate on the Reform Bill, the Conservative MP, Sir Charles Weatherell, taunted him with handing a 'begging-box' around his friends, a charge that O'Connell refuted.[117] O'Connell also objected to being referred to as a 'Catholic' Member of Parliament, explaining that, 'he sat there representative of his countrymen, Protestants as well as Catholics, and it was his duty to take care of the interest of one as well as the other'.[118] From the outset, Lord Edward Stanley proved himself to be an entrenched opponent of O'Connell, frequently interrupting him. Stanley did so with such frequency that during a debate on tithes O'Connell retorted 'I am glad that I have aroused the right hon. Gentleman from his torpor, and that he has begun to interrupt me so very soon in my speech.'[119] Privately, O'Connell concluded that Stanley's 'feelings are all anti-Irish, his entire turn of mind is bent to the protection of all existing abuses'.[120]

While championing both abolition and parliamentary reform, O'Connell spoke on a number of non-Irish issues, including the emancipation of Jews, stating that opposition to it was founded on 'principles of religious intolerance'.[121] His main preoccupation continued to be with having the Act of Union overturned. The tactics he employed in all this campaigns were similar to those used in gaining Catholic Emancipation and in the anti-slavery campaign. In March 1830, he submitted a petition for a repeal of the Union. He denied the accusation that it was sectarian or illegal, responding 'It would, indeed, be unbecoming in him to use any other than constitutional language on such a subject'.[122] The revolutions that took place that year in both France and Belgium convinced O'Connell that repeal could be won sooner rather than later. He advised one of his supporters in Ireland that 'The Union should now be agitated in every shape' and ended is letter by saying 'AGITATE! AGITATE! AGITATE!'[123] He followed this up by founding, on 23 October 1830 in Dublin, the Association of Irish Volunteers for the Repeal of the Union.[124]

O'Connell's activities were clearly disturbing some of his fellow politicians. According to one English member, Lord Althorp, an experienced Whig politician and leader of the Commons, 'There were times when the tactics of Mr O'Connell could not be otherwise than repugnant to a man of honourable feelings'.[125] He claimed that O'Connell's extremism on the issue of repeal and his confrontational tactics had alienated some of his supporters, including the popular Mr Shiel.[126] The radical English politician, Colonel Leslie Grove Jones, who sympathized with O'Connell's demands, informed him that:

> A *great horror* is entertained of you and more so with the Whigs than the Tories but all of the [Orange] Order or [those] connected with it are in full rage against you and you are abused and condemned generally.[127]

Regardless of the publically expressed dislike of O'Connell, at the end of 1830 the Whigs secretly offered him high public office in return for his acquiescence on a number of issues. O'Connell's refusal drew the fulsome praise of his wife:

> Thank God you have acted like yourself, and your wife and children have more reason to be proud of you now than they ever were ... You cannot abandon the people who have always stood by you, and for whom you have sacrificed so much ... Had you been betrayed into acceptance of the terms offered by Government you would die of a broken heart before six months expired.[128]

Apart from his fiery rhetoric, and his reputation in Britain as a rabble-rouser, O'Connell's commitment to legal, constitutional tactics remained, he even referring to himself as the 'Pacifier of Ireland', so determined was he to keep Ireland quiet and peaceful.[129] To this end, on 6 January 1831, he launched 'the General Association of Ireland, for the prevention of unlawful meetings and for the protection and exercise of the sacred right of petitioning for the redress of grievances'. The following day, the Lord Lieutenant of Ireland issued a proclamation banning the organization. A few days later, all repeal meetings were banned.[130] Clearly, the government was determined that O'Connell would not repeat the success of Catholic Emancipation.

In a private letter written in January 1831, Lord Althorp confided to Lord Spencer that, 'we shall be forced to adopt some very violent measures when Parliament meets. But O'Connell must be put down, whatever may be the means necessary to put him down'.[131] In the same month, O'Connell and five of his fellow repealers were arrested on the grounds that they had not conformed to the proclamation act. The charges were clearly specious, leading Thomas Wallace, a lawyer and supporter of the government, to contact O'Connell and offer him his legal services. He explained:

> In my opinion, the charge savours strongly of *illegality* and *oppression* ... To me it appears that he [the Lord Lieutenant] has misapplied the law to cases to which it was not applicable and has strained it in his proclamation – particularly the last – to an extent which *greatly* endangers public liberty.[132]

Some politicians had similar reservations, which they expressed privately. In the wake of O'Connell's arrest Althorp pointed out, 'Notwithstanding the unanimous opinion of our law authorities there [Ireland], I entertain some doubts of the legality of O'Connell's arrest ... the people of England can hardly be angry with us for having gone, perhaps, a little too far in resisting him.'[133] In May 1831, the government quietly let the charges drop, probably because they needed O'Connell's support in ensuring the passage of the parliamentary Reform Bill.[134]

Regardless of the disquiet that O'Connell had created, he continued agitating on behalf of repeal within Westminster. On 4 March 1831, he made a strong statement, warning:

> That if the Union was not repealed, Ireland would, indeed, soon cease to be a constituent part of the British Empire. It was necessary to the welfare and happiness of Ireland that she should have a separate Legislature.[135]

Nevertheless, the following day, he issued a letter to the people of Ireland asking that the repeal agitation be postponed until the parliamentary reform legislation had passed.[136]

The Whig government appeared unconvinced by O'Connell's appeal for calm. They used his fiery rhetoric and the unrest in Ireland, in the summer of 1831, to move for a renewal of the Irish Arms Bill. The Bill was proposed by Lord Stanley, who personally disliked O'Connell. It contained a number of draconian additions to the earlier legislation. Lord Althorp described it as 'one of the most tyrannical measures I ever heard proposed', and he privately worked to soften the measure.[137] His intervention proved unnecessary as the Bill was withdrawn. Later in the year, another offer was made by the Whig government to O'Connell, but again in secret. This time it was the position of Attorney-General, which was rejected by O'Connell.[138]

In 1832, the Whigs again secretly sought O'Connell's support, this time for the Reform Bill. The passage of the Reform Bill had facilitated the introduction of slave emancipation into the House, but repeal of the Union appeared to be no closer. In the early months of 1833, O'Connell decided against bringing a motion for repeal before Parliament even though he was urged to do so by some of his repeal MPs, led by Feargus O'Connor from County Cork.[139] In a vote on the issue, twelve voted not to bring forward a repeal motion in the current session, while ten abstained, demonstrating that O'Connell's decision was not a popular one.[140] O'Connell's determination not to promote a repeal agenda in Parliament was also criticized in Ireland, leaving him to question if he was losing his influence. In a long and frank letter to his trusted friend, Patrick Fitzpatrick, he confided:

> Alas! How little do men in Dublin know the precarious state of affairs. I am deprived even of my power of warning ... We are, however, now at the most portentous crisis of our affairs, and I perceive that circumstances are running away with my political influence. Why, if men thought me really honest, would they not admit that I am in a position to see more of the game than those who, residing in Dublin, cannot know one half of the circumstances on which political conduct ought to hinge? We are arriving at a crisis. God's holy will be done in everything.[141]

It was not only his fellow repealers who were causing O'Connell distress. Since his arrival in London most of the London press had been antagonistic to him. Led by the influential *Times*, they had given no, or little, coverage to his speeches in Parliament. O'Connell felt especially grieved that they had largely ignored the speeches he had made in favour of the Slave Emancipation Bill, which in his words had been 'concealed'.[142] During one debate on the Bill, he directed his fellow MPs to read *The Times* of that morning in order to see 'an excellent piece of scurrility'.[143] Despite being occupied with the details of the Slavery Emancipation Bill, O'Connell decided to challenge the press. He failed to get sufficient support to have the matter heard before the bar of Westminster, but commenced to use his privileges to have members of the press banned from attending the House. O'Connell was victorious and the press quietly backed down. He was jubilant at his success, confiding 'I believe I am the only man in either House of Parliament who would dare to beard so powerful a Press ... I am foolishly proud of that victory'.[144]

O'Connell frequently stated that the only obstacle to a repeal of the Union was the 'Orange faction', but that public opinion in Britain was moving in favour of it, largely because it was fed up of Irish immigrants and paupers.[145] In this he was mistaken as, despite his presence in Westminster, his goal of repeal remained no nearer to being achieved. Moreover, justice for Ireland appeared as elusive as ever. In 1833, as the Slave Emancipation Bill was passing through Parliament, more repressive measures were being introduced in Ireland. In February of that year, Habeas Corpus was suspended and a new Coercion Bill was introduced. O'Connell spoke out against both, but with no success.[146] He accused the government of being 'mean enough' to secretly ask *The Times* not to give full coverage to the parliamentary debates concerning its introduction.[147] He informed the House that:

> Often as he had endeavoured to direct its sympathies towards the wrongs of his country, unhappy, ill-fated Ireland, he never felt so painfully anxious as at that moment ... He would speak as he should feel if the liberties of Englishmen were threatened with destruction.[148]

As usual, O'Connell was interrupted many times. Despite his successes in helping the passage of the Reform Bill and the Slave Emancipation Bill, when it came to matters regarding Ireland, O'Connell's interventions achieved little.

O'Connell and America

While O'Connell was making a stir within British and Irish politics, his fame in anti-slavery was spreading across the Atlantic. In December 1832, a meeting was convened in New York by the Free People of Colour. They paid special tribute to O'Connell and read part of a speech he had made in the previous May in Exeter Hall. They also passed a resolution, stating:

> That we recognize in the Honourable Daniel O'Connell of Ireland, the champion of religious freedom, the uncompromising advocate of universal emancipation, the friend of the oppressed Africans and their descendants, and of the unadulterated rights of man.
>
> That we regret we are unable to make suitable returns for the disinterested friendship that he has manifested towards the cause of liberty and equality, to the terror of traffickers in human flesh, and that we should consider ourselves unworthy of the sympathies of the liberals, and traitors to our cause, if we should with-hold this public expression of our respectful attitude.
>
> That we tender to the Hon. Daniel O'Connell our sincere thanks and respect for his great exertions in the cause of the oppressed – hoping that when his labours of benevolence shall be finished on earth – when the oppressor shall cease from his oppression, he may receive the heavenly reward of Him who holds in his hands the destinies of nations.[149]

A copy of the address was sent to O'Connell.

The energy evident in the British and Irish anti-slavery movements was also apparent in the United States. On 1 January 1831, a newspaper was founded that was to be a major contributor to the cause of American abolition. The *Liberator* was the brainchild of William Lloyd Garrison, a journalist from Massachusetts, who had been born in 1805. In 1825, Garrison had joined the abolition movement, initially as a supporter of colonization; a position he soon came to repudiate. From the first edition of the *Liberator*, it was clear that the paper represented the new, more militant wing of abolition. His sympathy for slaves was so intense that some fellow abolitionists believed that he had to be a black man.[150] Garrison's admiration for O'Connell was unmistakable. In the first edition of his new newspaper, O'Connell's admonishment to American citizens was reprinted :

> Look at the stain in your star-spangled banner that was never struck down in battle. I turn from the American declaration of independence and I tell him that he has declared to God and man a lie, and before God and man I arraign him as a hypocrite.

Garrison went on to lament 'where is the O'Connell of this republic?'[151]

Overall, the American movement after the 1830s was more militant than earlier associations, it favouring immediate and uncompensated abolition. It was led by middle-class professionals although, as in the United Kingdom, it relied on its grass roots – particularly women - for support and finance. Garrison typi-fied the new type of American abolitionist, although he was at the extreme end in terms of his radicalism. Garrison and his supporters were not only interested in ending slavery. They also advocated women's suffrage, labour rights, temper-ance and the rights of Native Americans. In this sense they were close to the Enlightenment ideals of O'Connell. Garrison's uncompromising stand on aboli-tion meant that, unlike O'Connell, he had frequently to face physical danger. In October 1835, for example, his clothes were torn off and he was led through the streets of Boston with a rope around his middle. For his own safety, he was put in jail.[152] A further feature of American abolition after 1830 was the vis-ible involvement of black men, who were self-educated and articulate, including David Walker, Charles Remond Lenox and, later, Frederick Douglass. Whereas the earlier anti-slavery societies had been situated in all parts of the country, increasingly, they were located in the north.[153] Consequently, the anti-slavery debate became framed in terms of the North versus the South. However, the abolitionists did not have full support in the north of the country and so they needed friends elsewhere, particularly in Europe. The ending of slavery in the British Empire as a result of the 1833 legislation, meant that British abolitionists were greatly admired in America.

Garrison visited Britain in 1833. He told his wife, 'my spirit will be elevated and strengthened in the presence of Clarkson, and Wilberforce, and Brougham, and Buxton, and O'Connell'.[154] He had taken with him a copy of a 'Protest' to generate support for those fighting against colonization. His visit greatly increased support for and energized American movement. In December 1833, the first meeting of American Anti-Slavery Society was held in Philadelphia and it declared, 'We shall spare no exertions nor means to bring the whole nation to speedy repentance'. The society wanted immediate and uncompensated aboli-tion.[155]

The desire by American abolitionists to engage with abolitionists in the United Kingdom caused a dilemma for the latter group. Until 1833, the anti-slavery campaigns in Britain and Ireland had focused their energies on ending the slave trade, and then slavery itself, in the British empire. Did they have the right to interfere in the affairs of other nations? Following the passing of the Slavery Emancipation Act, some leading campaigners, including Macauley and Stephen, believed that their societies should now be wound up. Others continued to campaign to end apprenticeship in the West Indies, while also turning their attention to ending the institution of slavery in the United States. The latter angered pro-slavers in the United States. When, in 1834, Thompson visited America, he was refused accommodation in some hotels in New York. His tour had 'raised the spectre of a foreign plot to discuss the country, a theme that would dog the efforts of British abolitionists to promote the cause in the US in the future'.[156] Although O'Connell never visited the United States, after 1833 he continued to fight for the ending of slavery everywhere, whether on plantations in America or in the guise of apprenticeship in the West Indies. As usual, his unequivocal stand made him both loved and loathed in equal measure.

3 'SLAVERY UNDER ANOTHER NAME'

The 1833 Emancipation Act was a considerable victory for the British anti-slavery movement. It became effective on 1 August 1834 and, to mark that day, the London Anti-Slavery Society suggested that thanks be given to God as, 'Surely a day of such vast moment to the welfare of one part of the empire, and to the honour of the whole, ought not to pass unnoticed'.[1] For many supporters, the question was what to do next. In the preceding years, links with American abolitionists had been increasing, and a number had travelled across the Atlantic to seek support within Europe, but especially of Britain and Ireland, where a considerable success had been achieved. On the eve of his visit to the United Kingdom in 1833, William Lloyd Garrison had praised British abolitionists for 'fighting most manfully', adding, 'When I see what they are doing, and read what they write, I blush to think of my own past apathy and mourn in view of my poverty of thought and language.'[2] The support of British and Irish abolitionists was important to American abolitionists, but to what extent were they willing to interfere in slavery outside the British empire? Furthermore, following the passage of the 1833 Emancipation Act, George Stephen, the English abolitionist, believed that many of those who had helped to bring it about 'were weary and exhausted with labour and anxiety' and 'needed both rest and leisure'. A number of the most active had 'avowed that with Emancipation their co-operation ended'. He agreed that the anti-slavery societies should now wind up their activities.[3] O'Connell, however, showed no signs of slowing down. After 1833, he not only campaigned for the ending of the apprenticeship system, increasingly he agitated on behalf of the slaves in the United States. At the same time, he led the Repeal Party within Westminster, where he hoped a reformed Parliament would be more amenable to repeal than previous Parliaments had been.

O'Connell's activities during the passing of the Emancipation Act had showed him to be on the radical end of the anti-slavery movement. In the House of Commons, he had spoken forcefully of his opposition to both the £20,000,000 compensation and the system of apprenticeship, describing the latter as 'slavery under another name'.[4] His determination to oppose slavery in its various guises was evident in a number of other ways. In 1834, the black abolitionist Robert Purvis came to England. When visiting the House of Commons he was introduced to O'Connell, who hesitated in shaking hands with him. When O'Connell was told who Purvis was, O'Connell explained that he never shook hands with an American without first ascertaining his stance on slavery and on the American Colonization Society.[5]

On 1 August 1834, there was a dinner in London to celebrate the ending of slavery in the British empire. The guests included the Earl of Mulgrave, Lord Morpeth, Thomas Spring Rice, Lushington, Buxton and O'Connell. Some 'gentlemen of colour' were also present. O'Connell was one of the people who addressed the meeting, suggesting that his role in slave emancipation was being recognized. Buxton suggested that a celebratory meeting should take place every year on 16 May.[6] However, the celebrations were tempered by the realization that the 1833 Act had not resulted in the ending of slavery. Rather, slavery had been replaced with the apprenticeship system, by which the slaves were required to remain on the plantations, still indentured to their former owners, and to work for free. O'Connell immediately moved to the forefront of the protest to end apprenticeship. In 15 May 1835, he was present at the anniversary meeting of the London Anti-Slavery Society. The main focus of their work was now to be the apprenticeship system, although they also deprecated slavery in the United States. After O'Connell had spoken, there was 'loud applause'.[7] He had criticized the Emancipation Act for having 'taken the lash from master but given it to Stipendiary Magistrate'. Unlike some of his fellow abolitionists, O'Connell regarded the ending of apprenticeship as part of the wider call for the ending of slavery throughout the world. Many of his most forceful criticisms, therefore, were made of slavery in America. In his long speech, he expressed his abhorrence that America:

> which professed the most enlarged principles of liberty, [yet was] refusing to emancipate 2,000,000 of human beings from the degradation and horrors of slavery. The star-spangled banner of America was stained with Negro blood. They refused their slaves even the blessings of education, they enchained their bodies, and they would also enchain their souls. If they suffered this horrible system to continue, they would write themselves liars to their own declarations. He would proclaim them from the place on which he then stood blasphemers of their God and what some of them might think of still greater consequence, violators of their sacred honour.[8]

In what was to become a feature of his speeches throughout the next decade, he selected his fellow Irishmen who lived in America for particular and forceful condemnation:

> he had heard, with grief, that there were many Irishmen in the United States who were opposed to the emancipation of slaves, and that he believed what he heard to be too true, hoped that the wings of the press would convey across the Atlantic, to the

ears of those Irishmen, his detestation of their conduct. He was glad such Irishmen
had left their own country. They were amongst the objects of the curse of St Patrick,
who had banished all poisonous and venomous reptiles from the soil of Ireland.[9]

It was not just in England that O'Connell was making a mark on anti-slavery.
In September 1835, the Glasgow Emancipation Society held a public meeting
for the purpose of paying tribute to O'Connell and making him an Honorary
Member. When he appeared, he was greeted with 'hearty cheers'.[10] O'Connell
was then congratulated for his part in ending slavery in the British colonies. Part
of the reason for the Society honouring O'Connell was to compensate him for
'the contumely and reproach which the opponents of Universal Liberty, have,
with such profusion, showered upon you'. Those who had attacked O'Connell
were identified as being, 'the pro-Slavery press of Republican America, and the
British Anti-Liberal press'.[11] O'Connell responded by saying that much work
remained to be done, and that the 'most ardent' work remaining for him to do
was 'to diffuse over the whole globe a feeling in favour of the suffering Negro'.[12]
He welcomed the fact that the meeting was held in a Baptist Chapel, which
he regarded as being in keeping with the ecumenical nature of the movement.
O'Connell urged everybody to give assistance and 'he saw nothing to prevent
the Ladies from lending their aid'.[13] Inevitably, he criticized the apprenticeship
system and promised to oppose any further compensation being given for its
ending.[14] In regard to being censured in America, he retaliated by saying that,
'He invited the Americans to attack him, but he stood on the platform of humanity, and denounced them as the enemies of human liberty, foul detractors of the
democratic principle which he had cherished throughout his life'.[15] O'Connell
chastised Americans for not upholding the promises made in the Declaration of
Independence as, by not doing so, they 'had violated their honour', a theme he
referred to frequently.[16] He even said that he agreed with Sir Robert Peel – his
long-term adversary – who had categorized American aristocracy as being the
most detestable because it was 'the filthy aristocracy of the human skin'.[17] The
Glasgow Society asked O'Connell to agitate to divide the House on the question
of slavery, which he promised to do.[18]

On 1 February 1836, a large anti-slavery meeting was held in Birmingham,
the home of Joseph Sturge. The proceedings were later published as a pamphlet. The aim was to show the suffering of former slaves under apprenticeship.
According to Sturge, the meeting was enhanced by 'an address of extraordinary
power by Daniel O'Connell, whose fidelity to the cause of the slave never fal-
tered for an instant during his long and stormy public career'.[19] Like O'Connell,
Sturge was a fervent opponent of both apprenticeship and American slavery.[20] In
the following year, Sturge visited the West Indies and confirmed the worst fears
of his fellow abolitionists concerning the apprenticeship system. He reported

that its introduction had been 'a great violation of a solemn compact with the British people: that the bulk of the population still groaned under the worst evils of slavery; and that it was his duty to seek redress at the hands of the British public'.[21] Sturge's harrowing report helped to revive public opinion against apprenticeship.

Demands for the ending of apprenticeship were also made in Ireland. The Hibernian Anti-Slavery Society (HASS) had been founded in September 1837, to replace the Hibernian Negro's Friend Society. Its founding members were Richard Allen, Richard Davis Webb, both Quakers, and James Haughton, a Unitarian. James Haughton had been born in County Carlow in 1795. His parents had been members of the Society of Friends, but Haughton had become a Unitarian in 1834.[22] His politics were liberal, he supporting the 1832 Reform Act and O'Connell's demand for repeal. In addition, he was a committed supporter of temperance. Richard Allen was born in Dublin in 1803. He was a staunch Quaker, who was known for his non-sectarian views. He trained as a lawyer and from a young age showed a concern for humanitarian causes. He was Secretary of the HAAS, and of the Hibernian British India Society and the Hibernian Temperance Society. In 1842, Garrison's *Liberator* referred to him thus: 'Amongst the great men of this age and nation, there are few so deserving of the approbation of the Christian world'.[23] Richard Davis Webb, also a Quaker, was born in 1805. He was a successful publisher, allowing his printing business to be used to help fellow abolitionists. He was also involved in a number of reform issues.[24] Webb was initially suspicious of O'Connell's motives for supporting abolition, but he admired his skills as an orator.[25]

O'Connell, busy in the British Parliament, kept a distance from the day-to-day activities of the Irish society, although he spoke at some of its larger meetings.[26] Like O'Connell, the HAAS had opposed the compensation given to slave-owners. It also opposed apprenticeship, which had 'retained servitude without wages – merely transferring the whip from the Master to the Magistrate'. It argued that although the total abolition of slavery had been promised in 1833, the actual legislation had proved disappointing and 'hope found no refuge in its delusive and vicious enactments'. A speech made by the second Marquis of Sligo in February 1836 had shown how 'lamentable' the system was, and this had been confirmed by the research of Joseph Sturge.[27] Consequently, the Irish anti-slavery societies drew up 'a solemn Protest against it'.[28]

In September 1837, the Hibernian Anti-Slavery Society issued an 'Address to the People of Ireland'. They made the appeal with 'feelings of deep and bitter disappointment', on the grounds that:

> concurrent and incontrovertible testimony, derived from both official and private sources, demonstrate that every principle of humanity and justice is flagrantly and systematically outraged by the general treatment of the Colonial Negro population,

for whose emancipation our nation has liberally paid their Masters Twenty Million Sterling, with interest.[29]

In addition to opposing the apprenticeship system, they disagreed with the punishment of women by the whip and the treadmill. The Irish abolitionists also criticized the American President, Martin Van Buren, for having said that he would suppress the abolitionists, pointing out that the movement was continuing to grow in United States, there now being a total of 1,006 societies.[30] The resolutions of the Dublin Society were read at the meeting of the Anti-Slavery Society in London in November 1837. O'Connell, who had been asked to speak at the meeting, said that despite compensation of £20,000,000 being paid, former slaves in the West Indies were in a worse condition than before the payment. He promised that although it was his intention to support the newly elected Whig government, 'He would never support them in a measure so iniquitous as that of endeavoring to maintain the apprenticeship contract, which the planters themselves so completely abrogated'.[31] Following O'Connell's speech, the delegates then walked in procession from Exeter Hall, in the Strand in north London, to Downing Street, where a number of the delegates were invited into the Prime Minister's residence. There, they had a 'cordial' meeting. Lord Melbourne informed them that to interfere with the recent legislation would be very serious, but that he was 'fully conscious of the extent of influence represented by the delegates present'.[32]

The activities of the Hibernian Anti-Slavery Society intensified in 1838, with large meetings being held every month. The main focus was with ending apprenticeship.[33] In March, a large public meeting was held in the Rotunda in Dublin for the purpose of drawing up a petition on this subject. At the invitation of the Central Negro Emancipation Committee, they agreed to send three delegates to meeting in London on 27 March.[34] Those who attended the April meeting of HAAS in Dublin included the Mayor, Councillor O'Hagan, Torrens McCullagh Torrens and O'Connell. The meeting commenced by expressing its 'heartfelt regret' that a number of Irish Members of Parliament had not supported them more on issues to do with abolition. When O'Connell was asked to speak, he was greeted with 'great applause'. He started by stating that, 'I have long been the advocate of the Negro's freedom, and I look back to the zealous, though untalented efforts I have made upon their behalf'.[35] He pointed out that he had voted against the measure to give slaveholders £20,000,000, which he sarcastically referred to as 'the splendid generosity of the British nation ... for the single stimulating motive of humanity and benevolence'. He added that they had not got value for this money, but that, 'The British nation has been swindled'. O'Connell was particularly appalled by the condition of women apprentices, and the following week, he was going to support a motion in Parliament for the total emancipation of females in the West Indies. He hoped that all Irish members would vote for his, and Eardley Wilmot's, Bill to end slavery altogether. O'Connell concluded by reminding his audience of Ireland's anti-slavery history, stating 'No vessel for the purposes of the slave trade ever sailed from an Irish port' – whatever hardships people and merchants had endured 'they never stained their souls by the inhuman traffic in Negro slaves'. Daniel's son, Morgan, was then asked to speak, but he declined to do so. O'Connell reassured the meeting that his son would vote with him in the House of Commons on matters to do with slavery. The meeting ended with vote of thanks to the Marquis of Sligo.[36]

It was not only Irish men who were active in the abolition movement. The Dublin Ladies' Association had been formed in 1837 from the Hibernian Negro's Friend Society. In that year, under the direction of Catharine Elizabeth Alma, they issued two appeals to 'the females of Ireland' condemning the apprentice system. It warned that slavery had not disappeared, even though it 'may attire herself in the gay garb of a pretended freedom; or she may array herself in the mock garment of a legalized apprenticeship'. Unlike the male members of the HAAS, the Ladies' Association wanted to make a direct appeal to Queen Victoria, 'the youthful and philanthropic Sovereign of these realms'. In doing so, they believed the cause would be strengthened by women pleading to another woman on behalf of suffering women.[37] They again appealed to Irish women, to abstain from using sugar from the West Indies, pointing out:

> It ill becomes us, dear friends, the daughters of a country whose history glows with one perpetual struggle for liberty, whose poets have breathed its inspirations until the very breeze that wafts around our island seemed laden with the sound, and whose bards of other days touched this sweet chord so loud, so feelingly, that all our land responded to its tones.[38]

They concluded by asking their countrywomen 'to exercise that influence, which is so seldom and unacknowledged, with the other sex'.[39]

In April 1838, the Dublin Ladies' Anti-Slavery Society issued a further appeal to their friends and countrywomen. It berated Irish Members of Parliament who had not done more to bring apprenticeship to an end, saying:

> let us, the Irish of the nineteenth century, blush at our disgraceful position; for, as a people, we are identified with those who, notwithstanding all their boasted love of freedom here, by their recently recorded votes in the Commons on the anti-slavery question, added another link to the fetters of the friendless and heart-broken slave, and affixed a stain on the hitherto unsullied honour of their native country.[40]

They said that these men had not acted as 'the representatives of the wishes and feelings of the Irish people', adding a stinging rebuke:

Were we the mothers we should blush for them – were we the wives or mothers we should be slow to acknowledge the tie of kindred; for, surely such recreant conduct has broadly marked them out as the ignoble portion of a brave and freedom-seeking people.[41]

They ended by asking for more exertions, including numerous petitions, so that 'we may yet retrieve our shattered character'.[42] The appeal appeared to have succeeded. In 1838, 75,000 Irish women signed a petition to Queen Victoria in which they stated that apprenticeship was worse than slavery.[43]

In 1838, a Bill to end apprenticeship was introduced into Parliament. The outcome remained uncertain. The abolitionists made a direct appeal to the government. On 27 March, just before the issue was debated, 364 men met at Exeter Hall and then marched to the House of Commons.[44] Sir George Strickland proposed, and Joseph Pease introduced, a motion for apprenticeship to end on 1 August. Because Buxton was no longer a Member of Parliament, it fell to O'Connell and Lushington to argue for abolition.[45] During the subsequent debates, William Gladstone made a defence of the planters.[46] O'Connell's closing argument for immediate emancipation was described by Sturge as being 'admirable'. In it, O'Connell justified the resolution on the grounds of justice and humanity:

You have heard within the House the noise occasioned by the congregated Dissenters who besiege your doors. And who are they that have raised this cry of immediate emancipation? Are they idle and violent agitators, who delight in the convulsions if the State and disregard social order ...? No! They are the steadiest, soberest, most industrious, and most respectable men, differing from me in their religious form, but holding out in their conduct the happy spectacle of religious zeal united with religious charity. They are men who do not care for distance of country or difference of clime, but risk their health as scattered missionaries of humanity, and have travelled at their own expense to the remotest corners of the globe, in order to indulge the noble gratification of doing the work of their God by benefiting his creatures.[47]

His plea fell on deaf ears and the motion was defeated by fifty-four votes. Undaunted, the campaign continued and a new motion was introduced into Parliament asking for the immediate ending of apprenticeship. This time it was introduced by Sir Eardley Wilmot and the Hon. Charles Pelham Villiers. Whilst these debates were taking place in the United Kingdom, within the West Indies the former slaves and their supporters were undertaking a campaign of passive resistance. This climaxed on 25 July 1838, when Dr Jean Baptiste Phillipe, the first black member of the Council in Trinidad and Tobago, introduced a motion for the ending of apprenticeship. It was successful. Concurrent with this, the Slavery Amendment Act was being debated in the British Parliament, finally passing on 1 August 1838. It had succeeded by only three votes and, to the end, the Whig government had opposed it. O'Connell, who did not want to offend the Whig government with whom he had been in alliance since 1835, asked Irish members to vote according to their conscience.[48] Alarmed by the agitation taking place on their behalf in Britain, and the disquieting effect this was having on the black population, other colonial assemblies, including those of Barbados, Grenada, St Vincent, St Kitts, Nevis, Montserrat and the Virgin Islands, joined Trinidad and Tobago by declaring that their slaves would be set free on 1 August 1838.[49] In June 1839, in consequence of an Order in Council, Negro apprenticeship was abolished in the British island of Mauritius, resulting in the freeing of 25,000 slaves.[50] This marked the complete ending of slavery in the British West Indies: a victory achieved as result of fifty years of activities by the anti-slavery movement.

The ending of apprenticeship was received with joy by British and Irish abolitionists. James Haughton, who was in London for the occasion, spoke of it as a 'great victory'. He was aware that O'Connell been caught between supporting the Whigs and opposing apprenticeship, and informed his brother William that, in his opinion, O'Connell:

> ... is I believe an honest man, more candid and open than most great men; he is received here with enthusiasm, but as is the case at home, some mean minds cannot believe in his integrity, although his whole life has been devoted to man's freedom.[51]

To celebrate the end of apprenticeship, O'Connell was invited by Sturge to speak at a dinner in Birmingham.[52] O'Connell wanted to make his appearance at the occasion conditional on the launch of a new crusade to end universal slavery, but, in particular, slavery in the United States. His advice to Sturge was unequivocal:

> ... frame your announcement in such a way as to enable us to begin the work with the vile and sanguinary slaveholders of republican America. I want to be *directly* at them. No more side-wind attack: firing directly at the hull, as the seamen say, is my plan ... We will move Britain and all Europe against the vile union of republicanism and slavery; and I hope soon to see the day when not a single American will be received in civilized society unless he belongs to an anti-slavery union or body.[53]

The ending of apprenticeship, therefore, in O'Connell's view was to be succeeded by a campaign that took anti-slavery issues beyond the British empire with the United States as its main focus. O'Connell, who had been such a dominant figure in the movement in the preceding decade, was seeking to refocus the energies of the movements, with himself clearly in the vanguard.

O'Connell was not the only abolitionist who desired that their work should continue following the ending of apprenticeship. In 1839, the British and Foreign Anti-Slavery Society was formed in London. As its name implied, from the outset they were concerned with international slavery, rather than merely slavery within the British empire. Its founders included Thomas Clarkson, a veteran of the movement, who had also been associated with earlier societies, namely, the Committee for the Abolition of the Slave Trade (later the Society for the Abolition of the Slave Trade), founded in 1787, and the Society for the Mitigation and Gradual Abolition of Slavery throughout the British Dominions, founded in 1807.[54] Sturge was a founding member, as was O'Connell.[55] One of their first acts was to organize an international convention to be held in London the following year. Slavery in America was not their only interest. In July 1839, the British India Society was formed for 'the betterment of fellow subjects in India'. The inaugural meeting was presided over by Lord Brougham. O'Connell was one of the main speakers and he 'pleaded the cause with eloquence and power' on behalf of Indian slaves.[56]

Repeal to Repeal

Concurrently with his anti-slavery activities, O'Connell continued to campaign of behalf of Ireland. He was the leader of the third-largest party within Westminster and therefore could not be ignored, but his attempts to bring measures for the benefit of Ireland met with little success. On 22 April 1834, under pressure from his fellow repealers, he brought before Parliament a motion for the repeal of the Act of Union and the establishment of a domestic legislature in Ireland. He presented it in the form of requesting an enquiry into the state of Ireland under the Union. The opposition was led by another Irishman, and fellow anti-slaver, Thomas Spring Rice. In a speech of six hours' duration, Spring Rice started by informing the Commons:

> ... The question which we are really called upon to decide is, not the means by which the Union was carried, but whether it is expedient, with a view to the general interests of the empire at large, and of Ireland in particular, to repeal that Union. All the flourishes with which the Motion has been introduced, touching the events of past times, are but so much dust, which the learned Member has endeavoured to throw in our eyes to blind us, and to prevent our contemplating the real subject before us. That question is not the history of past times, but the real interest of the people of Ireland, and of the empire at large in the year 1834.[57]

Due to 'an indisposition', O'Connell was not present at the debate. His motion was eventually defeated, as O'Connell had expected, but the debate had been watched by the King, whose dislike of O'Connell was palpable. In a private letter to Lord Spencer written in April 1834, he stated that he had received the report on 'Mr O'Connell's introduction for a repeal of the Union, and as His Majesty does not take any interest in its success or that of any of his undertakings, he rejoices to learn that his speech upon this occasion was so bad and tiresome, although he may pity the sane portion of his audience'.[58] O'Connell's championship of issues such as parliamentary reform and anti-slavery had not diminished the dislike of him in Parliament – or elsewhere.

In 1834, both the Whigs and the Tories were in power briefly, but both administrations proved to be unstable with neither able to establish strong government. Following a series of discussions between O'Connell and the Whig Party in February 1835, an informal agreement known as the Litchfield House Compact was reached. In return for various concessions, which O'Connell referred to as 'justice for Ireland', he gave up his demand for repeal. O'Connell, however, always denied that he had stopped wanting a repeal of the Union and he denied going over to the Whigs, repeatedly claiming that they had come over to him.[59] O'Connell's decision disappointed some of his followers in Ireland. He was aware of these criticisms, explaining 'I may be blamed by some for supporting the present Administration instead of looking for the Repeal'.[60] He also informed his confidant, Patrick Fitzpatrick, 'I know of my own personal knowledge that the Government are determined to do all they can for Ireland'. He pointed to a number of reforms that had been promised, including standing up to the Orange Order, promoting Catholics of talent, abolishing tithes, and stopping the practice of jury packing. The recent appointment of a Catholic Attorney-General, the first for two centuries, whose 'ears will be open to the complaints of the Catholic Clergy as well as the Catholic laity upon every act of oppression and tyranny practiced against the poorest of the people', had provided O'Connell with the good intentions of the Whigs.[61] O'Connell further justified his actions by saying that if he had continued to campaign for repeal, the only outcome would have been to intensify the opposition of the Orange Order.[62] Because of their hatred for him, O'Connell and his family were being forced to fight six contested elections – each at enormous expense. These contests meant that O'Connell was constantly short of money, but he disclosed to Fitzpatrick, 'I sometimes almost despair. I must, I think, mortgage perhaps all my family property but do not breathe a word of this to anyone ... I will spend my last shilling in the struggle'.[63]

Regardless of O'Connell's uncertainties about his dwindling popularity in Ireland, he believed that he was gaining in popularity in England, 'it is only now that the people of England are beginning to understand me. I am growing exceedingly popular'.[64] O'Connell used his new position with the Whig Party to become more involved with a number of radical issues in Britain. In 1835, he campaigned in number of towns in Britain on the question of a reform of the House of Lords. In Manchester, 30,000 people, most of whom were tradesmen, turned out to meet him. In the evening he attended a dinner in his honour, with 300 people, 'and if it could hold three times as many it seems to me there would have been enough to fill it. I never was so well received in Ireland'.[65] However, being in alliance with the Whigs and Radicals did not diminish the negative way in which O'Connell was viewed by some of the press, and it intensified the dislike of the Tory press. The *Annual Register* offered its own explanation of O'Connell's treatment:

> He received dinners and preached his doctrines, at Manchester, Newcastle, Edinburgh and Glasgow ... Excepting those who were attracted by curiosity, all the respectable classes of society, even the middle ranks, kept aloof from is banquets and exhortations. Feasted and applauded by the ignorant rabble ... his language was excellently well adapted to gratify their prejudice and inflame their passions, but instead of being fitted to convince and convert the rational and sober-minded, it only excited disgust and some degree of alarm.[66]

O'Connell's unpopularity was evident in other ways. In 1835, there was an attempt to get him expelled from Brooks's, the London gentleman's club that had been founded for Whig supporters. The matter was discussed widely in the British press, with many favouring his expulsion.[67]

The antagonism of *The Times* to O'Connell continued. In an editorial dated 27 January 1836, the paper likening his coming to London as being similar to that of a 'pestilence' or a 'hostile invader'. It also criticized 'his tyranny' and referred to him as a 'foul-mouthed mountebank' who had done nothing to help Ireland. Nevertheless, they recognized that he was, at that time, 'a personage important to this country, and interesting as a subject of consideration just at present, in the exact proportion in which he possess an influence over the British government, and a consequent bearing upon the legislation of the empire'. Additionally, the paper criticized the Whigs whom, they believed, had betrayed Protestant England by allying with O'Connell.[68] Only a few months later, an editorial opened with 'We return to the disagreeable but necessary task of noticing Mr Daniel O'Connell', and after referring to him as an 'arch-vilifier', went on to outline 'the utter extinction of whatever influence he once possessed in England'.[69] In May, the paper included a long letter from an unknown author, 'M. Burke', who claimed he had followed O'Connell's career for decades and want to show what a charlatan '*King* Dan' was. One of his criticisms related to O'Connell's support for Garrison and his attacks on America, which were 'constant, unwarrantable and unmanly'.[70] In the same year, the paper published a series of nineteen letters written by 'Runnymede' that made fun of Whig supporters, including O'Connell. The letters had been written by the Tory politician Benjamin Disraeli who disliked O'Connell intensely and had even challenged Morgan O'Connell to fight a duel on his father's behalf.[71]

The Times had long been opposed to O'Connell's role in abolition and frequently used it as a vehicle for attacking him. Following an anti-slavery meeting in Exeter Hall on 23 November 1837, the paper described some of those present as 'humanity-mongers who agitate merely with the view of preserving the profits of their quack practice'. It then made a lengthy attack on O'Connell:

> That such persons as these still exist may be easily proved; for some 'auxiliary delegates' of this slavery speculation have actually invited Mr Daniel O'Connell to speak to-day at Exeter Hall! *Similes similibus gaudent.* [sic] The manner in which Mr O'Connell fleeces the unhappy peasantry of Ireland – his extortion of the penny from the ragged man, and the half-penny from the starving man – the blood that has been shed in consequence of his accursed agitation in Ireland, – are known to everybody. And yet *he,* even DANIEL, is to be the great gun to-day at Exeter Hall, – the thing that is
> 'At once to stink and shine'
> We rejoice that these 'auxiliaries' of the hero of 'deaths' heads and cross bones' have so soon appeared in their real character. We doubt, however, whether their speculation in a pecuniary point of view will turn out as well as they expect. A vast proportion of the subscriptions for anti-slavery purposes come from females; and that the ladies have taken the alarm at the notion of such a person as O'Connell being obtruded upon them to-day, is sufficiently manifest by the following placard, which we are told has been very extensively circulated:
> ENGLISH WOMEN!

The paper went on to claim O'Connell had made a speech in Ireland in September 1824, published in the 'Catholic Miscellany', in which he had ridiculed English morality, even claiming that many Englishwomen had children after only a month of marriage. *The Times* appealed to all English women not to 'consent to be insulted by Mr O'Connell, or sanction his speaking on the platform of Exeter Hall. Call upon your husbands, fathers, brothers, to shield you from this insult'.[72]

It was not just the conservative *Times* that disliked O'Connell. His fellow Irishman and former repeal colleague, Feargus O'Connor, frequently attacked him for being insufficiently radical. O'Connor, a former repeal MP, had become one of the leaders of militant Chartism. He dismissed O'Connell's frequent criticisms of the compensation paid to slave-owners, by asking 'where is the value for the Irish Rent?'[73] This was a reference to the fact that O'Connell continued to draw much of his income from his Irish supporters, many of whom were poor, and it was a criticism frequently made by his enemies. In 1837, during the general election campaign, O'Connell stood for Dublin. A petition had been circulated asking voters not to support O'Connell, or the Liberal candidate Robert Hutton. O'Connell narrowly defeated his conservative opponent, but one consequence of having to contest these elections was that he was constantly short of money.[74]

Sections of the British press and a number of his own countrymen may have despised O'Connell, but he had aroused curiosity in an unexpected quarter. On 21 February 1838, when the apprenticeship campaign was reaching its climax, Daniel O'Connell met the young Queen Victoria at a royal levee. They each appeared excited by the meeting. The eighteen-year-old woman noted in her journal after the encounter that he was 'the only person who I wanted to see', adding that he was 'very tall, rather large, has a remarkably good-tempered countenance, small features, small, clever, blue eyes, and very like his caricatures'. She also observed that he was wearing a wig, something he had taken to doing as he got older. She was captivated with her Irish subject, and it was mutual. The enchantment proved to be short-lived. Only six months later, O'Connell insulted the American Ambassador in London over his support for slavery. In the Queen's eyes, O'Connell was now a political liability who was damaging Britain's relationship with America.[75]

While O'Connell was proving an irritant within Britain and Ireland, he was achieving heroic status elsewhere. In August 1838, there were celebrations in Haiti to mark 'Emancipation Day' in 1804, the day it had gained independence and had become the first black republic to do so. A toast proposed by Jules Anni-bal Courtois was to:

> Lord Brougham and Daniel O'Connell. Friends of Liberty and universal emancipa-tion, they have valiantly fought with slavery and its partisans – and triumphed. They have nothing more to do but to celebrate their victory and receive the applause which their noble efforts have earned'.[76]

At the same time, O'Connell's stature was continuing to rise in the US, includ-ing amongst former slaves. In 1838, the narrative account of James Williams was published. The title page included an extract of a speech made by O'Connell in 1833:

> Oh the slave, who toils from the rising sun to sundown – who
> labors in the cultivation of a crop whose fruits he may never reap –
> who comes home at nightfall weary, faint, and sick of heart, to find
> in his hut creatures that are to run in the same career with himself,
> – will you not tell him of a period when his toil shall be at an end?
> Will you not give him a hope for his children? [77]

Experienced American abolitionists continued to find O'Connell's words inspirational. Edmund Morris Davis, a leading campaigner in Philadelphia and son-in-law of James and Lucretia Mott, after reading an anti-slavery appeal made by O'Connell to the people of Britain, asked, 'Can it be possible that anyone, who reads and ponders on it, will consent to remain idle?'[78] Not all who heard O'Connell were as impressed. His outspokenness was starting to concern some Irish-Americans. In February 1838, five of his admirers in Philadelphia wrote to him requesting that he tone down his attacks on American slavery. The request fell on deaf ears.[79]

By the end of the 1830s, O'Connell was growing sceptical of ever achieving justice for Ireland, despite having served for ten years in the British Parliament. Nor had the 1832 parliamentary reform act or his alliance with the Whig Party brought much lasting benefit to the Irish people. In 1838, he launched a series of letters to the people of Ireland. In them, he made a number of demands, which included reducing the power of the Orange Order; an impartial system of justice; abolition of the tithe and more equitable voting rights for Irish people. O'Connell warned that if Parliament refused or delayed in redressing these grievances, he would agitate to get a restoration of the Irish legislature.[80] These letters marked the first step in O'Connell's relaunch of his repeal association. At the end of the year, O'Connell undertook a tour of Ireland to agitate for Irish equality. Simultaneously, he was assuring the Whigs that he would continue to support them.[81] While getting a new campaign underway in Ireland, O'Connell was also causing upset in the transatlantic debate on slavery.

The Stevenson Affair

By the end of the 1830s, O'Connell had become one of the most famous transatlantic opponents of slavery; at the same time, he remained one of the most controversial. This became evident at the end of 1838, when O'Connell became embroiled in a controversy with the American Ambassador to Britain, Andrew Stevenson. Newspapers on both sides of the Atlantic reported the incident, but with an increasingly partisan twist, which made it difficult to tease out the truth. The resulting events were considered of sufficient importance for both the British Foreign Office and the United States Congress to offer opinions on it. Amongst other things, the episode showed how polarized the debate between pro-slavery and abolition had become.

The occasion of the incident was in August 1838 when O'Connell, together with Joseph Sturge and Dr Stephen Lushington, spoke in Birmingham to mark the fourth anniversary of apprenticeship. Even before he arrived at the meeting, O'Connell had informed Sturge of his desire to set about ending universal slavery, with a particular focus on the United States.[82] The plans for the Birmingham meeting were lavish, commencing with 3,000 schoolchildren processing through the town, observed by a crowds of approximately 13,000 people. In the evening, O'Connell joined a number of eminent abolitionists, including Sturge and Lushington, in the Town Hall.

During his speech, Dr Lushington criticized Americans, who prided themselves on their liberty yet continued with slavery. O'Connell was the final speaker of the evening. His appearance earlier in the day had been greeted with cheers.[83] He also spoke about American slavery, his core message being that Americans, including even the venerated George Washington, were hypocrites for allowing slavery. Still criticizing America, he added:

> I believe their very Ambassador here is a slave-breeder; one of those beings who rear
> up slaves for the purpose of traffic. Is it possible that America would send here a man
> who traffics in blood, and who is a disgrace to human nature? .. I was going into the
> House of Commons the other evening when a tall, gentlemanly looking man, yellow
> and lank, addressed me.

The 'stranger', to whom O'Connell referred was from Alabama, and had wanted to go into the House of Commons. When O'Connell had asked if he was a slave-owner, he had replied 'yes', to which O'Connell had responded, 'Then I will have nothing to do with you. That is what we should all do. Universal Europe should proclaim that any man who is the holder of slaves is degraded in his moral character, and not fit to associate with honest men'. He then gave the stranger some examples of American cruelty to slaves. The stranger was, in fact, the American Ambassador to Britain. Accounts of O'Connell's speech in Birmingham were reported in a number of British newspapers. His speech and the subsequent dispute were then reprinted in many American newspapers, from New Orleans to New England, although interpretations of the incident varied greatly.[84]

Andrew Stevenson, Ambassador to Britain and a wealthy landowner and slaveholder in Virginia (not Alabama), had been the target of O'Connell's attack. By the 1830s, as the demand for slaves rose in the south-west, some areas, including Virginia, had acquired a reputation of raising slaves in order to sell them. The 'slave-breeders' had been a frequent target of O'Connell's scorn.[85] Stevenson had been appointed Ambassador in June 1836, but even before his arrival at St James's Court in London, the British government had been aware of his views on slavery. Henry Fox, the British Minister in Washington, had warned Lord Palmerston, the Foreign Secretary:

> Mr Stevenson is a citizen of Virginia, and himself a large slave proprietor; and he
> appears, I am very sorry to say, to partake fully of the irritable and excited feeling,
> which are daily beginning more and more the slave holding citizens of America, with
> reference to that calamitous subject.[86]

In 1808, the United States had banned the slave trade, but unlike many European countries, they had refused to allow a right of search on any of its vessels. Palmerston had hoped that Stevenson might assist him in negotiating a mutual right of search treaty, but the American had made it clear that he fully supported his country's opposition to the right of search.[87] In August 1839, the *Leeds Mercury* (an admirer of O'Connell) reported on correspondence between Palmerston and 'the minister of the United States in this country (Mr Stevenson)'. The paper concluded:

> It appears that Lord Palmerston, on behalf of the government, has altogether refused
> to enter into a proposed convention by which American slaves in vessels driven by
> stress of weather, or otherwise, on shorein [*sic*] out colonies, would have been pre-

vented from acquiring that freedom which is identified with British soil. The tone of the correspondence on the side of Lord Palmerston is as dignified and truly British as on Mr Stevenson's it is insidious and unworthy the representative of a free people.[88]

Therefore, even before his much-publicized encounter with O'Connell, Stevenson had indicated his personal and professional support for the institution of slavery.

When Stevenson read the press accounts of O'Connell's speech, he was furious.[89] Assisted by his friend, General James Hamilton of South Carolina, he put in place plans to challenge the sixty-three-year-old O'Connell to a duel if the reports were not denied.[90] The dispute was immediately carried out in the public eye. Stevenson wrote to O'Connell on 9 August demanding to know if the report in the *Spectator* was correct. The following day, O'Connell responded saying that he had 'no hesitation in saying that the paragraph you have selected is not a correct report of what I said on that occasion ... and having another report since, as well as from distinct recollection, I repeat that the report is not correct'. O'Connell, while not apologizing, appeared to be providing the Ambassador with a way to 'pursue or drop the matter as he pleased'.[91] The differences in the two reports were relatively minor and of inference, rather than substance – O'Connell said that rather than Stevenson '*is* a disgrace to human nature' he had said '*would be* a disgrace'. Stevenson responded to O'Connell the following day, saying:

> presuming that you intended your reply as a disavowal of the offensive expressions contained in that part of your reported speech which has allusion to myself, and to which your attention was called, I am satisfied with the answer you have given. As an incorrect report of your speech has been made public through the press, I beg to inform you that I deem it due to myself that the correspondence which has taken place should also be published.

Stevenson then arranged for the correspondence to appear in the London *Times* and the *Morning Chronicle* on 15 September.[92] Publicly, O'Connell remained unrepentant, continuing to attack American slaveholders and slave-breeders in the British press.[93] Possibly, O'Connell realized that this disagreement was worth exploiting and he was, therefore, reluctant to apologize.[94]

The interest of the public in this affair was clear, although the responses were polarized along pro- and anti-slavery lines. Some of Stevenson's supporters felt that he had been too restrained, but rejoiced that he had stood up to O'Connell publicly. The American Minister in Paris congratulated Stevenson on the grounds that 'You have fairly put the braggadocio down'.[95] A similar sentiment was expressed in the Massachusetts paper, the *New Bedford Mercury,* which announced, 'the agitator was compelled to eat his own words as reluctantly as Bottom was compelled to swallow the leeks in the play, to the great amusement, no doubt, of the English public'.[96] An alternative view was offered in a poster that included O'Connell's original speech and his subsequent correspondence.[97] The poster, which sympathized with O'Connell, averred that Stevenson had been easily satisfied. It pointed out that for some years Virginia had made its money by breeding slaves for other states, providing examples of some adverts. It closed with a letter from O'Connell, sent from Derrynane and dated 13 September 1838, to the editor of *Morning Chronicle,* which it titled, 'Mr O'Connell's Vindication'. In it, O'Connell informed the editor that the correspondence which the paper had published – at Stevenson's insistence – had been, 'almost one-sided correspondence which took place between us'. O'Connell asked for the editor's courtesy in inserting his remarks. The letter accused Stevenson of having:

> with the gravity of a diplomat, put to use the single question, viz., whether the report was correct or not; it being thus impossible that he should get any other reply to that question than the report was not correct ... no apology had been called for or made ... But as I made Mr Stevenson no apology, he determined on making one to himself, and accordingly he wrote a second letter, and in it assumed that I had made a disavowal of offensive expressions. Now this was either fancy or diplomacy, I care not which; but it was as gratuitous on his part as the reality would have been unnecessary on mine.

O'Connell challenged Stevenson to disavow:

> if he pleases, a thing most offensive in the sight of man and in the presence of God ... That it is which stains the character of the American slave-holder and leaves the breeders of slaves the most despicable of human beings ... My sole object in my speech in Birmingham, and my present object is, to rouse the attention of England and of Europe to all that is cruel, criminal, and in every sense of the word, infamous, in this system of negro slavery in North America. My deliberate conviction is that until the system is abolished, no American slave-holder ought to be received on a footing of equality by any of the civilized inhabitants of Europe.[98]

It was not only in Britain that the disagreement received attention. O'Connell's actions were condemned by pro-slavery newspapers in the United States. The American press had been keeping an eye on O'Connell for some time. Following a speech he had made in Exeter Hall in May 1835, there had been some anti-Irish riots in a number of cities, and O'Connell's actions had been blamed by those who instigated them.[99] In relation to the Stevenson affair, the *New York Gazette* accused O'Connell of making slanderous assertions.[100] The anti-abolition *New York Herald* made a number of outrageous assertions of its own. In an unfounded personal attack on O'Connell, they described him as a 'heartless, unprincipled, cowardly wretch', and his response to Stevenson as 'abusive filth', adding:

> We would advice O'Connell not to make a tour of the United States, for the sake of his numerous children and concubines. Will our readers believe that this same moral rascal, O'Connell, once made a public boast that he never spared a man in his anger, or a woman in his lust. His wife once, in order to shame him, collected together six young women, whom he had seduced, and employed them about his house in various menial capacities.[101]

In the Southern States, papers including the *Richmond Enquirer* and the Washington-based *National Intelligencer* gave full coverage of the unfolding saga. They were overwhelmingly sympathetic to Stevenson and angry with O'Connell for his attack on the slaveholding states. The *Richmond Enquirer* was especially keen to come to the defence of Stevenson and did so by delivering a philippic on O'Connell, which started by affirming, 'We have no expressions adequate to describe the indignation we feel'.[102] It continued:

> Nothing can exceed the gross prejudice which this man has conceived against the Southern States, unless it be the infamous calumny which he has uttered against Virginia, and the course language in which he has given it utterance ... we pronounce Daniel O'Connell's attack on the Virginia character to be a wanton and an infamous libel.[103]

The paper condemned O'Connell's character, pointing to the fact that he took 'rent' from the people of Ireland, averring 'No apology he can make; no service he can render to poor old Ireland, can conceal the meanness of the transaction'.[104] For the next three months, the paper provided full coverage of the incident, publishing O'Connell's correspondence to prove what a scoundrel he was, and Stevenson's correspondence, which they believed justified his actions.[105] It also included a letter from James Hamilton, a friend of Stevenson who had been in London during the incident, attacking O'Connell. Its language was unrestrained, describing O'Connell as being 'as false to his friends, as he is mean and treacherous to his enemies' and the 'most copious fountain of low vituperation anywhere to be found in her majesty's dominions'.[106] Regarding challenging O'Connell to a duel, Hamilton stated that O'Connell was 'beneath the notice of a gentleman ... but, both Mr Stevenson and myself, knows what Virginia asks and expects of her sons', and they would have 'endeavored in this contingency to have made ourselves as *ugly customers* as possible, to the immaculate patriot and his disciples'. Moreover, if O'Connell had been killed in the duel, he believed:

> ... my escape would have been connived at by the English people; for, I should have entitled myself by this act to their everlasting gratitude, for expelling *in self defence*, one of the greatest pests with which, in His inscrutable wisdom, the Almighty has been pleased to inflict on the British Empire – a man, who, having extorted rent money from the poor deluded paupers of his own country, is selling for a large-sized lump of Whig patronage in Ireland, the interests of a people he has dishonored and betrayed. [107]

The *Charlottesville Advocate* offered a different perspective on the actions of Stevenson and his friends. Describing what had happened as 'exceedingly small business', it averred, 'Ambassadors are sent abroad to take care of the interests of their country, not to fight duels with unprincipled blackguards'.[108] A similar interpretation was offered by the *New Bedford Mercury*, 'A man, who like

O'Connell, has been voted by a large majority of the House of Commons a calumniator, is beneath the notice of a gentleman'.[109] The pro-slavery *New York Star* viewed the incident as damaging to the Irish-American vote, claiming 'Van Buren would have recalled Stevenson the moment he found him picking a quarrel with Dan, and thus endangering his alien voters in this country'.[110] The attention paid to this incident demonstrated that O'Connell had become a serious irritant to those who supported slavery in the United States.

The unfolding events were followed by the two main American abolitionist newspapers, the *Emancipator* and the *Liberator*. The former produced 'an elegant broadsheet' containing all of the correspondence and 'O'Connell's triumphant vindication'. It was accompanied by an engraving of the Liberator. The cost was $1 for a hundred copies, or 6c. for a single. The paper urged 'friends of freedom' everywhere to buy them, but especially 'sons of Erin'.[111] In regard to the correspondence, Garrison opined, 'No upright man can peruse it without feeling a thrill of horror shoot through his veins; for its language is that of a ruffian and an assassin'.[112] The attacks on O'Connell drew support from an unlikely source. Hamilton's description of O'Connell as 'the Irish Caliban' even led the British Foreign Office, rarely sympathetic to O'Connell, to express concern that the accusations in the letter were too extreme.[113] Undaunted, Hamilton wrote a further letter accusing O'Connell of lying, prompting the *Liberator* to ask 'Sons of the Green Isle! What say you to the abuse of your friend and countryman?'[114] Hamilton's letters continued to cause outrage in abolitionist newspapers, with the *Liberator,* the *Emancipator,* and the *New York Evangelist* in the vanguard of defending O'Connell's integrity.[115]

The Stevenson incident was discussed in the American Congress at the end of 1838. Even American newspapers were surprised by this development. A Philadelphia paper referred to it as 'a very remarkable motion, and one that will not fail to create a sensation in Great Britain'. It had been brought before Congress by John Quincy Adams, a former President, who was known for his anti-slavery views. He asked for the papers relating to the Stevenson–O'Connell affair to be put before a committee of the House.[116] His purpose was to ascertain:

> Whether Andrew Stevenson, envoy extraordinary and minister plenipotentiary from the United States at London, is or has recently been engaged in a public newspaper controversy involving his personal integrity, and the honour of this country, whose representative he is, with Daniel O'Connell, a member of the parliament of the United Kingdom of Great Britain and Ireland.[117]

Adams accused Stevenson of, in his capacity as an Ambassador, having violated the law of nations. Adams wanted to ascertain if the House should intervene to impeach Stevenson. He was opposed by George Washington Hopkins, Representative for Virginia, who warned him that 'no good could result from a discussion upon such a subject'.[118] The House voted by 140 to 57 not to continue. However, as one Philadelphia newspaper pointed out, '57 votes are quite a strong support'.[119] Adams did not give up. A few days later, he put forward a resolution asking the President if he had recalled Stevenson to explain his behaviour, and whether Captain Matthew Perry, who had delivered the challenge for a duel, had been rebuked. Again, the majority of the House was opposed to his suggestions.[120] Undaunted, he raised the matter a few weeks later, an action that resulted in a letter threatening to kill him if he brought the issue up again.[121]

The matter was taken up in the American Senate by Henry Clay, a Whig politician from Virginia, who claimed to be no friend of slavery, but was a vehement opponent of abolitionists, whom he believed were putting the Union in jeopardy. In February 1839, Clay delivered a speech in the Senate, which was subsequently published in a number of newspapers. In it, he referred to the incident between O'Connell and Stevenson and opined that the latter should have maintained a 'contemptuous silence'. He referred to O'Connell as an agitator who 'would exclude us from European society – he who himself can only obtain a contraband admission, and is received with scornful admission into it!'[122] Clay was supported by a number of papers who mounted personal attacks on O'Connell's integrity. The editor of the *Philadelphia Gazette* denounced O'Connell as a 'political beggar' adding that 'his weakness of mind is almost beyond calculation'.[123] Feelings were running so high that there was even talk of an alleged 'conspiracy against the life of Daniel O'Connell'.[124]

Clay's attack drew criticism, in turn, from the poet and anti-abolitionist, John Greenleaf Whittier. Whittier castigated the American politician for holding 'the great Liberator of Ireland' up to scorn. Whittier speculated that Clay's attack had been motivated by his desire to win the support of slaveholders and Irish voters in the forthcoming presidential election.[125] O'Connell's political activities rendered him, in Whittier's eyes:

The leading politician, the master mind of the British Empire. Attempts have been made to prejudice the American mind against him by a republication on this side of the water of the false and foul slanders of his Tory enemies ... his heart and soul and mind have been directed to this suffering country and the cause of universal freedom. For this he has deservedly a place in the heart and affections of every son of Ireland.[126]

For the anti-slavery Governor of New York, William Henry Seward, O'Connell was simply, 'the remarkable man of the age'.[127] Overall, the Stevenson incident demonstrated that O'Connell's role in anti-slavery had attracted transatlantic notice and notoriety at the highest political level. It also provided a microcosm of divisions that existed within American politics. The New York *Morning Herald* published an editorial in October 1838 warning that the country was in danger, 'This happy land is on the verge of a deep gulf'. The trouble was identified as '*abolition* – and *abolition alone* that now agitates the country and preys on its vitals'. They believed that abolitionist voters had made a secret agreement with the Locofoco Party (an offshoot of the Democratic Party), and if they were successful in the forthcoming elections, it would 'inevitably lead to a dissolution of this glorious Union in less than five years'.[128] The abolition question was no longer marginal within American politics, but as people were forced to take a position on it, attitudes were becoming more polarized. O'Connell's interventions, while inflaming opinions on the issue, kept the debate in the public eye on both sides of the Atlantic.

As the 1840 Presidential election moved closer, the attacks on O'Connell became more personal. He was accused of supporting abolition simply to strengthen his own role in the British Parliament and by doing so, 'hold the balance of power in the British Empire'.[129] The *Morning Herald* went on to claim:

Mr O'Connell cares nothing for Mr Stevenson – nothing for slavery – nothing for the United States – nothing for the West Indies – nothing for our slave population. He only wants the abolition votes in England, and plays a deep and profound game to wield the balance of power of a mighty empire.[130]

However, according to the historian Howard Temperley:

To thoughtful people, whether they supported slavery or not, the Stevenson-O'Connell issue was a reminder that the South's position was becoming increasingly more isolated ... so far as the English speaking world was concerned, the South was henceforth to be on its own. Time was working against it and to the advantage of its opponents.[131]

O'Connell, so long the scourge of the British Parliament, as a result of the Stevenson incident demonstrated that he had become a major player in the transatlantic struggle to end slavery.

Divisions

Following the ending of apprenticeship in 1838, abolitionists were able to focus more attention on slavery in the United States. As in Britain, the abolitionist movement in America had been revived in the 1830s, with its two main centres being Boston and New York. In 1833, the American Anti-Slavery Society (AASS) had been established in Philadelphia, to work for the immediate and total abolition of slavery. Its founders included William Lloyd Garrison, who was based in Boston, and Arthur and Lewis Tappan, who were wealthy New York merchants. The importance of establishing contact with abolitionists in the United Kingdom was a priority of the new organization. Garrison already had a considerable presence in the movement as a result of founding the *Liberator* in 1831. Only weeks after the AASS was formed, Garrison travelled to Britain, he explaining to a female supporter that:

> There, my spirit will be elevated and strengthened in the presence of Clarkson, and Wilberforce, and Brougham, and Buxton, and O'Connell, and their noble coadjutors – there I can tell the story of the black man's wrongs, in this land of liberty and light, to hearts that will melt with pity, and devise liberally for his recue – there I shall doubtless be permitted to address those of your own sex who are animated with zeal for the overthrow of slavery.[132]

Slavery was increasingly intruding into national politics in the United States. This was evident in the inaugural speech of Martin van Buren who, upon becoming president in 1837, stated:

> The last, perhaps the greatest, of the prominent sources of discord and disaster supposed to lurk in our political condition was the institution of domestic slavery. Our forefathers were deeply impressed with the delicacy of this subject, and they treated it with forbearance so evidently wise that in spite of every sinister foreboding it never until the present period disturbed the tranquility of our common country.[133]

He warned that during his Presidency he would be an 'inflexible and uncompromising opponent' of all attempts to interfere with slavery in the States where it existed and that, 'no bill conflicting with these views can ever receive my constitutional sanction'. This approach, he believed, was in keeping with the spirit of the 'venerated fathers of the Republic, and that succeeding experience has proved them to be humane, patriotic, expedient, honorable, and just'. He went on to castigate those who disagreed for their 'reckless disregard of the consequences of their conduct'.[134] The President's speech was widely reported. In Ireland, it was criticized by the Hibernian Anti-Slavery Society, who asserted that his criticisms had had the opposite impact because, 'so far from subduing the Abolitionists, it has provoked them to renewed and extended action'.[135]

The American Anti-Slavery Society was also spreading rapidly and, by 1838, incorporated over 1,350 societies. Its growth disguised the fact that there were some substantial differences between the leaders of the Society. Garrison was known to be a progressive on many issues, while the Tappans were more socially conservative. In particular, the Tappans did not feel that anti-slavery should be mixed up with the woman question, whereas Garrison regarded them as inseparable.[136] Like O'Connell, Garrison combined fiery rhetoric with a commitment to non-violent methods. In 1838, Garrison persuaded the AASS to adopt the 'Declaration of Sentiments', which had reaffirmed its commitment to peaceful tactics.

The differences came to a head in 1839, leading to a split in the American Anti-Slavery Society. It was precipitated by Garrison calling for a new American government that outlawed slavery and gave blacks equal rights within the United States. He also wanted women to have a more prominent role in the abolition movement. Some members of the AASS considered these proposals as too radical. Lewis Tappan and his followers left and became the American and Foreign Anti-Slavery Society, also referred to as the 'New Organization'. Garrison led what was called the 'Old Organization'. For supporters in Ireland and Britain this division caused some problems. In Britain, the newly-formed British and Foreign Anti-Slavery Society tended to favour the more conservative society led by Lewis Tappan.[137] Irish abolitionists were also divided about whom to support. Overall, they tended to favour Garrison, although there were some exceptions. While the Cork Ladies' Society tended to favour Garrison, a ladies' society in Ulster favoured the newer group.[138] There were divisions even within family groups – while Richard Webb remained close to the Garrisonians, Maria Webb favoured the anti-Garrisonians.[139]

At the end of 1839, an unexpected ally made a public statement in support of the abolitionist cause. On 3 December, Pope Gregory XVI issued *In Supremo Apostolatus*, which 'condemned slavery and the slave trade and forbad all Catholics from propounding views contrary to this'.[140] However, the way in which it was written meant that its message could be interpreted in a number of ways. The origins of the Papal Letter lay with the British Foreign Secretary, Lord Palmerston. Despite various treaties concerned with ending the slave trade, thousands of Africans were continuing to be taken into slavery in Cuba and Brazil. Britain alone was unable to police this traffic and in the late 1830s sought the cooperation of the United States, who had stood aloof from the earlier treaties. Palmerston's overtures were rejected.[141] He then appealed to the Papacy, where his suggestion was more warmly received. Aware of the sensitivities on this issue, Gregory and his Cardinals decided not to address the letter directly to any particular country or statesman, but to make it a general appeal.[142] The Pope's Letter was particularly welcomed by Irish abolitionists, especially O'Connell and the

Catholic doctor, Richard Madden. Madden, at that time, was acting as an expert witness in the *Amistad* trial, concerning a slave rebellion on board a schooner of that name. He had first become involved in Irish anti-slavery in 1829 and, unlike O'Connell, he was to gain first-hand experience working with slaves.[143] Using a theme that was later frequently employed by O'Connell, Madden claimed that the Roman Catholic Church had a long history of being opposed to slavery.[144] Pope Gregory's letter caused problems for members of the Catholic hierarchy in the United States. At a conference in Baltimore, where the Letter was first read, bishops from the slaveholding states formed a majority. Led by John England, the Cork-born bishop of Charleston, they interpreted the letter as condemning the slave trade, not slavery itself. Bishop England even praised large slaveholders for being amongst the most devout Catholics in the United States.[145] To explain the position of the Catholic Church in America on domestic slavery, he wrote a series of letters for publication. Like Bishop Hughes in New York, he argued that slavery was legal under the American system of government and that abolition, without multiple precautions, would be dangerous.[146] Overall, the Catholic Church hierarchy in America interpreted the Pope's intervention in a conservative and limited way and, more importantly, in a way that would safe-guard the status quo. For them, the Letter raised the thorny question of loyalty: was their allegiance to America or to Rome? Moreover, the reception of the Pope's Letter, like the much-publicized incident between O'Connell and Stevenson, revealed how entrenched and polarized the slavery debate had become in the United States.

Regardless of division with the transatlantic abolition movement, the 1830s had been a significant decade in the struggle against slavery. In Britain, substantial gains had been made on behalf of the slaves. Furthermore, the problems apparent in the United States were briefly overshadowed by a decision to hold an international anti-slavery conference in London. The proposed convention, which was an initiative of the British and Foreign Anti-Slavery Society, was a symbol that the cause was now a truly international one in which transatlantic cooperation was crucial. And as the convention was to show, O'Connell was the undisputed leader of the transatlantic struggle to end slavery. While O'Connell was championing the cause of the slave, he was also masterminding a new campaign to bring about a repeal of the Act of Union.

4 'MURDERERS OF LIBERTY'

The ending of apprenticeship completed a long phase of struggle in the anti-slavery movement. In its wake, there was a desire by activists to extend their achievement beyond the British empire and to work to end slavery internationally. In 1839, Joseph Sturge, an English Quaker, founded the British and Foreign Anti-Slavery Society. At a meeting at Exeter Hall on 17 and 18 April, the principles of the new society were laid out, with an emphasis on employing only peaceful methods to end slavery and the slave trade.[1] Many of the former campaigners were involved in the new association, including Thomas Fowell Buxton, Dr Stephen Lushington and Daniel O'Connell. Sturge was anxious to establish relationships with Lewis Tappan in New York, rather than with William Lloyd Garrison in Boston. Tappan had been one of the founders of the American Anti-Slavery Society, but he had found himself increasingly at odds with the radical politics of Garrison. The differences resulted in his departure to form the American and Foreign Anti-Slavery Society. Sturge hoped to work with the new American association, but only if they felt able to commit to his peace principles.[2]

Sturge's philosophy was 'to bring what had been gained in aid of what yet remained to be accomplished'.[3] Clearly, much remained to be accomplished in the anti-slavery struggle. The British and Foreign Anti-Slavery Society immediately became involved in a number of issues that demonstrated that the struggle was far from over. The continuation of apprenticeship in the West Indies was to prove particularly contentious. Despite the official ending of apprenticeship, the 1833 legislation was not being implemented the way that had been intended. The local legislatures in the West Indies passed a number of laws on marriage, vagrancy and policing that were aimed at former slaves, and with a view to keeping them from enjoying full freedom.[4] Many anti-slavery societies took up this cause and petitioned the government. They demanded that the government 'immediately take steps for enforcing in the Colonial legislatures a strict adherence to the provisions of the Negro Emancipation Act'.[5] The government received so many appeals that the Colonial Office introduced three Orders in Council to ensure that emancipated population of the West Indies obtained their legal rights.[6]

Concern with winning abolition in the West Indies and the United States overshadowed the far less public campaign to end slavery in the British East Indies, that is, India. The 1833 Act had abolished slavery throughout most of the British empire, but it had excluded territories in Ceylon and those controlled by the East India Company. India had a long tradition of slavery. No census of slaves there had ever been taken, but by 1840, estimates varied between 800,000 and 900,000.[7] William Adam, a Scottish missionary who corresponded with Buxton on this issue, informed him that not only was slavery flourishing in India, but that the slave trade had also continued regardless of the 1807 legislation. He described slavery a 'hydra-headed monster' and 'one of the heads of this monster is British India'.[8] After 1839, both the British and Foreign Anti-Slavery Society and the Hibernian Anti-Slavery Society took up the issue of slavery in India. The London Society submitted a series of articles to the *Morning Chronicle* in order to draw public attention to the matter.[9] O'Connell became active in this campaign and was consulted for advice and support by other campaigners.[10] His involvement drew praise from the English abolitionist, Elizabeth Pease. She commended O'Connell for the fact that he had, 'most generously left his urgent engagements in Ireland last week to attend a meeting here on behalf of British India'. During his speech, O'Connell had stated that slavery in India was 'the most important question that he had ever advocated'. He promised to go to future meetings to give the cause further help.[11] The campaign had some success as in 1843 slavery was abolished in both Hindu and Muslim India by the Indian Slavery Act V.

Appeals were also made to O'Connell to campaign for an ending of slavery in Cuba. Cuba, a major producer of sugar, was a Spanish colony, renowned for the cruel treatment of its slaves. Richard Madden, an Irish doctor and abolitionist, had lived in Havana in the 1830s where he served as a Judge Advocate on behalf of the British Government to ensure that slaves were not being imported. Upon returning to Ireland, he became involved with the Anti-Slavery Society in Dublin. James Haughton introduced him to O'Connell.[12] Shortly afterwards, Madden wrote to O'Connell himself, including a present of slave chains that had been taken from a ship off Cuba. He explained:

> to bring chains to Ireland is like carrying coals to Newcastle and to offer them to you whose employment for the last thirty years has been in breaking them is perhaps a Cuban compliment. I do pray you shake them in the ears of the English people and to stir their hearts if it be possible and move them to put a stop to the work of a rapine guns in Africa and Cuba in the face of agents of the British government and in the teeth of the treaties entered into for its suppression of the most prosperous and daily expanding trade.[13]

Madden first-hand knowledge meant that he was one of the main speakers at the 1840 International Anti-Slavery Convention, and in the following year, he was an expert witness in the Amistad trial.

The early 1840s coincided with a number of debates over whether sugar duties should be maintained or abolished. For abolitionists the debate presented a quandary. Sugar duties protected the monopoly of former slaveholders in the West Indies, but they also protected the jobs of the now free plantation workers. For the public, abolishing sugar duties would bring cheap sugar into the United Kingdom, but the trade would probably move to areas that still produced sugar with slave labour. In 1841 and again in 1844, bills were introduced into Parliament for reducing the duty on sugar. For O'Connell, the matter was not clear-cut. He was torn between wanting cheap sugar for the Irish people and not wanting to encourage slavery. In the end, he supported the Whig bill for a reduction in the sugar tariff.[14] In 1844, when the Tory government proposed a further reduction in sugar duties, O'Connell was less equivocal. He advised Sturge about the stand to be taken, leading the latter to describe him as a 'master of logic'. O'Connell posited that the question was not one of 'political economy', but one of humanity. He argued:

> It would be, in my mind, the most absurd of all absurd things to give 20,000,000*l.* sterling to get rid in our own colonies of all the cruelties necessarily incident to slavery, and then immediately after to open our markets to slave-grown sugar of other countries, and thus to hold out a bonus to other countries to continue and increase all the horrors of negro slavery.[15]

On the question of denying cheap sugar to British people, his answer was 'Yes, I will, if the cheapness of the sugar is to be procured by shedding the blood of the negro.'[16] O'Connell's reasoning drew praise from Richard Webb who said he had handled the matter as 'perhaps only an able lawyer can'.[17] It was not until 1846 that an act was passed to equalize sugar duties within the British empire.[18] It had a devastating impact on the West Indies. O'Connell was absent from Parliament on the day of the vote.[19]

In addition to these campaigns, in the early months of its existence, the Anti-Slavery Society was occupied organizing the first international Convention in London and 'To this conference they earnestly invite the friends of the slave of every nation and of every clime'.[20] The Convention was to commence on 12 June 1840, but as early as June 1839, anti-slavery societies were choosing their delegations.[21] O'Connell was chosen to represent the Glasgow Anti-Slavery Society. However, even as he was representing Britain on the world stage, O'Connell was being treated with scorn by some of his fellow abolitionists.

On 1 June 1840, shortly before the Convention, a meeting was held in Exeter Hall to discuss the welfare of Africa. It was presided over by Prince Albert, and

Sir Robert Peel, leader of the Conservative Party, was present. Buxton was one of the main speakers. The hall held 4,000 people, but demand for admission was so great that 6,000 tickets had been issued.[22] When O'Connell entered the hall, there was an 'interruption' to the meeting and the audience 'clamoured' for him to speak.[23] When he eventually got to his feet, the organ started playing. Those responsible for starting the music were alleged to have been Sir Thomas Acland and Sir Robert Inglis, two Conservative MPs. The resulting controversy was played out in the columns of the main newspapers. In the subsequent days, letters complaining about O'Connell's treatment were published in the *Morning Chronicle*, a paper sympathetic to him and to abolition.[24] One letter stated that 'a great shame was acted in not allowing him to speak'. Another suggested that many of the big names who spoke that day had only attended due to the presence of the Consort.[25] Another correspondent pointed out 'for the sake of hearing one particular man speak at that meeting, the boldest and most enlarged philanthropic measure that was ever propounded is to be sacrificed'.[26] Irish liberal newspapers were indignant at O'Connell's treatment, pointing out that the presence of Sir Robert Peel, O'Connell's longstanding adversary, may have led English Tories to behave in this way.[27] A number of British abolitionists were angered at O'Connell's treatment. George Stephen, a leading anti-slavery campaigner, demanded to know who had given the order to play the organ, and he condemned the 'party feeling' shown towards O'Connell, 'whose services in the anti-slavery cause had been most zealous'.[28]

Unwittingly, O'Connell had again become the object of controversy in the anti-slavery struggle. O'Connell, when responding the various newspaper articles, showed himself to be a peacemaker. In a letter to the *Morning Chronicle* he stated that:

> It is a pure mistake. I did not rise to speak: I rose to go away. Notwithstanding the many and general calls made on me to speak during the business I declined to come forward, as I would not speak without the assent of the chairman, I assuredly had no notion of 'privateering after the war' by speaking after the business was conducted. The ordering the organ to play up, and thus 'bothering' the crowd that remained, was therefore quite a gratuitous offence against the meeting rather than against me.[29]

O'Connell, an admirer of Queen Victoria, added that his primary motive for going had been to show respect for the Consort as this was his first public meeting. He had also wanted to ensure that Ireland was represented on such a memorable occasion:

> I also attended the meeting that Ireland might, in the presence of the illustrious Prince, be represented, at least by silent acquiescence, in the great work of annihilating slavery. I still think the voice of Ireland should not have been excluded at such a meeting. If I were not deemed a suitable advocate, some other, a better Irish advocate,

might easily have been selected. But it was an occasion on which Ireland ought to have been represented, and her voice heard. The accents of that voice might have been rude and uncouth, but her heart would have been upon her tongue, and there would have been no hypocrisy in the ardour of her aspirations in the cause of liberty and religion. I therefore insist on behalf of my despised, but blessed be God, still undergraded country, that she has been wrongfully despoiled of her share in a glorious struggle.[30]

O'Connell used this occasion, and the public attention it had attracted, to remind the readers that anti-slavery was 'deeply indebted to Ireland'. He explained:

When that cause was first introduced by the venerable Clarkson, and afterwards taken up by the venerable Wilberforce, they made no way in Parliament – that is, they were in continual minorities, until the Whigs came into office in 1806; when the majority in favour of the abolition of the slave trade was literally Irish – all the Irish in the house having voted for it.

As the letter continued, O'Connell seemed to become more irked at his treatment. He pointed out that all the Irish members had voted for emancipation in 1833, 'no matter what religious or political opinions'. On these grounds, he believed that:

Ireland was treated ungratefully and insultingly, when she was excluded from her just participation in this effort of humanity. Truly, we had as good a right to be heard as even your right rev. prelates, who never, I believe, voted for negro emancipation; or as Sir Robert Peel, who, I am convinced, never voted for it, but, on the contrary, belonged for more than twenty years to a party, and a party in power, that constantly opposed the striking off the negro's fetters, and would not even take the lash from the back of the negro female![31]

O'Connell wondered if his treatment had been due to 'the paltry under-working of either national, or religious, or (what would be infinitely more degrading than either) personal malignity'.[32] The *Bristol Mercury*, which followed the incident, praised O'Connell's response as being made with 'the best temper, but the most stinging effect'.[33] Furthermore, if O'Connell had been silenced in Exeter Hall, nothing could diminish his stellar performance in the Anti-Slavery Convention just a few days later.

Anti-Slavery Convention

To hold an international anti-slavery convention had been the idea of the newly formed British and Foreign Anti-Slavery Society. Even before the Convention met, some tensions were apparent, especially amongst the American delegates. Many of the delegates were members of the Society of Friends and a few years earlier there had been a schism, with some of the more radical members following Elias Hicks. Orthodox members referred to them as 'Hicksites'. James and Lucretia Mott were followers of Hicks, and some orthodox members of the Convention suggested that they should no longer describe themselves as Friends.[34] Additionally, there were a number of differences between the radical wing led by Garrison, and the more moderate wing under Lewis Tappan. These came to a head over the question of women; those who disapproved of women having an equal place in the society left and formed the American and Foreign Anti-Slavery Society. The leadership of the British and Foreign Anti-Slavery Society made it clear that they supported women remaining separate. The split in American abolitionism revealed some of the divisions within British and Irish anti-slavery. The BFASS sympathized with those who had left the AASS, while the Hibernian Anti-Slavery Society and the leading Scottish societies supported Garrison. Many women's associations took the side of the more militant Garrison.[35] O'Connell, who was a member of both the British and Foreign Anti-Slavery Society and the Glasgow Emancipation Society remained on good terms with all of the American abolitionists. Yet, the radical programme of Garrison's society – from the equality of women to workers' rights – was unsuited to O'Connell's more moderate approach to social reform. Initially, however, he seemed closer to Garrison than to Tappan. The Convention offered an opportunity for some of these rifts to be healed.

Before the Convention commenced, abolitionists from America and the West Indies, together with a number of 'emancipated Africans', toured Britain. In May, the delegation from Jamaica spoke at an anti-slavery meeting in Birmingham, at which Sturge was present.[36] In the days preceding the opening of the Convention, the committee of the British and Foreign Anti-Slavery Society hosted three tea parties. Generally women were not allowed in the rooms, 'but as several had crossed the Atlantic, to manifest their interest in the cause of the slave, and to give their aid to such measures as would promote his liberation, it was concluded by the committee to deviate from their custom on this occasion'.[37]

Delegates to the Convention came from all over Britain, from Aberdeen to Truro.[38] Delegates from the other side of the Atlantic, included the West Indies' representatives William Knibb and John Clark, who were, according to Sturge, 'to represent the noble band of missionaries who have so long and bravely battled with the monster slavery on its own soil'.[39] Edward Barrett, Henry Beckford and Samuel Prescod from Barbados also attended.[40] Delegates from the American Anti-Slavery Society included William Lloyd Garrison, Wendell Phillips and Charles Lenox Remond, a black abolitionist. The AASS was also represented by a number of women including Lucretia Mott. Mott admitted that on the voyage over, she and her husband James, had talked with others about 'the haters of O'Connell'.[41] Henry Brewster Stanton and his new wife, Elizabeth Cady Stanton, both of whom were progressives on issues such as women's rights and universal suffrage, attended. James Gillespie Birney, a former slave-owner, was a delegate. He had left the American Anti-Slavery Association as he did not agree with equality for women. Instead, he had joined the newly formed, anti-slavery Liberal Party and had been chosen to contest the Presidential election in the following November.[42]

Among those assembled were seventeen delegates from Ireland, representing Dublin, Cork and Belfast. They included James Haughton, Dr Richard Madden, the Reverend James Morgan (a Belfast Presbyterian minister), William Martin (a Quaker and temperance advocate), William Torrens McCullagh Torrens (a young Dublin lawyer), Richard Webb and Richard Allen.[43] O'Connell, whom the Dublin *Freeman's Journal* described as 'this great champion of the negro', represented the Glasgow Emancipation Society.[44] The paper described the assemblage as including:

> the sooty African, the swarthy coloured man, the intrepid American abolitionist, the indefatigable West India missionary, accompanied by two newly-emancipated negroes, whose language, whose deportment, whose whole bearing show that they value liberty, and that they thirst to extend to others what they have themselves received.[45]

When a list of the delegates was published, it showed that those present included twenty members of the British Parliament, 100 clergymen of all denominations, and deputations from France, Spain, Switzerland, Canada, the United States and the West Indies. Most of the American delegates came from Massachusetts and Pennsylvania.[46] In total, approximately 600 attended.[47] This included a large number of members of the Society of Friends.[48]

The first meeting of the Convention was held on Friday 12 June, at the Freemason's Tavern, Queen Street, London. The area was cordoned off, and the whole outside space was filled, mostly with women. Before proceedings commenced, it was moved by William Allen and seconded by James Gillespie Birney that Thomas Clarkson, the eighty-year-old veteran of anti-slavery, be appointed President. This was agreed to unanimously. Because of his age, there was to be no applause, but delegates stood when he entered. In his opening address, he praised his fellow abolitionists who were now dead, including Wilberforce.[49] Sturge read the opening address on behalf of the President. In it, Clarkson had pointed out that he was the only surviving founder of the anti-slavery committee of 1787.[50] Clarkson warned the audience 'you have the most difficult task to perform'. The preliminaries were then agreed on: four vice-chairmen and a number of secretaries were appointed. After these arrangements had been made, the meeting became embroiled in a controversy. A motion was submitted by Wendell Phillips of the AASS that women be admitted as delegates. His own wife was a delegate of the Massachusetts Society.[51] The proposer was asked to withdraw the motion, but he refused to do so. This led to a discussion of over two hours' length, after which the motion was 'overwhelmingly' defeated on the grounds that it would be contrary to English custom.[52] Consequently, women could only observe the Convention from a designated gallery. James Mott later recorded his disapprobation with the outcome:

> One of the first acts of a Convention, assembled for promoting the cause of liberty and freedom universally, was a vote, the spirit and object of which was a determination that the chains should not be broken, with which oppressive custom has so bound the mind of women.[53]

The discussion about women was omitted from some of the reports of the day.[54]

O'Connell had not been present at the opening of the meeting. When he entered the room, there was 'a simultaneous burst of applause which had to be quietened'. This was followed by a warm greeting between O'Connell and the chairman.[55] Shortly afterwards, O'Connell, at the request of the President, addressed the meeting. When he rose to speak, there was 'much cheering'.[56] He said how important the Convention was and criticized nations who were still involved in slave trade. When he finished, O'Connell turned to Henry Beckford, a liberated slave and 'took off his hat and bowed to him'. [57]

James Canning Fuller, a Quaker who was the delegate for the New York State Anti-Slavery Society, spoke after O'Connell.[58] He complimented O'Connell, but made an appeal to him on the grounds that:

> He believed that he [O'Connell] could do more to pull down slavery in America than any other individual. To the Americans, there was a particular charm about Mr O'Connell's name, and his influence in that country was greater than that of the whole Convention. If Mr O'Connell would issue an address to his countrymen in America the effect would be felt throughout the length and breadth of the land.

O'Connell responded to this request by saying that if such a plan was thought desirable, he would not lose a moment in the preparation of such an address. The meeting continued till after 4 o'clock, but both Clarkson and O'Connell had left at about 1 o'clock: Clarkson due to poor health, O'Connell in order to return to Parliament where he was engaged in fighting another battle.[59]

For Joseph Sturge, the day's proceedings had been a triumph:

> It was, indeed, a remarkable assembly ... no man whose heart could be touched with sympathy for the wrongs of the oppressed, or with admiration for that noblest kind of heroism which seeks its rewards in the triumphs of humanity and mercy, could gaze along those thronging benches, without an emotion of singular interest and respect ... There might be seen as the veteran champions of the cause of the slave in the British Parliament, Buxton and Lushington, and O'Connell, and Villiers.[60]

The debate on women, however, had revealed some divisions in the international movement. The response of the American male abolitionists varied. Wendell Phillips spoke on behalf of the women, while William Lloyd Garrison, who had arrived a few days later, adopted a strategy of silence. According to one of the women present, Maria Waring, the Irish delegates were supportive of the women being treated equally.[61] Not all Irish men supported the women delegates: the Reverend James Morgan from Belfast did not like woman question even being raised. O'Connell was initially ambivalent on the issue, agreeing that the admission of women would lay the Convention open to ridicule. A few days later, Lucretia Mott wrote to O'Connell, as one of 'the most distinguished advocates of universal liberty', asking him his opinion on women delegates.[62] O'Connell's response was long and frank. He admitted that had been opposed to the idea of women delegates on the grounds that the Convention would be ridiculed. On further consideration, however, he 'recognized that this was an unworthy, and indeed a cowardly motive, and I easily overcame its influence'.[63] He added:

> My mature consideration of the entire subject, convinces me of the right of the female delegates to take their seats in the Convention, and of the injustice of excluding them. I do not care to add, that I deem it also impolitic; because that exclusion being unjust, it ought not to have taken place, even if it could also be politic.[64]

He concluded with an apology, admitting, 'I have a consciousness that I have not done *my* duty in not sooner urging these considerations on the Convention. My excuse is that I was unavoidably absent during the discussion on the subject'.[65] For the remainder of the Convention, O'Connell was one of the small group of men who visited the women in their allotted space in the gallery.[66] Lucretia Mott described him as 'excellent and amusing'.[67] Elizabeth Cady Stanton was more fulsome in her praise; 'he was tall, well-developed, and a magnificent looking man, and probably one of the most effective speakers Ireland ever produced'.[68] Garrison and some of his supporters from the AASS had only arrived after the Convention had commenced, and they were shunned by some of the delegates. Garrison and Remond chose to sit in the ladies' gallery.[69] The exclusion of the women proved to be pivotal in the subsequent creation of the American women's movement.[70]

O'Connell attended the Convention on Saturday and when he entered the hall he was greeted with 'loud cheering'. He delivered another lecture on the evils of slavery.[71] On Sunday, there was no gathering. On Monday, O'Connell again lectured. In what the *Leeds Mercury* described as a 'powerful speech', he spoke in support of a motion by James Gillespie Birney demanding that the American Congress guarantee indemnity to escaped slaves.[72] O'Connell averred that the actions of the American government in not doing so were in violation of the Constitution, adding 'there was not a single word in the declaration of independence of the US which allowed or sanctioned the accursed principle that man can have property in his fellow-man'. He added that he had 'no hope of touching the sense of justice, of those who, for the sake of lucre, commit robbery and murder, and plunder'. He concluded by praising American abolitionists. Throughout his speech, he was greeted with cheers.[73]

On Tuesday, Birney was in the Chair and the debate focused on slavery in the French colonies. One of the speakers was Adolphe Crémieux, a French-Jewish lawyer. He spoke in French which was then translated. His speech made clear his admiration for O'Connell:

> I feel overpowered by the thought that an Israelite should appear in this assembly, where he has been received with so much favour, to demand, with enthusiasm equal to yours, the abolition of slavery. Gentlemen, all liberties are united, and all persecutions hold together. Persecute and you will make slaves, proclaim the equality of all and you make citizens. It is thus your O'Connell (loud cheers) – whom we should envy to England if the glory of England at this moment was amalgamated with that of France in this great work – in demanding complete equality for Ireland, proclaimed at the same time the principles of humanity and justice, and has rendered for the future all persecution impossible against men who conquered equality for themselves (loud cheering).[74]

Crémieux's remarks were judged by a minority of the Convention to be controversial. The Reverend J. H. Johnston, a vicar from Wiltshire, protested that the comments regarding Ireland 'were totally unconnected with the subject of slavery or the slave trade'. Johnston was shouted down, to which he responded that he understood that it was the wish of the Convention to be always united, and to embrace the whole community of England of all parties. He was again shouted down and he was asked to withdraw his comments by Dr Bowring on the grounds that Crémieux was from a foreign country. Johnston was prevented from making any further comments due to the commotion in the hall. It was left to O'Connell, the unwitting object of this controversy, to intervene and ask the meeting to give Johnston a hearing. Johnston responded that he was satisfied with the explanation, but he hoped no more political issues would be discussed. However, the next speaker, Justine Jeremy, praised O'Connell for his championship of Jewish Emancipation, and pointed out that all Catholic members of the House of Commons had supported him. He added:

> A Jew was there that day espousing and supporting the cause of negro freedom, and the Catholics had espoused and supported the cause of Jewish emancipation, and they had himself there, a firm and good protestant, supporting and maintaining the cause of liberty of every sect, colour and nation'.[76]

O'Connell was the focus of attention by foreign delegates, and not merely for his anti-slavery activities. He did join in the debate, but kept it focused on the topic of French slavery. He asked that there should be an address sent to the French people, 'impressing on them the injustice and the impolicy of any longer tolerating the existence of slavery in their colonies'.[77] On Wednesday, 17 June, the Irish delegate Dr Madden spoke about slavery in the Spanish colonies, a topic on which he was an expert.[78] His speech was then translated into Spanish for circulation in Spain and its colonies.[79] Madden, like O'Connell, was a Catholic, but unlike O'Connell he had witnessed slavery first-hand, having been a stipendiary magistrate in Jamaica and then travelled to the United States. O'Connell spoke on the Friday about how to protect the free Negro. He warned that 'laws were as vain as the idle wind if they were to be administered solely by the masters'.[80]

The Convention was painted by the society artist, Benjamin Haydon, a task that took him over a year to complete. Haydon, who had no interest in the abolition movement, had originally been reluctant to accept this commission. He later admitted that:

> On entering the meeting, at the time appointed, I saw at once I was in the midst of no common assembly. The venerable and benevolent heads which surrounded me, soon convinced me that materials existed of character and expression in the members present, provided at any one moment of pictorial interest should occur.[81]

The portrait was notable for including the freed slave, Henry Beckford, in the front row, which was one of the first times that a British artist had painted a former slave in a positive light.[82] Placing Beckford in the heart of the conference had been Haydon's idea and he had suggested to various delegates that in the portrait he would have them seated together. Haydon did this out of mischief – in his words, as a 'touchstone', because 'A man who wished to place the Negro on a level must no longer regard him as having been a slave and feel annoyed at his sitting at his side'. A number of the delegates, however, did object to being placed next to Beckford.[83] Haydon also included a number of women in the portrait, sitting with the men.[84]

In the portrait, O'Connell was located on the back benches, although in a prominent position. Haydon had first painted O'Connell in 1834, for a parliamentary portrait. On that occasion, O'Connell had appeared 'rolled in a morning gown, a loose black handkerchief tied around his neck ... a wig and a foraging cap bordered with gold lace'.[85] When they met a few days later, O'Connell was wearing 'his best wig, and looking in great health and vigour'. The artist added, 'O'Connell has a head of great sentiment and power, but yet cunning'.[86] It was not until 1841 that O'Connell was painted for inclusion in the portrait of the Convention. Haydon observed that, 'He is grown older, considerably, but there is in his face inexpressible good nature'. As they had done seven years earlier, they good-humouredly talked about repeal, with Haydon expressing his opposition to it.[87]

Overall, the Convention was considered a great success. Following its conclusion, it was decided that a medal would be produced to commemorate the meeting, with the figure of Clarkson on one side.[88] But if Clarkson was the venerated elder of the Convention, O'Connell was the international star. He had proved to be one of the most frequent speakers at the Convention even though, as James Birney, who met O'Connell for the first time, acknowledged:

> Mr O'Connell was also a member of the conference, and altho' Parliament was in session at the time, was daily present at the antislavery meetings, partaking in the proceedings.[89]

O'Connell's speeches were consistently greeted with cheering. Garrison, a long time admirer of O'Connell, reported that:

> When O'Connell made his appearance, the applause was absolutely deafening. He made a speech of great power, and denounced American slave-holders in blistering language – at the same time paying the highest compliments to American abolitionists.[90]

O'Connell's fame amongst American abolitionists had been apparent from the outset of the conference. Even those who were unable to attend wanted to have some association with him. The English abolitionist, Elizabeth Pease, had been asked by fellow abolitionists in Boston to acquire a number of his autographs, to be sold at the next fundraising bazaar. Pease reported:

> It was my good fortune to be in his company more than once last week – and he kindly wrote me thirteen cards, ten of which I enclose to thee – he is the most good-natured, kind-hearted person you can conceive – and I hope at some future time I may be able again to avail myself of his kindness, for your benefit.[91]

The Convention was groundbreaking in a number of ways. By involving dissenters, freed black men, middle-class women, Irish Catholics and Jews in one of the most pressing issues of the day, the meeting showed how both British and international politics were changing.[92] Representatives of black Americans were pleased with the outcome, praising 'our beloved friend Garrison. They also praised 'the great agitator, Daniel O'Connell, the man whose fame will be sung by some future Moore, in strains sweet as fell from mortal lips.'[93] Regardless of the successes of the Convention, divisions had been apparent, although they had been mostly channelled into the debate on women delegates. An unlooked for consequence of the Convention was the emergence of an organized women's movement in the United States. The rejection of women as delegates led Lucretia Coffin Mott and Elizabeth Cady Stanton to organize the Seneca Falls Women's Rights Convention a few years later.

Overall, the conference had favoured the more moderate approach of the British and Foreign Anti-Slavery Society and the American and Foreign Anti-Slavery Society. When writing to his family, Garrison expressed his disappointment, 'On the score of respectability, talent, numbers, it deserves much consideration; but it was sadly deficient in freedom of thought, speech and action, having been under the exclusive management of the London committee, whose domination was recognized as absolute.'[94] For him, one positive outcome had been 'I have shaken hands with O'Connell repeatedly'.[95]

Following the Convention, the divisions in transatlantic anti-slavery hardened. While Garrison maintained good relationships with the Hibernian Anti-Slavery Society, the more conservative British and Foreign Anti-Slavery Society did not sympathize with his radical politics, and as a result, financial support to his organization dried up. John Collins of the Massachusetts Anti-Slavery Society, who toured England in the wake of the Convention, was horrified by the depth of antagonism to Garrison and his supporters. He reported despondently at the beginning of 1841:

> I do not know as I can promise another farthing. I would as soon go among the Southern slave-holders to solicit aid, as among the abolitionists of Great Britain. So much has been done by Prest, Birney, Stanton and *Van Buren,* John Scoble, as they, in the capacity of philanthropic gentlemen, travelled all over the kingdom to prejudice the mind of the leading abolitionists of the country, that we are shunned by them as we should have been by the rankest pro-slavery men of our country.[96]

The Convention had provided an opportunity for international slavery to share a forum, although actual unity remained ephemeral.

Post-Convention Ireland

Following the Convention, three groups of American abolitionists toured Britain, lecturing in various locations. While in London, Garrison shared a platform with O'Connell. At this stage, it appeared that O'Connell was closer to the approach of the Garrisonians than to that of the supporters of Tappan. Garrison and his group, which included Remond, then visited Scotland and Ireland.[97] In Ireland, Garrison stayed with the Webb family, where he was visited by O'Connell. At the end of his tour, he attended a large gathering in Dublin during which O'Connell made a withering attack on slavery.[98] Lucretia and James Mott also visited Ireland. In Dublin they were entertained by James Haughton and Richard Webb. On their way to Belfast they 'passed miserable huts, and poor villages, with wretched looking people, mostly barefoot'.[99] From there, they travelled to Belfast.

A positive outcome of the Convention was that it revived abolitionist activities in Ireland. In October 1840, the Hibernian Anti-Slavery Society convened a public meeting in Dublin, which was its first for almost two years. The prominent American abolitionists, James Birney and Henry B. Stanton, and the English abolitionist, John Scoble, were present. Richard Allen, the secretary, reiterated the fact that, like the British and Foreign Association, the Hibernian Society was committed to using only moral and peaceful means to end slavery and they did not approve of using an armed force under any circumstances. Birney, a former slave-owner, spoke from first-hand experience of the way in which slaves were treated by their masters. He said that the movement against slavery in various European countries would bring it to an end in America.[100]

Birney and Scoble next travelled to Belfast, although Birney became delayed visiting relatives in Cootehill. In November 1840, Scoble attended an anti-slavery meeting in Belfast, described as being the largest ever. It was held in a Presbyterian hall, and a large number of Protestant ministers were present. The Reverend Thomas Drew, an evangelical Anglican minister who was also a member of the Orange Order, was in the chair.[101] Drew commenced the meeting with a prayer. He then pointed out that this was not a political meeting but one of 'charity and love'; however, he followed this by pointing out that 'Ministers of the Established Church had not been put sufficiently in the foreground of slave emancipation'. Drew asked for England, Scotland and Ireland to exert 'moral pressure' on the American government. The theme of pressuring religious ministers in the United States, 'their transatlantic brethren', to join the cause was taken up by other speakers.[102]

Birney and Scoble were not the only visitors to Ireland. In 1841, Remond visited the country. Remond, a black abolitionist from Salem, Massachusetts, was renowned for his oratory. Those who opposed him did so in unexpected ways. Mary Ireland, a member of the female Anti-Slavery Society in Cork, informed a friend in Boston of a rumour that Remond was, a white man 'who had assumed the Ethiop tinge to suit a purpose'.[103] Nonetheless, he attracted large crowds: in Belfast each of his lectures was attended by over 3,000 people. Remond made a lasting impression in Cork, which he visited in November. He was still being praised when Fredrick Douglass travelled to the city four years later.[104] Remond also lectured before the Hibernian Anti-Slavery Society in Dublin. He was preceded by Richard Allen who spoke about slavery in British India. Allen, like many abolitionists, had come to believe that American and Indian slavery were linked, and that ending slavery in the latter would be a death blow to the former. Remond agreed with this, pointing out:

> In British India is to be found the instrument which will put to death American slavery. If British India may produce, in as great excellence and abundance, those things which are mow imported from America at the expense of slave toil, why should not British give preference to the former country? It is only consistent with her well known love of liberty that she should do so.[105]

Remond flattered his Irish audience, describing them as 'men who in the year 1841 have the name of philanthropists,' while referred to himself as 'an advocate of a cause, which, above all others, be, and ever has been, dear to the Irish heart'.[106] However, Remond's most fulsome praise was reserved for O'Connell:

> When Mr O'Connell, and now that I have mentioned his name, let me take occasion to say how deeply I venerate that good and mighty man, who has put himself forth as the undaunted and fearless champion of liberty and the rights of man in every clime the sun adorns ... I was about to say something with reference to a man who is justly dear to all your hearts, but you interrupted me in the middle of my sentence, and I am now sure that I have not forgotten all that I intended to utter.[107]

Remond concluded his panegyric on O'Connell by retelling the story of O'Connell's encounter with the American Ambassador, Andrew Stevenson. Stevenson, in his opinion, 'was not fit to have had a local habitation amid a free people.'[108] Overall, Remond was happy with the three months that he spent in Ireland, commenting that he was 'pleased to say as my belief that I have been instrumental in awakening much interest for the furtherance of the good cause'.[109]

O'Connell and Ireland

O'Connell had undoubtedly been the star of the London Convention. Yet while he was attracting international attention within the anti-slavery movement, he was also gaining notice for his decision to revive the repeal movement. Throughout 1840, O'Connell had been fighting a number of issues relating to Ireland. He had become increasingly disenchanted with his pact with the Whigs and with the idea that an alliance with a British political party could bring genuine benefits to Ireland. These fears were confirmed in 1840 when Lord Stanley introduced into Parliament an Irish Registration Bill that disadvantaged Irish voters. Stanley's Bill had been opposed by a number of Irish members. John Grattan described it as, 'impolitic, unwise, and unjust, and its effects would be to annul the Emancipation Act of 1829, by destroying the ten-shilling voters, who were principally Catholics'.[110] In March 1840, a public meeting was held in Dublin to appoint a committee to consider the Bill's impact.[111] Agitation over the Registration Bill coincided with a renewed campaign to bring about a repeal of the Act of Union. In April, O'Connell launched a National Association, which was later renamed the Loyal National Repeal Association. His second-in-command in this endeavour was his son, John, also an ardent abolitionist. From this point, his pact with the Whigs was unofficially over. Instead, O'Connell started to build a movement modelled on the earlier, successful Catholic Association. At the end of May, O'Connell informed his long-term supporters that repeal was the 'one hope – one chance – one remedy' to redress the grievances of Ireland.[112] Irish abolitionists were divided on the question of repeal. James Haughton supported O'Connell and joined the Repeal Association, but Webb and Allen remained opposed to it.

Only the day before the Convention, O'Connell had been involved in a dispute in the House of Commons regarding the Irish Registration Bill, which he described as 'a bill to trample on the rights of the people of Ireland'.[113] The subsequent debate was heated, with O'Connell being prevented from speaking, leading him to describe his opponents as 'beastly' and 'bellowing'. Whenever he attempted to speak, he was drowned out with whistling, jeering and even singing. The Conservative politician, Benjamin Disraeli, described O'Connell's behaviour on the day as being 'insanely savage'.[114] The Whig politician and fellow abolitionist, Thomas Macauley, offered a more balanced view of the debate, writing that, 'O'Connell raged like a mad bull ... I for one, while regretting and condemning his violence, thought it much extenuated by the provocation'.[115] O'Connell was defended by an English Whig MP, Hedworth Lambton, who declared 'in my humble opinion, it is disgraceful for an assembly of English gentlemen to tyrannize over one member of this house'.[116] When O'Connell had left the Convention on the afternoon of its first day, he had immediately attended the House of Commons. There, he gave notice that in relation to the Registration of Voters bill he would be asking the committee to define the right of voting.[117] Shortly after the Convention ended, O'Connell travelled to Ireland and addressed repeal meetings in various parts of the country, including as far west as County Mayo.[118]

The revival of the repeal movement was carried on concurrently with O'Connell's anti-slavery activities. At the Convention, O'Connell had publicly agreed that he would send an Address to Irish immigrants in America. He was reminded about this promise over the following months. The American abolitionist James Birney had toured the United Kingdom following the Convention. In Ireland, he attended a repeal meeting in Dublin in October 1840. Despite being extremely busy, O'Connell met with Birney and assured him that the address was 'neither forgotten nor neglected'. Birney believed that the subsequent delay in preparing an address was 'doubtless, owing to the judicious change of the original plan, and the time required for obtaining the signatures of sixty thousand of his countrymen'.[119]

In 1841, O'Connell was elected Lord Mayor of Dublin, making him the first Catholic to hold this position since the seventeenth century. O'Connell carried out this role while escalating the repeal campaign and continuing to be a prominent spokesman on transatlantic slavery. In the same year, he was appointed chairman of a Watch Committee, established to oversee emigration from Ireland to the West Indies in an effort to ensure that the Irish were not inadvertently replacing black with white slavery.[120] O'Connell had also emerged as a leading parliamentary champion of the agitation for a repeal of the Corn Laws.[121] He was now aged 65. Amelie Opie, an English Quaker abolitionist, was present at an anti-slavery meeting on 14 May 1841 and offered an objective assessment of his physical appearance. The meeting had proved to be a fractious one as some Chartists had climbed onto the platform and had only been removed by police intervention. The last speaker:

> at length, generally called for, rose O'Connell, in his might and his majesty, and the magical music of his voice hushed the jarring elements to peace. He is a marvelous person! ... he had a lady with him, his own dear daughter ... He certainly must have been ill, though he looks blooming; for he is excessively shrunk; but he looks the better for it. He spoke admirably, but I thought his voice less powerful than usual. Tonight he holds, at the Crown and Anchor, a meeting for Repeal. He said several unguarded things, but still the charm predominated.[122]

Opie next visited the Reform Club and the first person that she met there was O'Connell:

> To be sure we had a cordial meeting and a shaking of hands ... he would make such a fine drawing! He had wrapt a cloak round his manly form; and his loss of flesh (of which he had far too much) makes his neck look longer; and his cheeks being less round, his face appears less flat; the nose is much handsomer than I thought it was. I reckon on hearing him again on 17th, at the Aborigines Protection Society.[123]

O'Connell's expertise and oratorical skills meant that he was in great demand. The London Convention had inspired a number of follow-up meetings and, in 1842, the French abolitionists planned a meeting in Paris and they issued a special request to O'Connell. They hoped that ending slavery in the French Colonies would expedite its downfall in Cuba and Brazil. The London Anti-Slavery Committee had appointed a delegation to attend, but Sturge impressed on O'Connell that:

> The freedom of *millions* may under Providence in no small degree depend upon thy being at this important meeting, and I hope thou wilt excuse my pressing they attendance in the very strongest manner that I can. Great as no doubt will be the sacrifice, I do believe thou wilt have an ample satisfaction in making it.[124]

O'Connell did not travel to the French conference. Even for a younger man, his schedule would have been punishing, but O'Connell showed no signs of slowing down.

Irish-America

In the years after 1840, O'Connell continued to be as controversial a figure in the US as he was in Britain, but for different reasons. His unequivocal condemnation of slavery touched a raw nerve in a country that remained ambiguous as to what role slaves should have in its society. Patriotism and loyalty to the American Eagle also contributed to an unwillingness to condemn slavery. Initially, the founding of a new repeal movement in Ireland was of interest to Irish immigrants in the US who sought to combine being American citizens with being Irish nationalists. In addition to providing moral support, Irish-American repealers proved to be an important source of revenue for the Repeal Association. However, the combining of anti-slavery and repeal caused problems for O'Connell and his son John, in Ireland. After 1840, the repeal movement spread in the United States and money continued to be sent to Ireland, from both slave-holding and non-slaveholding states. O'Connell's acceptance of all of this money made some of his fellow abolitionists uneasy. At the end of October 1840, the *Dublin Chronicle* included a report of a repeal meeting in Dublin in which John O'Connell allegedly said that 'communications had been made to them [the Repeal Association] that, if they kept apart from the anti-slavery movement, sums of money would pour into the funds of the association to advance its purposes', but this offer had been 'scorned'. When asked by Dr Madden to name the source of the offer, he had refused.[125] John O'Connell later denied the accuracy of this particular report, but he admitted that if the Association continued to support slavery, it was likely that contributions would stop from parts of America.[126]

The controversy over accepting contributions from America continued and by 1842, it was dividing repealers in both Ireland and America. In May, James Haughton appealed to O'Connell to stop taking contributions from American repealers who continued to condone slavery. O'Connell responded that his policy was to persuade rather than alienate these people.[127] In October 1842, the usually gentle Haughton again wrote to O'Connell, pleading:

> I know you hate slavery; your whole life has been one continuous act of opposition to the iniquity in all its forms. Now is the critical moment for Ireland. We must either rise in the esteem or sink into the contempt of the good and free-hearted in America. I conjure you to put an end to the unholy alliance between Irishmen and slave-dealers in America ... The work of your life will be marred and destroyed by such an unholy contamination.[128]

Linking slavery with the aims of the newly formed Repeal Association was something with which repealers in America were not comfortable. Gerrit Smith from New York, who had been a founder of the American Liberal Party, questioned O'Connell about his accepting money from people who upheld slavery, adding:

I am far from saying this is wrong ... But that you should allow your opinion of American abolitionists to be modified by what their pro-slavery revilers say of them, very naturally instills the fear that, after all, slavery is not so unutterably bad in your eyes but that you can confide in the testimony of its advocates against men whom scarcely any earthly testimony should suffice to convict of a want of integrity.[129]

At a repeal meeting in Dublin in 1842, O'Connell spoke of the importance of having American sympathy, comparing it to the support provided during the agitation for Catholic Emancipation. He added that although the enemies of Ireland did not like American involvement in repeal, 'it was to be recollected that the part of America from which they received the largest contribution was unstained with any species of slavery'. During the meeting, the receipt of money from Boston, Buffalo and Cincinnati was noted.[130]

Within Irish-America, there was some frustration with O'Connell's frequent attacks on American slavery. The New York *Truth Teller*, for example, admired O'Connell and supported repeal. This paper was an organ of the Irish-born John Hughes, who had been Bishop of New York since 1838. Within the United States, Bishop John Hughes was one of the most powerful leaders in the Catholic Church. As a young pastor in Philadelphia in 1829, he had written a sermon giving thanks for Catholic Emancipation, which he inscribed to Daniel O'Connell.[131] In July and August 1841, the *Truth Teller* had serialized the publication of 'Memoirs, Private and Political of Daniel O'Connell'. It also included a weekly column entitled 'Repeal! Repeal! Repeal!', which commenced with the axiom 'The American cock crowing on the other side of the Atlantic shall awaken Ireland from her dreary slumbers and bid her arise to enjoy a day of light and happiness'. In November 1841, the *Truth Teller*, published a long address written by O'Connell in which he praised Irish-Americans.[132] However, the newspaper did not support abolition: nor did Bishop Hughes. Hughes believed that Africans were better off as slaves in the United States than as free men in Africa, if slave-owners behaved responsibly. His solution, therefore, was to urge slave-owners to greater charity towards their slaves.[133] Like many American church leaders, Hughes hated abolitionists. His hatred was partly irrational: it arose from the fact that the movement had been started by Protestants, notably English Protestants.[134] Part of his opposition was based on his dislike of the extremism of the abolitionists and their liberal agenda on topics such as women's rights.[135] Although O'Connell's pronouncements against slavery continued, the paper simply ignored them. Hughes, while remaining an admirer of O'Connell and a supporter of repeal believed:

His [O'Connell's] thinking on the slave question was never organized into a coherent system of ideas. His expressed thoughts were usually ambiguous, sometimes contradictory and always filled with the tension which frequently characterized northern intellectuals who attempted to reconcile the harsh realities of slavery with their lofty principles of humanity.[136]

It was increasingly apparent that O'Connell, whose main contact with the US had been through American abolitionists, did not understand the complexities of opposing slavery for those who resided in the country. Nor he did realize that even the Church hierarchy there remained ambivalent on the slave question. Moreover, not only was abolition disloyal to the American constitution, it was increasingly regarded as a hazard to the union of the country. A number of slaveholders had threatened to withdraw from the Federal Union if slavery was prohibited. Interference with the American Union was an extremely sensitive subject. While lecturing in Ireland, Remond had referred to this issue and to the fact that slaveholders used the dissolution of the union as a threat to silence their opposition. Remond believed it was an empty gesture as:

> the moment when the American Union is dissolved, that instant the power of the slave-holder is prostrated in the dust. Hopeless, helpless, friendless, they become an isolated class of beings, having nothing to depend on but their own strength, and that is weakness indeed.[137]

However, support for disunion came from an unlikely source – Garrison. Inspired by O'Connell's movement to end the union with Britain, Garrison became an advocate of breaking the union with the slave states in America.[138] He declared:

> For my own part, I avow myself to be both an Irish Repealer and an American Repealer. I go for repeal of the Union between England and Ireland, and for repeal of the union between the North and the South. We must dissolve all connection with the murderers of fathers, and murderers of mothers, and murderers of liberty, and traffickers in human flesh, and blasphemers against the Almighty, at the South ... Why have we not dissolved the union in form, as in fact? [139]

In 1842, Garrison announced the American Anti-Slavery Society was making 'the repeal of the Union ... [its] grand rallying point'.[140]

Clearly, O'Connell's activities and his influence were continuing to cause trouble at the heart of the slave world, and these rumblings were to become an uproar in 1842, following the receipt of the Address to Irish Americans.

5 'FOREIGN INTERFERENCE IN DOMESTIC AFFAIRS'

By the beginning of the 1840s, O'Connell had achieved an unparalleled role in the transatlantic anti-slavery movement, with even his detractors admitting the power of his words and his presence at any abolition gathering. The London Convention in 1840 had consolidated his position as an influential leader in the transatlantic struggle. It had also been the occasion on which he had promised publicly to publish an appeal, in the form of an address, to Irish-Americans, calling on them to oppose slavery. The timing was improprietous for O'Connell, coinciding with the relaunch of the repeal movement and his election as Mayor of Dublin, both of which combined with his usual parliamentary duties that required him to be in London. Nonetheless, at the beginning of 1842, the arrival of the 'Address from the People of Ireland to Their Countrymen and Countrywomen in America' was announced in Boston. The response was polarized: abolitionists were delighted with it, but Irish-Americans, who disliked being singled out on such a controversial issue, were embarrassed by it. The Address, rather than bolstering support for abolition, embroiled O'Connell in a further transatlantic controversy that was not entirely of his making.

The Address was an outcome of O'Connell's involvement in the London Convention. Despite becoming indelibly linked with his name, the Address had actually been written by two of the founders of the Hibernian Anti-Slavery Society, Richard Davis Webb and James Haughton. It was taken to the United States in December 1841 by Charles Lenox Remond, following the completion of his tour of the United Kingdom.[1] It had been signed by an estimated 60,000 Irish people, with O'Connell and Father Mathew, the two most famous Irishmen of the period, heading the list of signatures. Mysteriously, Mathew's name had not been there at the end of 1841, yet it appeared on the Address when it arrived in Boston early in 1842.[2] In April 1842, Richard Allen sent a further 10,000 Irish signatures to the United States.[3] The Address was short – less than two pages, and was accompanied by a letter from Haughton. Unusually for a document of this time, the Address appealed to men and women equally: a tacit acknowledgment of the contribution that women had made to the various anti-slavery campaigns. However, by foregrounding the involvement of the man responsible for winning Catholic Emancipation and that of a Catholic priest, it may have appeared to be appealing to the Catholic Irish only. The Address opened:

> Dear Friends:
>
> You are a great distance from your native land! A wide expanse of water separates you from the beloved country of your birth – from us and from the kindred whom you love, and who love you, and pray for your happiness and prosperity in the land of your adoption ...

It explained:

> The object of this address is to call your attention to the subject of slavery in America – that foul blot upon the noble institution and the fair fame of your adopted country. But for this one stain, America would indeed be a land worthy your adoption; but she will never be the glorious country that her free Constitution designed her to be, so long as her soil is polluted by the foot-prints of a single slave ...
>
> The American citizen proudly points to the National Declaration of Independence, which declares that all mankind are born free and equal, and are alike entitled to life, liberty, and the pursuit of happiness. Aid him to carry out this noble declaration, by obtaining freedom for the slave.
>
> Irishmen and Irishwomen! Treat the coloured people as your equals, as brethren. By all your memories of Ireland, continue to love liberty – hate slavery – CLING BY THE ABOLITIONISTS – and in America you will do honour to the name of Ireland.[4]

Despite the late appearance of the Address, its arrival caused much excitement amongst American abolitionists. James Birney, who had met with O'Connell in London and in Dublin, said 'It is just such an address as I should expect from the clear and comprehensive mind of Mr O'Connell'.[5] At a meeting of the Anti-Slavery Society in Boston, Garrison announced its arrival. Wendell Philips then made a resolution that:

> We rejoice that the voice of O'Connell, which now shakes the three kingdoms, has poured across the waters a thunder-peal for the cause of Liberty in our own land, and that Father Mathew having lifted, with one hand, five millions of his own countrymen into moral life, has stretched forth the other – which may Heaven make equally potent – to smite off the fetters of the American slave ...
>
> We receive, with the greatest gratitude, the names of the sixty thousand Irishmen, who, in the trial hour of their own struggle for liberty, have not forgotten the slave on this side of the water; that we accept, with triumphant exultation, the Address they have forwarded to us, and pledge ourselves to circulate it through the length and breadth of the land, till the pulse of every man, and especially every man who claims Irish parentage, beats true to the claims of patriotism and humanity.[6]

Privately, a number of Boston abolitionists were disappointed. They had hoped that the Address would contain 100,000 signatures, leading John Collins, an agent for the Massachusetts Anti-Slavery Society, to ask of Richard Webb, 'How soon will the other 42,000 reach us?'[7] Collins was part of a committee to organize a meeting of Irish-Americans to present the Address. He had already called to see the editor of the *Pilot,* the leading Catholic and Irish newspaper in Boston. Collins believed that the *Pilot* was 'the thermometer of Irish feeling in this country'. The editor was Irish-born Patrick Donahoe, a supporter of O'Connell and of repeal.[8] Although opposed to slavery, Donahoe had informed Collins, 'It would not do for them to take hold of the question of abolition'.[9] The response of the editor was a mirror of the dilemma facing all Irish-Americans. Even if they opposed slavery privately, openly siding with the abolitionists was not acceptable – a fact that their compatriots in Ireland did not always understand.

Garrison appeared impervious to some of these concerns. He viewed the Address as an important tool in 'breaking a stupendous conspiracy, which I believe is going on between the leading Irish demagogues, the leading pseudo democrats, and the Southern Slave-holders'. He believed that the Irish were all Democrats because the Democratic Party feigned to support Irish repeal – but that this was only a ploy to keep them from supporting abolition. Cynically, to secure Irish support, they were 'sending donations over to Ireland, to stop O'Connell's mouth on the subject of slavery, and to bring their united strength to bear against the anti-slavery enterprise'. Garrison believed that if O'Connell and other supporters in Ireland remained true 'it will put down at the South this pretended sympathy for Ireland'.[10]

On 28 January 1842, the Address was presented in Faneuil Hall in Boston. An estimated 3,000 attended of whom 1,200 were thought to be Irishmen. Garrison, who was in the chair, described it as being 'a voice ... from good ould Ireland', which drew shouts of 'Hurra for Dan O'Connell', 'God Bless Father Mathew; and 'Hurra for repale [*sic*]'.[11] He then criticized Democrats for supporting repeal and sending donations to Ireland, accusing them of only doing so to get the Irish-American vote.[12] Garrison also likened the oppression of Ireland with the oppression of slaves. He averred that:

> England, in true slave-holding style, says that Ireland cannot take care of herself and therefore *she* will look after the interests of the Emerald Isle ... But Ireland has made up her mind, that she will no longer be the vassal of England, to be subjected to famine, oppression and misrule. Success to her in every righteous effort to secure her emancipation.[13]

Similar sentiments were echoed by Wendell Phillips, who invoked the memories of Henry Grattan, Robert Emmet, John Curran and Edmund Burke. Fuller, himself an Irishman, then appealed to his compatriots on the grounds that 'Oppression drove you here and you came for universal liberty.'[14]

George Bradburn, who had met O'Connell at the Convention and had then visited Ireland, made a vituperative speech against the South. He informed his Irish-American listeners that, 'Daniel O'Connell and also Mathew gave him charge of the American Irish, and to tell them and to beseech them, as they hated oppression, and loved freedom in the largest sense of the term, not to give their votes to any man who was not known to be a thorough-going abolitionist ... let not the blood be found on your garment for voting against the oppressed ... I appeal to your patriotism in the name of an Emmett [*sic*], of a Curran, of O'Connell, of Father Mathew'.[15] Again, abolition was tied in with repeal, with Bradburn introducing a resolution:

> That this meeting most cordially wishes Old Ireland success, in all her righteous efforts to redeem the Emerald Isle from every species of British oppression, and especially in the grand movement of Daniel O'Connell, for the repeal of the fraudulent act of Union between his country and England.

The enthusiasm apparent at this meeting was short-lived as opposition to the Address, especially in the Irish-American press, was swift and ferocious. In a letter to Richard Webb, his friend in Ireland and one of the organizers of the Address, Garrison admitted:

> Our meeting in Faneuil Hall to unroll the Irish Address, with its sixty thousand signatures, was indescribably enthusiastic, and has produced a great impression on the public mind. I am sorry to add, and you will be not less ashamed to hear, that the two Irish papers in Boston sneer at the Address, and denounce it and the abolitionists in true pro-slavery style. I fear they will keep the great mass of your countrymen here from uniting with us.[16]

That Garrison had underestimated the strength of feeling against the Address was soon evident. Moreover, the most vocal opposition came not from the abolitionists in the South, but from the North, including from fellow Irishmen. The *New York Herald*, when reporting the arrival of the Address, stated that it was a dangerous tactic to 'enlist the Irish to join the bloody crusade against the South, by the use and means of a direct, positive foreign influence' and not one that those who opposed abolition would tolerate it. Mischievously, the paper wryly asked 'Where is Father Hughes?'[17]

The concerns of the *New York Herald* regarding the interference of an outsider in the internal affairs of America were quickly confirmed, with even papers that supported O'Connell condemning the Address. In Boston, the condemnation was led by the *Pilot*, a local newspaper with a large circulation amongst Irish immigrants. One article suggested that O'Connell really did not understand the issues involved and could not be fully aware of the extremities of the abolitionists. It warned him that if he continued to ally with the Northern abolitionists, he would alienate much 'chivalorous' support for repeal in the South.[18] However, the Boston *Pilot* made an important observation – a point that Donahoe had made already to Collins: Irish-Americans were not pro-slavery, but nor were they pro-abolitionist.[19] For Garrison, however, it was not possible to be neutral on the issue of abolition. Garrison and his followers used the columns of the *Liberator* to refute all of the *Pilot*'s assertions, claiming that their purpose had been 'to destroy the electrifying effect of the Address which has been sent over from Ireland'. To demonstrate how fully O'Connell understood and sympathized with the abolitionists, large portions of his speeches at the London Convention were quoted.[20] More damning criticism of the Address was to come. An article in the *Boston Catholic Diary* commenced by admitting that slavery was 'unjust', but added, 'the zealots who would madly attempt to eradicate the evil by the destruction of our Federal Union, and thus spread devastation and anarchy throughout the land, are infinitely more reprehensible than the most tyrannical slaveholders'.[21] Criticism was directed at both O'Connell and Father Mathew:

> The illustrious Liberator and the Apostle of Temperance have an indisputable right to affix their signatures to any document which may appear to them equitable, but their autograph, or even an exhortation from the eloquent lips of either, implies no right to shackle the opinions of the Irishmen of America. We respect – we revere – those men as the greatest benefactors of our native land, but as dictators over the reason and mind we deny and repel the assumption of such authority.

The *Boston Catholic Diary*'s most severe criticism was reserved for the Boston abolitionists who had sought to 'pervert' the views of O'Connell and Mathew and 'flatter Irishmen into the frenzy of abolitionism – to hold us up as the target for Southern pistols and the sheath for Southern bowie-knives'.[22]

Even more pointed attacks followed. The *New York Courier and Enquirer*, under the headline 'Foreign Interference' claimed that O'Connell had 'transmitted to "his agents" in this country "an appeal" signed by himself and 60,000 other "malcontents"'.[23] It also included a letter from the outspoken Bishop John Hughes of New York, who had written to the *Courier* suggesting that the Address was not authentic, and now challenged:

> Should it prove to be authentic, then I have no hesitation in declaring my opinion that it is the duty of every civilized Irishman to reject and repudiate that address with indignation. Not precisely because of the doctrine which it contains – but because of their having emanated from a foreign source, and of their tendency to operate on questions of domestic and national policy. I am no friend of slavery, but I am still less friendly to any attempt of *foreign origin* to abolish it. The duties of naturalized Irishmen, or others, I conceive to be in no wise distinct or different from those of native born Americans. And if it be proved that an attempt has been made by this Address, or any Address, to single them out in any question appertaining to the foreign or domestic policy of the United States, in any other

capacity than that which is common to the whole population, I then think it will be their duty to their country and their conscience to rebuke such an attempt come from what foreign source it may, in the most decided manner and language that common courtesy will authorize.[24]

The article went on to say that just as Irishmen had no right to interfere in the affairs of America, so did Irishmen in America have no right to interfere in the affairs of Ireland. The dilemma felt by Irish-Americans was evident in the response made by the *Truth Teller*. Initially, the paper had described the *Courier* article as a 'misrepresentation in low language, and unworthy of any respectable paper'. In its editorial, the paper defended the right of Irish-Americans to care about Ireland and to support repeal.[25] The *Truth Teller*, however, was caught between its admiration for O'Connell and its reluctance to become involved in the slavery controversy. In an addendum to the editorial the *Truth Teller* stated:

> Since the above was in type we have read with profound attention the letter of our eminent and venerated Bishop; and it is with feelings of self-congratulation we coincide with him in doubting the authenticity of the 'appeal' to which are now attached the names of Daniel O'Connell and Fr Mathew. We were satisfied the moment we saw this document that it contained internal evidence of a spurious character. Daniel O'Connell is too wise, too good a tactician, to stultify himself by invoking American sympathy for Ireland, and then throwing amongst us an appeal of discord. The letter, however, which we submit to our readers from an ever-active and pious Prelate, is another proof of his zeal in the cause of truth, and of his sensibility in all cases, of even a chance of misconstruction of his motives and his conduct, either spiritually or temporally'.[26]

After questioning the authenticity of the Address, Hughes called on his fellow Irishmen to 'repudiate the address with indignation'.[27] Hughes's assertion that Irishmen had no right to interfere in the affairs of America was criticized by some abolitionists. James Birney pointed out Hughes's inconsistency in supporting Irish repeal and thereby interfering in the affairs of Britain.[28] In a letter to the *Free Press,* Birney challenged Hughes to produce evidence of the Address's inauthenticity. He countered:

> It seems abundantly strange that one so intelligent as the Right Reverend gentleman, and so well informed as he ought to be, must be, as to the sentiments of Mr O'Connell, Father Mathew, and Dr. Madden, and the Irish *at home universally,* on the subject of slavery, and in the absence of all evidence, should deny the genuineness of so remarkable a document ... It is no light thing in anyone, and it is a very serious thing for him, who stands before the country clothed with the influence of a diocesan teacher of Christian ethics, recklessly to impute a base fraud to his neighbours and fellow citizens.[29]

Hughes was not the only Bishop to condemn the Address. Bishop England of Charleston was equally dismissive. Their response was not simply motivated by their dislike of abolitionists. They were equally motivated by a desire to prove their loyalty to their adopted country, because 'American bishops knew that they too had to take every opportunity to counteract charges that they were being directed by influences outside the state'.[30]

The reaction to the Address resulted in a re-evaluation of O'Connell's influence on Irish America. Privately, Birney suggested that O'Connell had misunderstood the Irish in America:

> Mr O'Connell seemed to think that all was necessary to be done to insure from his American countrymen such a course in their future , as he felt confident was in strict unison with their unperverted feelings and judgment in every conflict between freedom and slavery, was to bring them seriously to reflect, to exhort them faithfully but affectionately to turn from their error; and to tell how much they have grieved their fathers and mothers and brothers and their whole kith and kin left behind, by dishonouring the case of liberty now everywhere associated with the name of Irishman.[31]

Edward Davis, a leading abolitionist in Philadelphia, urged that more proof of the authenticity of the Address be provided in order to silence its detractors. In particular, he desired that O'Connell should send a further address 'in his own burning and enspiriting words to his fellow countrymen here'. Davis qualified this by adding, 'He knows not his influence in this country, how much those who hate him even, would give to know what he has to say. He owes it to the slave to use the influence he has'.[32]

The idea that the Address was not authentic was taken up by some repeal groups. The Baltimore Association had a lengthy and heated discussion on this topic. In the course of it, a resolution proposed by Richard McNally encapsulated the unease felt by many Irish-Americans with the Address, while criticizing O'Connell for allowing repeal to become mixed up with other subjects. McNally referred to the Address as 'a paper purporting to be by Daniel O'Connell, Theobald Mathew, R. Madden, and sixty thousand other Irishmen, and addressed to the Irish born citizens of those us, has lately made its appearance in this city'. The meeting then passed the following:

> Resolved. That the Repeal Association of Baltimore seeing in this paper undoubted evidence of forgery or fraud, unhesitatingly pronounce it a fabrication, intended for the most base and insidious purposes, and denounce it in the strongest and most indignant terms, as a fire-brand thrown between Irishmen and their native fellow-citizens.
>
> Resolved. That Irish born citizens of the Repeal Association of Baltimore hold themselves bound in this, the country of their adoption, to the preservation of its institutions, its tranquility and its integrity, by every duty, every bond, by which their native-born fellow-citizens conceive themselves bound; and that they are prepared in

affection, interest and obligation, to defend with their lives and property its institutions, its tranquility and integrity.[33]

Resolved. That on the part of their countrywomen, the Irish men of this Association repel, with feelings of disgust and abhorrence, the call made upon them by the authors of this vile and base foundation.

Resolved. That the Irish born citizens of the Baltimore Repeal Association repel this address, from whosoever it may emanate, what source, or from what motive or cause so it may.

Resolved. That neither the interest of the Association, nor the obligations and feelings of its members, recognize any power nor will they tolerate, on any pretext whatever, any such foreign interference in the domestic concerns, state policy, or government of the United States, under whose laws, institutions and union, they have found security and political privileges, and in the preservation of which institutions, and the integrity of which union, they can alone hope to transmit this security, and these political privileges, to their children.

A second speaker called on all Irishmen to distance themselves from the abolitionists, 'those desperate fanatics, who, to abolish Negro servitude, would wreck and crush a world of freedom. Those who would charge us with tardiness in repelling this appeal, do so falsely and maliciously, for so far as the repeal societies are concerned, the question was settled at the Convention in Philadelphia'. He went on to accuse the Irish who supported abolition of being disloyal Americans on the grounds that:

> Irish adopted citizens have sworn allegiance to this country – upon the Evangely of Almighty God they have promised to support her Constitution, maintain her institutions, and defend her against foreign aggression, and all enemies whatsoever. This they are ready to do under every circumstance ... No consideration, no reward, no hope, though that hope was to make Ireland as free and happy as the country we live in, could tempt Irishmen to pluck a feather from the proud eagle beneath whose wings they found shelter and protection – a home and freedom (great applause).[34]

Similar protests were expressed by repeal groups elsewhere. Repealers in Pottsville, Pennsylvania, objected to having been addressed 'in terms other than those of American citizens'. Additionally, they rejected any suggestion that they were in alliance with the abolitionists and they objected to O'Connell's inference that black people were the equal of white people. Their much-publicized protests were, in turn, criticized in Ireland, where they were condemned by a number of newspapers and during a meeting of the Repeal Association in Dublin. The Pottsville repealers reacted by describing the Irish press as 'a guardian of vice and blackguardism'.[35] In Britain, James Grahame published a pamphlet in which he speculated about Irish-American support for slavery and cited the Pottsville repealers for typifying Irish emigrants who had felt compelled to adopt American prejudices.[36] Overall, the commotion caused by the Irish Address was a plain reminder of the fragility of the transatlantic abolition movement, and the intransigence of the opposition to it.

The reactions to the Address were tracked by Garrison's *Liberator,* which reprinted some of the most critical articles. Garrison was particularly angry with the response of the Boston *Pilot,* which he accused of attempting to 'destroy the electrifying effect of the Address'. He added:

> We should like to look at the countenance of Daniel O'Connell while he is perusing this selfish, base and libelous article in the Pilot. It will cause a glow of honest indignation to mantle his cheeks, and exhort from his lips words of the sternest condemnation. It will excite the scorn of every free spirit in the Emerald Isle.[37]

But the arrival in April 1842 of a further 10,000 signatures to the Address led to further attacks in the press. The Boston *Pilot* referred to the actions of the Irish abolitionists as a 'crusade against the American Union'. It suggested that O'Connell and Mathew had only signed the Address reluctantly. The *Liberator* countered these attacks by quoting a letter from Richard Allen, describing O'Connell and Mathew signing the Address:

> [O'Connell's] full, beaming and cordial face warmly welcoming Us ... and the vigour with which he snatched the pen, and endorsed his name to the Irish Address, not in a corner, but at the head of the sixty thousand ... could they have seen the cordiality with which Father Mathew walked into my house, and laid down the roll with his own name attached to it.[38]

Nonetheless, there were some concerns that when O'Connell and other Irish abolitionists heard about the response to the Address they would distance themselves from it. John Collins was convinced that this would not be the case and reassured Webb:

> The repealers of Ireland must not be afraid that it will diminish their friends at all from this country, as everyone knows that O'Connell and all the Irish of Ireland are abolitionists and will be honoured by all for their fidelity to the cause of human freedom, but will be thoroughly disposed of if they are made to succumb for a few paltry dollars. I have no fear of O'Connell backing out. I know some of the trying position he occupies at home among his own friends as he denounces American slavery while he needs the money of the Irish of this country to sustain his repeal operations. This exhibits on his part – a fineness of principle – a decision of character worthy of the man.[39]

James Canning Fuller, who had originally asked O'Connell to prepare an Address, contacted him in March 1842, saying that he had witnessed the reception of the Address in Boston, but 'the foes of liberty, with shame it be said that some of them are Irishmen, are by all means they can devise endeavouring to destroy the good produced, indeed, to destroy the credibility of the Address itself'. He urged O'Connell to write an even stronger address to Irish-Americans and if he could get Father Mathew to sign it 'no mortal can tell how powerful the action it might induce for the overthrow of slavery'.[40] However, when Garrison and Remond presented the Address in Albany on 21 April 1842, they were disappointed with its reception. By then, it appeared that O'Connell was adopting a more pragmatic approach to involving Irish America in the abolition struggle. He promised that Irish repealers would not interfere directly or indirectly with American slavery. This may have pleased Irish-Americans, but it dismayed American abolitionists.[41]

Why was the opposition to the Address so vehement? For the historian Benjamin Quarles, 'The fear of labour competition from Negroes was the dominant reason for the coolness of the Irish American toward the abolitionist movement'.[42] Economic considerations were clearly important. When the Irish had arrived in the United States in large numbers in the nineteenth century, they had taken the menial jobs that had previous been done by urban black people. In doing so, they demonstrated that they were aware of 'the advantage conferred by their skin colour'.[43] However, for Maurice Bric, financial considerations were secondary to those of identity. Irish-Americans were, at the time, engaged 'in forging a new identity and "ethnicity" in America, Irish-Americans were not prepared to be blindly guided by a leadership that they had left behind in Ireland'.[44] They 'did not want to be caught up in these debates', but nor did they 'welcome anybody who questioned their loyalty to their new homeland and, however innocently, presented them as "un-American"'.[45] The political ferment caused by the Address proved to be 'an important milestone in defining new relationships within the Irish Diaspora'.[46] Noel Ignatiev agreed that the Address was a watershed in the creation of an Irish-American identity, as it was, 'The first time Irish Americans as a group were asked to choose between supporting and opposing the colour line. Their response marked the turning point in their evolution toward membership in an oppressing race'.[47]

The timing of the Address was significant. The 1840s coincided with an increase in immigration to America; it also coincided with a growth in American nationalism. Even before the influx of poor Famine immigrants, a nativist movement was taking root that was anti-immigrant and anti-Catholic. William Orne White, a young Harvard graduate, was caught up in the anti-Irish sentiment. In his 1840 Commencement speech on 'The Irish Character', White declared: 'The sin of the Irishman is ignorance – the cure is Liberty'.[48] However, Irish Catholics continued to be a particular target for nativists as the anti-immigrants riots in Philadelphia in 1844 demonstrated. Repeal meetings had also been attacked by nativists.[49] John Collins of Massachusetts believed that O'Connell's blistering attacks on slaveholders had increased their anger not only against abolitionists, but also against Irish immigrants. In Collins's opinion, 'The Irish were suffering much in consequence of his course'.[50]

Initially, nativists had belonged to secret societies, but nativism took a more structured and sinister turn with the creation of the Native American Party or 'Know-Nothing Party' in the 1840s. By directing the address to Irish-Americans, this group had been singled out as being distinctive and apart from other people in America. Moreover, this approach had identified them as a group that was willing to criticize American institutions, while accepting American hospitality. In the eyes of native-born Americans and nativists, the Address represented a test of loyalty at a time that anti-immigrant feeling was increasing. The expectations placed on them by O'Connell were high at a time when nativism was spreading in influence. Clearly, the Address had touched a raw nerve amongst the Irish in America. Moreover, it alienated them from O'Connell just when their support for repeal was needed.

Divisions

O'Connell was shocked by the strength of opposition to the Address, which had been expressed by repeal societies as far apart as Louisiana and Albany. O'Connell responded to the criticisms by reiterating his dislike of slavery. The Address, however, had highlighted the difficulties faced by O'Connell's supporters in the United States, who wanted to draw a clear line between repeal and abolition. In April 1842, a Repeal Convention was held in Philadelphia. It made a decision at the outset not to discuss slavery or abolition. The *Truth Teller* praised the Convention for its display of Irish patriotism.[51] Significantly, while supporting O'Connell's campaign for repeal, the paper continued to ignore his involvement with abolition. The desire to separate the issues had widespread support. In May 1842, the paper published a letter from a Democratic politician, Colonel R. M. Johnson of Kentucky, in which he expressed his support for Irish repeal, adding:

> I am happy to discover that the Irish population are acting worthy of the patriotism and good sense by which the great mass have always been actuated, and I shall rejoice to see the subject of repeal kept separate from the irritating, unconstitutional subject of abolition.[52]

A similar plea was made by William Stokes of the Philadelphia Repeal Association who:

> referred in a very forcible manner to those mad fanatics who have made an abortive attempt to blend the dark cause of abolition with repeal ... As the subject of abolition is forced upon us, we must boldly meet it not by flight but by conflict. We are not abolitionists, nor are we opposed to abolition – we go in for the abolition of Irish

slavery – all other minor considerations sink into utter significance. Tell these men if they really desire something to gratify their appetites, they can find it in England, without crossing the Atlantic. They can pick up millions of white slaves there.[53]

An even stronger attack was made by the Albany Repeal Association, and their letter to the Repeal Association in Dublin was reprinted in the *Truth Teller*. The Albany repealers criticized abolitionists for being 'inflammatory', and blamed them for retarding the ending of slavery. They believed that the repeal associations throughout America were 'disturbed' by the linking of repeal with this question, especially as it originated 'mainly, if not exclusively in Ireland'. Furthermore, the recent appearance of the Address in Albany had 'given offence to several of the best and warmest Americans and ... Irish Americans'. In a long and detailed refutation of O'Connell's support for abolition, the Albany repealers reiterated the argument that slavery was constitutional and that any foreign interference was 'presumptuous and unwarrantable'. They also questioned 'Why should Irish citizens be thus designated as a distinct body?' The letter warned:

> With us no question can be agitated so alarming in its tendencies as the question of slavery; and I am certain nothing could more effectively alienate the sympathies of American Repealers than this new address, presented as it has been without any mitigating circumstances, and hence I regret to say that every Irish American citizen must regard it, to speak in the mildest terms, quite gratuitous, irrespective of its impolicy.[54]

In an argument that was to become commonplace, the repealers argued that the condition of slaves compared favourably with the condition of the people of Ireland:

> They are not only happier than the emancipated blacks in the free states, but thousands of nominally freemen in England and misgoverned Ireland would gladly exchange places with them. They are well clothed and fed, and can enjoy the air and light of heaven free and untaxed ... I know a land where but lately was my home in which these atrocities have been consummated. Unhappy Erin, fatherland. No, Sir, the slaves of America partake of all necessaries and comforts of life in abundance. They are visited by no periodical famines.[55]

The letter concluded by stating 'those who discountenance abolitionists are the real friends of Ireland'.[56] The letter from the Albany repealers was followed swiftly by one from the Lord Mayor of Albany. He regarded the previous letter as an apology for slavery and so he could not agree with it. The Mayor had signed the Address from Ireland, but this did not mean that he subscribed to 'a particular abolition society'. He believed that abolitionists were men like themselves and should not be demonized.[57] The letter from the Mayor demonstrated the complexity of the anti-slavery question and the determination of repealers in America to distinguish between opposing slavery and supporting abolitionism.

Whilst O'Connell's participation in the Irish Address was causing ructions in the United States, within Ireland things were generally peaceful. Some English observers believed that this was because O'Connell was not willing to take on the new Tory Prime Minister, Sir Robert Peel.[58] The Tory Party had won a landslide General Election in 1841 and their victory had effectively put an end to any hope of a further alliance between the Whigs and O'Connell. Yet in the months following the election, the repeal movement had been languishing. Nonetheless, O'Connell remained busy. In addition to his parliamentary and mayoral duties, he remained committed to various humanitarian campaigns. He had also commenced writing a two volume history of Ireland.[59] At this point, O'Connell disclosed to a correspondent in America that he was too busy to answer letters even though he was working all day and was not sleeping at nights.[60] He also confided in an Irish colleague that, 'Everybody writes to me about everything; so that I really do not read all the letters I receive'.[61] O'Connell, now almost seventy, appeared to be worn out. In 1842, though, the repeal campaign was refreshed by the founding of the popular *Nation* newspaper by three young members of the Repeal Association.[62] The youth and inexperience of the contributors to the *Nation* led to some of O'Connell's older supporters labelling them as 'Young Ireland'. However, a new era in Irish nationalist politics had begun. O'Connell seemed revitalized. Only a few months later, he declared 1843 to be 'repeal year'. In that year, O'Connell was going to challenge the British government, similarly to the way that he had challenged them for Catholic Emancipation. However, linking repeal and abolition together meant that O'Connell was not only challenging Peel's government, but all those who supported repeal but did not support abolition.

Repeal

O'Connell had declared 1843 was to be repeal year. It also proved to be the year in which O'Connell made some of his most strenuous attacks on slavery that propelled him into a number of transatlantic controversies, each of which proved to be both acrimonious and long-running. In January, O'Connell decided that he was going to spend less time in London on parliamentary duties.[63] The following month, after a three-day debate at the Dublin Corporation, O'Connell persuaded his fellow councillors to submit a petition to Parliament asking for a repeal of the Union.[64] The Lord Lieutenant of Ireland, Thomas de Grey, was alarmed at the rapid spread of support for repeal within such a short space of time. In a private communication of 6 May, he informed the Prime Minister, 'the burst of audacity which has broken out within this very short space of time, [is] astounding'. He warned, 'matters are looking so serious, that delay or temporizing will be ruin'.[65]

The Prime Minister, Sir Robert Peel, a longstanding adversary of O'Connell, had been responsible for steering Catholic Emancipation through Parliament, but he was adamant that the Union was inviolable. He reacted to de Grey's concerns by making a statement in the House of Commons, concurrently with one being made in the Lords by the Duke of Wellington, announcing the government's determination to preserve the Union and to 'use all the authority of the Government in support of it'.[66] Peel's willingness to take on O'Connell was indicated a few days later by his support for the dismissal of Irish magistrates who supported repeal. The explanation provided an insight into the intransigence facing O'Connell:

> Her Majesty's Government have recently declared in both Houses of Parliament their fixed determination to maintain the Union; it becomes the duty of the Members of the Government to support that declaration. The allegation that the numerous Repeal meetings are not illegal does not diminish their inevitable tendency to outrage; and, considering the subject in all its bearings, it is the opinion of the Lord Chancellor, that such meetings are not in the spirit of the constitution.[67]

In the same month, the government introduced a new arms bill, which limited the possession of firearms, and made the carrying of unregistered firearms punishable by transportation or imprisonment.[68] There was also a rumour that the government desired to prosecute O'Connell, but was held back by the belief that no Irish jury would convict him.[69]

In the midst of O'Connell's repeal agitation, a second international convention was held on London, again organized by the British and Foreign Anti-Slavery Society. It opened on 13 June 1843 and, as had been the case three years earlier, Thomas Clarkson was elected President. It was held in the Freemasons' Hall and at one end of the room, Benjamin Haydon's image of the previous convention was hung.[70] Approximately 300 delegates attended the 1843 Convention, making it smaller than the first one.[71] O'Connell may not have been present, but a number of speakers referred to him and his contributions.[72] The Rev. J Blanchard, for example, described him as 'the most eloquent of men, a man in whom whole generations of Irish orators seem condensed'.[73] Clarkson also paid his own tribute to O'Connell. He compared the hatred of abolition in the Southern States of America with the antagonism that the British movement had initially faced, pointing out, 'For many years, the only support which the cause received in the House of Commons was from William Wilberforce, Sir Thomas Fowell Buxton, Dr Lushington and Daniel O'Connell. I mention the latter name because it is due to him'.[74] Given that O'Connell was being criticized in the British press and in Parliament for his repeal activities, it was a brave tribute.

In August, the Queen's speech on the proroguement of Parliament condemned repeal agitation in Ireland and reconfirmed the determination to maintain the Union and the Empire.[75] Despite the unwavering actions of the government, O'Connell appeared optimistic that his tactics were working, informing a colleague in Cork at the beginning of September 'Believe me, the Repeal is nearer than you think'.[76] Matters came to a head in October. O'Connell had convened a mass meeting to be held on 8 October, two miles outside Dublin, in the village of Clontarf. The location was symbolic as it was the site of the battle won by the last high king of Ireland, Brian Boru. The meeting was also to be the culmination of an arduous year of public events and meetings, with the aim of exerting moral force on the British government. Peel's government had proved intransigent, leaving O'Connell no closer to achieving repeal than he had been a year earlier. On 7 October the Lord Lieutenant issued a proclamation prohibiting the meeting to be held in Clontarf. At that stage, thousands of troops were stationed in Dublin. For some British newspapers, this amounted to a 'declaration of war' against the Irish politician.[77] O'Connell complied with the ban and called on his followers to respond peacefully. A few days later, he was served with an arrest warrant in his home. In the intervening period between the calling off of the Clontarf meeting and O'Connell's prosecution, he had, on behalf of the Repeal Association, issued an address to fellow repealers in Cincinnati and thus embroiled himself in more controversy.

O'Connell's trial took place at the beginning of 1844. He was informed of the date while spending time at his beloved home in Derrynane, County Kerry, and he responded, 'What a tasteless fellow that Attorney-General was not to allow me another fortnight in these mountains. I forgive him everything but *that*'.[78] O'Connell was found guilty by a handpicked jury of trying to change the government and constitution of the country. On 30 May, he was sentenced to one year in prison with a fine of £2,000. It was a harsh punishment on somebody who had sought throughout his life to abide by the law. A number of his associates, including his son John, were sentenced to nine-month imprisonment and a fine of £50. Only two weeks before he was sentenced, on 17 May, O'Connell attended the anniversary meeting of the British and Foreign Anti-Slavery Society in London. He had been urged to attend by Sturge, as one of the things they were going to discuss was the news that John Brown, who had led a slave uprising in the United States, was to be hanged. Sturge also wanted O'Connell's opinion on the latest government proposal regarding colonial sugar duties. O'Connell, despite facing probable imprisonment, attended.[79] However, the fact that he remained a divisive figure with the British abolition movement was evident. Lord Brougham could not attend to preside, so he was replaced by Samuel Gurney. O'Connell sat on the left of the Chairman, but his appearance 'was received with cheers, interrupted with hisses and other marks of disapprobation. The cheers, however, predominated, and continued for some time'.[80] Undaunted, O' Connell spoke at length on a number of issues, including those raised by Sturge.[81]

O'Connell and his fellow repealers were imprisoned in Richmond Bridewell in Dublin. He had informed a friend, 'I shall endure it without shrinking or compromise, come what may'.[82] O'Connell's conviction and imprisonment aroused sympathy for him and his movement. The amount of Repeal Rent collected increased. A number of dinners were held in his honour to protest against his harsh treatment. Guests at a dinner at Covent Garden in London on 12 March included Lords Shrewsbury, Camboys and Dunboyne and 'that hearty cheer which reverberated through Covent Garden Theatre on Tuesday last has never had a parallel in any other country'.[83] O'Connell, who had always known how to turn a negative situation to his advantage and to court public opinion, responded to the news of the various tributes by suggesting that a day of 'humiliation and prayer' be appointed on the grounds that 'if universally adopted it would have a magnificent effect on the enemy, besides being in its own nature most desirable'.[84]

In prison, the aged O'Connell was treated well, being allowed many visitors and additional comforts. Richard Webb, who took the English Chartist Henry Vincent to visit, commented positively on O'Connell's appearance:

> I never saw him more ruddy and cheery. His face is almost as rosy as if he were a boy of six years old. His eye is bright and his port erect ... he receives visitors three days in the week for three hours each day. The place of reception is a large and handsome garden full of fruit trees, vegetables and flowers – on these occasions, a word or two is all he has to spare for chance customers – so many come and so many more are kept waiting till these are served.[85]

O'Connell's autograph had always been a valued commodity amongst abolitionists, but during his incarceration it became even more treasured; the energetic English abolitionist, Elizabeth Pease, urged her friends in America to chase their Irish colleagues to collect the desired signatures.[86]

The arrest and imprisonment of O'Connell had further, unexpected consequences. William Smith O'Brien, a Protestant landowner and an MP, who had for so long resisted formally joining the repeal movement, did so on 20 October. O'Connell appointed him as his deputy during his absence. As a consequence, O'Brien rose to international prominence within the movement, with repealers in the United States thanking him for the way in which he managed the Association during O'Connell's absence.[87] Increasingly, O'Brien sided with the more radical Young Ireland group, and became their unacknowledged leader following the premature death of Thomas Davis in 1845.

O'Connell served a shortened sentence as the verdict was quashed on an appeal to the House of Lords. The prisoners were released on 6 September. Following release, O'Connell returned to his former activities, telling a meeting of the Association in October that repeal was 'merely a question of time'. Nonetheless, although he toyed with the idea of federalism, the repeal question had lost its vitality, and divisions were becoming apparent. O'Connell's dwindling power became evident in 1844, over the government's decision to introduce a Charitable Trusts Act, which overwhelmingly favoured Catholics. O'Connell opposed it; the majority of the Catholic hierarchy supported it. As the government had intended, O'Connell had lost the support of the moderate wing of the Catholic Church.[88] Yet O'Connell still seemed energetic on a number of issues, including the government's decision to introduce non-denominational colleges into Ireland. His interest in the condition of Jews continued. In 1846, he supported the removal a number of religious disabilities against Jews, including getting the British government to repeal the ancient *De Judaismo* law, which prescribed a special dress for them.[89] He explained, 'Ireland has claims on your ancient race, it is the only country that I know of unsullied by any one act of persecution of the Jews'.[90] At the same time, O'Connell remained as vocal as ever on the slave question. Again, his forceful interventions caused consternation on the other side of the Atlantic. The reaction demonstrated that his personal support was weakening and that the sympathy aroused at his imprisonment was now dissipating. Moreover, in 1845, the year that O'Connell reached seventy, a previously unknown disease attacked the potato crop in Ireland. It appearance marked the onset of a devastating famine.

6 'AMERICAN SYMPATHY AND IRISH BLACKGUARDISM'

In the same year that O'Connell was fighting to bring about a repeal of the Act of Union, he made some of his most blistering attacks on slavery. Even as the repeal campaign had been gathering momentum, O'Connell had intensified his attacks on American slavery. His actions were clearly making an impact in America. The *Pennsylvania Freeman*, an admirer of O'Connell, reprinted a number of his speeches delivered before the Repeal Association in Dublin. It opened by saying:

> O'Connell has become almost as much of an 'Agitator' in the United States as he is in his own country. His frequent and just denunciations of our republican inconsistency and despotism, have thrown our people into paroxysms of excitement, and given a fresh impetus to the anti-slavery discussion.[1]

As much as he was admired in the United States, he was despised in equal measure. A newspaper in Maryland published correspondence alleged to be from O'Connell, in which he had attacked the author, Charles Dickens. This article was reprinted in an Irish newspaper, the *Pilot*. O'Connell was furious. He informed the Irish editor:

> There is a species of outrageous rascality which has been seldom attempted in this country, and seems reserved for the vileness of a great portion of the newspaper press in the United States – that portion of it which seems to exceed in every species of infamy even the basest of the base, the London *Times*.
>
> I am surprised that you did not take notice that this forgery was published in a slave-holding state – a state in which there is that moral contamination about the press which, I think you ought to know, would preclude me from having any communication with it.[2]

But O'Connell's relationship with American repeal associations – particularly his acceptance of American money, on the grounds that these who gave it loved Ireland more than they loved slavery – was causing some dissatisfaction within Ireland. O'Connell had first received a donation from America in the spring of 1841, from Philadelphia. For some time, the Philadelphia Repeal Society was the largest in the country with over 3,000 members in 1841. As repeal societies became established in the main cities of America, donations to Ireland increased.[3] In October 1842, Haughton had written to O'Connell, now Mayor of Dublin, saying:

> I know you hate slavery; your whole life has been one continuous act of opposition to the iniquity in all its forms. Now is the critical moment for Ireland; we must either rise in the esteem or sink into the contempt of the good and the freehearted in America. I conjure you to put an end to the unholy alliance between Irishmen and slave dealers in America; you can do more to effect this great good than any other living man ... do not lose your moral power (the only power which can enable you to gain your object) by the acceptance of further sympathy or aid from American 'soul-drivers'. The work of your life will be marred and destroyed by such an unholy contamination.[4]

O'Connell ignored this advice and continued to accept American money. He was criticized by Irish abolitionists, many within his Association continuing to believe that abolition and repeal should be kept separate. O'Connell was caught in the middle of these conflicting approaches. In March 1843, money was received from Robert Tyler, whose father was President of the United States. Again, James Haughton objected, suggesting that the money be refused. O'Connell was forced to defend his actions publicly at a meeting of the Repeal Association, saying that accepting such money did not mean that his views on slavery had changed.[5] Privately, O'Connell tried to reassure Haughton that he was willing to accept American sympathy and money 'for the peaceful furtherance of our good and just cause'. He added, 'All I object to is the hollow sympathy and blood-stained money of American slave-holders'.[6] At a meeting of the Repeal Association, O'Connell explained that 'his public opinion was one thing, and his duty to the Irish public another', adding 'He was not at liberty to sacrifice the interests of the Irish people, and if he were at liberty, he would not do it. He would not feel justified in depriving them of American sympathy, in consequence of his opinions on the subject of slavery'.[7]

O'Connell's desire not to jeopardize the income from the United States seemed further evident when, in early 1843, the Repeal Association announced that John O'Connell and Tom Steele would be going to the United States to collect money for the movement; they simultaneously announced that they would not become embroiled in the slavery issue while there. When hearing of this decision, Garrison retaliated.[8] He attributed the decision to the fact that 'Ever since a *southern breeze* from America first fanned the brow of O'Connell, his allusions to slavery and slaveholders, it has been observed, have been in a subdued tone of reproof – no *thundering* of indignation, but, comparatively, a mere muttering of displeasure'.[9] He warned the O'Connells that the announcement had 'kindled into fury the abolition blood'.[10] In the event, the visit did not take place, but it indicated that O'Connell realized that expressing support for anti-slavery in Ireland was very different from supporting it in the United States.

Furthermore, a speech made by O'Connell on 10 May, in which he attacked slavery unequivocally, led Garrison to declare joyously, 'O'Connell himself again!' Regardless of differences, Garrison did not want to lose the support of his most committed champion.

O'Connell's commitment to the cause of abolition became clear only a few weeks later, on 10 May 1843, at a specially convened meeting of the Repeal Association, and it was to have both immediate and long-term repercussions on the transatlantic debate about slavery. The meeting was called to consider a letter from the Pennsylvania Anti-Slavery Society in which they sought to reject the criticisms made of O'Connell by some Irish-American newspapers and repeal societies in the previous months. In addition, they provided a graphic description of the horrors of slavery. O'Connell was delighted to get such unequivocal support.[11] His response was characteristically forceful, although he said that he was speaking on behalf of all of the Repeal Association. James Haughton, his fellow abolitionist, was in the Chair. O'Connell suggested – controversially – that there was no evidence 'that the negro is really inferior as a race' and suggested that the two races could mix together as equals. At the same time he proclaimed, 'shame upon every man in America who is not an anti-slavery man'.[12] O'Connell's most pointed criticisms were reserved for Irish-Americans, he demanding that they 'come out of such a land'; if they chose to remain and condone slavery 'we will recognize you as Irishmen no longer'. He further proclaimed: 'Those who commit, and those who countenance, the crime of slavery I regard as the enemies of Ireland, and I desire to have no sympathy or support from them (cheers).' He reinforced this statement by saying that he expected donations from America to dry up, but he would refuse to accept any more 'blood-stained money'.[13] Even by O'Connell's standards, his speech was searing. Irish-Americans who supported repeal could no longer be equivocal on the abolition question.

O'Connell's response to the Pennsylvanian repealers was reported in a number of American newspapers. According to the *New York Freeman*, his words had been uttered 'in his own sweeping, unsparing way, upon slavery as it exists in America; in short he pronounced against it a philippic as eloquent as it is severe'.[14] Inevitably, there was an angry response, with some Irish-Americans denying that O'Connell was speaking for them. Part of the anger derived from the fact that they believed O'Connell had no right to interfere with a domestic institution. Many regarded his speech as insulting and proof of his lack of knowledge on the question. Moreover, according to the *Richmond Enquirer*, the most influential newspaper in Virginia:

> Daily his privacy is invaded by the Garrisons, the Tappans, the Leavitts ... his ears, ever open to the cry of distress, are filled constantly with their statements. We need not say that they are infinitely more disgraceful to this country than anything ever uttered by O'Connell – that they are a tissue of horrors enough to rouse the indigna-

tion in a man's heart ... Statements like this ... tell Mr O'Connell what they would not dare to publish here – are the grounds upon which he relies, he speaks.[15]

In addition to blaming American abolitionists for misleading O'Connell, the paper sought to separate the cause of repeal from the cult of O'Connell. It averred:

The indiscretion and madness of an individual cannot extinguish the rights of a whole people. The worst folly of Daniel O'Connell cannot destroy our sympathies for the oppressed people of Ireland. Because he is grossly unjust to us, we cannot be unjust to him.[16]

At the beginning of August, the *New York Freeman* reported that supporters of repeal in the South were 'beginning to get over Mr O'Connell's speech'. It gave the example of the Savannah Association, which had supported O'Connell in his campaign for Catholic Emancipation, and which now informed the paper that, 'A melancholy damp was thrown over this glorious cause through the entire South, by the unfortunate expressions said to be uttered by Mr O'Connell, at first published and then widely circulated by our enemies'. After reflecting on the matter, a few repealers had decided to meet 'at all hazards', although the numbers attending subsequent meetings had been much depleted.[17] In the weeks following O'Connell's speech, it became even more apparent how much his words had upset his Irish-American supporters. The Natchez Repeal Association held a meeting to discuss O'Connell's recent speech and, despite continuing to support repeal, they agreed to dissolve and give their funds to a local orphan asylum.[18] The *Baltimore Saturday Visitor* chastised the Natchez repealers for being 'shallow' in their support of repeal, adding:

The opinions of O'Connell, in regard to slavery, were well known to the whole South, years ago. Now, the fact is just plainly this: the Southerners so acting, prove that they are afraid of offending public opinion at home; that they are miserable cowards, and never were repealers from principle ... the cause of Freedom is one thing – O'Connell's opinion of slavery another – and the man or association of men who cannot see this and *feel* it, we pity sincerely. But we fear these Southern *pseudo*-repealers do see it, while they act as above – therefore not deserving pity.[19]

A meeting held in New Orleans, reported as the largest ever, protested in 'strong but decided language' at O'Connell's speech. The proceedings of the meeting were sent to the Repeal Association in Dublin and the New Orleans society adjourned until they received a response.[20] Repealers in Washington were divided on the issue. The Secretary announced his resignation over O'Connell's speech and sent a copy of his resignation letter to the *National Intelligencer*.[21] Those who opposed O'Connell held a meeting in the City Hall and passed a number of forceful resolutions, including, 'That the Irish and the friends of

Ireland in America here, have no sympathy or connection, nor never had any, with the abolitionists of this country, or their coadjutors abroad, in the matter of domestic slavery existing in various States of this Union'. Another was passed 'condemning and deploring the error of Mr O'Connell'.[22] In Philadelphia, some repealers withdrew from the local Association and formed their own society. At a subsequent meeting, a Catholic priest, Dr Moriarty, roundly condemned the abolitionists, particularly those in Philadelphia, 'as meddlers and busy bodies, and the founders of all the trouble in which the repealers here and elsewhere in the United States found themselves at the moment'.[23] The Repeal Association in Binghamton, New York, while expressing their commitment to the cause of Irish independence, passed a resolution saying:

> That we greatly admire the energetic, noble, persevering and law-abiding stand taken by Daniel O'Connell on behalf of his oppressed countrymen, and that we ardently hope his wisdom to *guide* may be equal to his power to *agitate*. But while we admire the stand he has taken and frankly concede to him the right to express as freely his sentiments concerning the institutions of our country, as we of his, we cannot but consider is language in a late speech, while referring to the subject of slavery, as uncalled for, and highly embarrassing to his friends on this side of the Atlantic.[24]

A number of newspapers suggested that the speech would kill the American support for repeal, just as it had started to spread. Papers, including the *Atlas,* the *Express*, the *Richmond Whig,* and the *Journal of Commerce* each declared repeal to be dead.[25] The *New York Freeman's Journal* took a more measured view, believing that the reason for the speech appearing in so many American newspapers was due to 'the exuberant zeal' of British officials, and those who were hostile to repeal had ensured its circulation.[26] The paper suggested that:

> constructions have been forced upon it, and inferences extracted, which its author never dreamt of, and would be the very first to repudiate; it has been garbled and distorted, presented piecemeal, the explanatory portions being dishonestly omitted; and only those retained which were calculated to damage the cause; in a word, nothing has been left undone which a perverse ingenuity could devise, or an unprincipled hostility execute.[27]

At the beginning of August, a repeal rally to be held in New York led the *New York Freeman's Journal* to warn that a 'great deal' depends on this meeting, on the grounds that:

> For weeks past the enemies of Ireland have been clamoring that the Repeal cause was dead, that Mr O'Connell's speech had destroyed it, and so on ... This, of course, is all false ... but nevertheless it remains for New York to dispel the last shred of the weak fabrication, to show our friends and foes both, that the young giant of the West is as fresh for the struggle as ever.[28]

A more revealing test of support for O'Connell came in September 1842, at the National Repeal Convention that was held in New York. Members from the two Philadelphia Repeal Associations attended. The election of Robert Tyler as President indicated that the groups opposed to abolition were in the ascendancy. During its three-day meeting, the issue of slavery was not discussed.[29] It appeared that O'Connell's powerful denunciations had only served to polarize the American repeal movement.

If O'Connell's speech on 10 May had divided Irish-American repealers, it delighted abolitionists in Ireland and America. James Haughton admired it on the grounds 'it will do great good to the cause of freedom and humanity'.[30] Gerrit Smith sent a long and animated letter from New York, explaining:

> The fears of American abolitionists have become excited – had, indeed, begun to run high – that American slaveholders would prove themselves able to gag, even Daniel O'Connell. But your late speech which has blistered these tyrants from head to foot and filled this land with their howlings and execrations, has put an end to all those fears.[31]

He warned O'Connell that his speech had angered repeal societies, while their 'expressions of great bitterness toward yourself and the abolitionists in general, has done much to develop the atrocious and horrible proslavery character of these Associations'. The letter closed by saying:

> If you knew the immeasurable influence of your example on our endeavours to terminate American oppression, you would pardon me for enclosing my letter with the earnest prayer that Daniel O'Connell may have grace given him from God to stand firm in the cause of Liberty – of American as well as Irish Liberty.[32]

O'Connell's attacks on slavery continued throughout the summer of 1843. On 5 August 1843, Haughton wrote to O'Connell praising him on a speech he had made on the previous day. Just over a week later, Haughton, having heard from his friends in America, wrote:

> The pro-slavery party there are in great rage in consequence of O'Connell's recent denunciations of their horrid system, and our anti-slavery friends are greatly rejoiced. My valued friend O'Connell has nobly sustained his high character; he is a fine fellow; his enemies, who know not how to imitate his virtues, have only eyes to see his faults: these like spots on the sun are blemishes, but they are lost in their brightness of his many good qualities'.[33]

O'Connell had declared 1843 to be 'repeal year'. However, twinning repeal with slavery brought problems and dilemmas. Not all Irish repealers supported abolition, and many Irish-American repealers desired that the two issues should be kept totally separate. O'Connell had caused controversy and division with his speech on 10 May, and he caused even more when he attacked Garrison, the leader of the American Anti-Slavery Society.

O'Connell was not only being lambasted in words. He was being lampooned in a number of political cartoons. One entitled 'American Sympathy and Irish Blackguardism', which appeared in 1843, depicted an imaginary encounter between O'Connell and Robert Tyler and his father. Although the American context was different, many of the images had become commonplace in British cartoons of O'Connell. He was depicted wearing knee-breeches, and a hat decorated with a republican cockade. He was smoking a clay pipe, holding a club marked 'Agitation' and a sack for 'Repale Rint'. He announced to Tyler, 'Arrah! give up your Slaves. I'd rather shake hands wid a pick-pocket than wid a Slave Holder, and if we ge our repale we'll set em all free before you can say Pathernoster – I don't want any of your blood-stained money!' Meanwhile a bemused black servant looked on, who made it clear that he loved his servitude.[34] Another cartoon of the same year, entitled 'O'Connell's Call and Pat's Reply', also demonstrated a familiarity with O'Connell's recent speeches on slavery. The image contrasted the well-being of the Irish in America with their poverty and lack of status in Ireland. In the Irish scene, O'Connell is standing on a shore holding an 'Agitation' club and calling through an 'Abolition' horn. He says, 'Over the broad Atlantic I pour forth my voice saying come out of such a land you Irishmen or if you remain and dare continue to countenance the system of slavery that is supported there, we will recognize you as Irishmen no longer'. A prosperous looking labourer on the opposite shore answers:

It is a mighty far voice you have Mr. O'Connell – I love **Ireland** as well as you do, but this is my adopted Country and the birthplace of my Children. By industry and economy I am become prosperous – my Children are receiving the benefit of a good education, and the highest situations in the State are open to them. Here we can express our opinion's freely without the fear of bayonets or policemen. I have sworn to defend its laws and the interests of its union and will do so with the last drop of my blood.[35]

The illustrator of both was the cartoonist Edward Williams Clay, who had gained a reputation in Philadelphia for lampooning black abolition societies. This arose from his conviction that whites were superior to blacks.[36] Clay's images were a further indication that in the United States O'Connell had become more hated and feared than any American abolitionist.

Texas

Despite his time spent in prison in 1844, O'Connell seemed as committed to anti-slavery as he had ever been. At the beginning of the year, he confided in Haughton:

With respect to the principles of President Tyler, on the subject of negro slavery, I am as abhorrent of them as ever I was; indeed, if it was possible to increase my contemptuous disgust of slave-owners and the advocates of slavery, my sentiments are more intense now than ever they were, and I will avail myself of the first practical opportunity of giving utterance to them, especially in connexion with the horrible project of annexing Texas to the United States. But at the present moment the public mind is so engrossed here by other topics of local interest, that an anti-slavery speech would excite no attention as it ought.[37]

The Texas issue that O'Connell was referring to had been causing consternation for a number of years to abolitionists both there and in Europe. It related to American expansionism, sometimes referred to as its 'Manifest Destiny'. It caused problems because the expansion of territories also, in some cases, meant the expansion of slavery. This issue came to a head over the acquisition of Texas. Since 1821, Texas, which had an ambivalent attitude towards slavery, had been part of Mexican territory. Slavery was gradually abolished and finally outlawed in all Mexican territories in 1829, although an exception was made of Texas, which was given until 1830 to abolish slavery. It tried to avoid doing so by converting slaves into indentured servants. In 1836, the Republic of Texas was created and legislation governing freed blacks was introduced. However, the 1830s coincided with the expansion of cotton production and during this decade the number of slaves increased from approximately 5,000 to over 11,000.[38] Throughout the 1830s, the annexation of Texas had been proposed, but it was rejected on the grounds that it would lead to war with Mexico.

In 1840, to the horror of abolitionists, the British government recognized the independence of Texas. The Hibernian Anti-Slavery Society was one of the first organizations to condemn this action. They informed Lord Palmerston that the government's action would 'retard, to a serious extent, the progress of human freedom, by acknowledging a rebel people, who have made the perpetuation of slavery a part of their constitution.[39] In a formal protest that was reprinted in the London *Times,* the HASS asked 'of what avail is it to have sacrificed £20,000,000 of the national treasure to release one part of the human family from bondage, if the right hand of fellowship is given to men who have declared that they will uphold the foul system to their last breath'. They believed that Britain could have influenced Texas to adopt a more liberal constitution and by so intervening would have 'at least preserved an important moral position and won her honour, which was undoubtedly pledged to the overthrow of slavery throughout the world'.[40] The Foreign Office responded by pointing out that if Britain had refused to recognize Texas, it would not have induced Texas to abolish slavery, whereas recognizing Texas could not be construed as giving support to slavery, rather 'the greater intercourse between Great Britain and Texas, which will probably result from that treaty, may have the effect of mitigating rather than aggravating the evils arising from the existence of slavery under the laws of the republic'.[41]

The British and Foreign Anti-Slavery Society was concerned about Texas. In 1841, they asked O'Connell if he would be willing to convene a public meeting, with the London Anti-Slavery Society paying part of the expense.[42] O'Connell opposed the absorption of Texas on the grounds that it would augment the number of slaveholding states in America. The *Freeman's Journal* took a more cynical line – thinking that if it caused a conflict between Britain and the US, the former was more likely to grant repeal as a way of conciliating Irish opinion.[43] The *Nation* welcomed the dispute, viewing it as strengthening the United States while annoying the British government.[44]

It was not until 1843 that President John Tyler openly supported annexation. Two years later, under the newly installed President Polk, the Republic of Texas was absorbed in the United States, resulting in the Mexican War of 1846–8. After 1845, President Polk, himself a slaveholder, had also made the goals of his administration the acquisition of Oregon, California and New Mexico. The annexation was condemned by abolition groups in Europe and in the US. O'Connell informed his friend James Haughton that he regarded with 'horror' the annexation of another slave state to the American Union and the 'human misery' that would follow.[45] At a meeting of the Repeal Association, O'Connell was publicly critical of the actions and words of President Polk, accusing him of 'arrant cowardice' on the grounds that he had avoided using the word 'slavery' but had referred to it as a 'domestic institution'. In words directed at the President, he declared:

> Mr Polk, it is huckstering in human flesh. It is a loathsome and execrable system that makes man the property of his fellow. It is buying and selling man, created after the image of God ... as though he were the beast of a field that grazes, and not a deathless being marked out for immortal redemption.[46]

O'Connell used the occasion to make a wider point about American involvement saying that 'I want no American aid if it comes across the Atlantic stained with negro blood; and from my soul I despise any government which, while it boasts of liberty, is guilty of slavery, the greatest crime that can be committed by humanity against humanity'.[47] O'Connell also criticized the British Foreign Secretary, Lord Palmerston, for recognizing Texas and he accused the British authorities of 'political cowardice' when it came to American politics. More controversially, O'Connell asserted that if Ireland was given her independence, she would gladly fight for Britain against America in defence of Oregon and thus would see 'the honour of the British Empire maintained – and the American Eagle, in its highest pride of flight, brought down'.[48]

O'Connell's stance angered some in Young Ireland who viewed his words as being unnecessarily offensive to their allies in the United States.[49] Moreover, in a political stand-off between Britain and America, he was giving his support to the former – his adversary in the struggle for repeal. Even the gentle Thomas Davis felt moved to write:

> I don't think it would be quite just towards myself, and to those who concur with me, If I did not to some extent express my dissent from the opinion put forward by my Illustrious friend in reference to the American slaveholders. I condemn slavery as much as it is possible to condemn it ... but I am not prepared to condemn the Americans to the extent to which my illustrious friend goes, or silently to hear the amount of censure which he so conscientiously and so consistently with his opinions casts upon them.[50]

O'Connell's comments caused consternation amongst supporters of repeal in the US. The Repeal Association of Norfolk and Portsmouth in Virginia criticized O'Connell for saying he would be willing to assist Britain 'in the destruction of this free and happy country'.[51] They described his language as, 'bitter' and 'uncalled for'. Their comments showed how supporters of repeal were balancing their love for Ireland with their patriotism for America.[52] They concluded by agreeing to dissolve their association so they could not be accused of harbouring unpatriotic feelings towards America. As they pointed out in one of their resolutions,

> as American citizens, whether native or adopted, we feel ourselves bound by the most sacred and solemn ties of patriotism, by the blessings which we enjoy, by the love of our free and glorious republic, and by our solemn oaths and deep-rooted obligations for the blessings which we have inherited or acquired, to cheerfully and steadfastly protect and support the American eagle in its onward and upward flight, against every foe.[53]

The New Orleans Repeal Association decided to break up and give their funds to two local charities.[54] The Baltimore Repeal Association also decided to dissolve and give the funds in hand to the local Hibernian Society. The *Brooklyn Eagle* cautioned against such an 'injudicious movement', explaining

> It is well known that Mr O'Connell's peculiar sentiments in regard to the United States are far from being reciprocated by his fellow countrymen; and if they fail to rebuke them openly, it is because they are not willing to be diverted from their grand object by extraneous and secondary matters.[55]

It appeared that a number or repealers were making a distinction between supporting repeal and supporting O'Connell. As usual, some of O'Connell's harshest critics were from the Northern states of the United States. The assault was led by Orestes A. Brownson, editor of the *Quarterly Review,* who accused O'Connell of deceiving the Irish people and not really believing his own criticism of the United States but doing it to win the support of British abolitionists.[56] A critique of O'Connell in the *Brooklyn Eagle* suggested that he was 'grossly ignorant' and no longer in touch with the views of repealers in the United States. The suggested that his words showed:

> The pernacity with which even great men adhere to the most transparent blunders when the truth is within their reach. We have no doubt that Mr O'Connell is sincerely opposed to slavery, but not more so that nine-tenths – yeh, ninety-nine hundredths – of the very people he denounces in such coarse and sweeping terms. Yet he ought to know that, viewed merely with reference to the physical condition, the slaves of the South are vastly better off than the *white* slaves of Great Britain ...
>
> But we reckon that the orator reckons without his host. Indeed we are certain that the great body of his countrymen in the Unites States, however warmly they may incline towards him for his exertions in the cause of Repeal, will be the last to adopt his sentiments on the question of slavery. And it will take more than his *ipse dixit* to convince us that any considerable portion of them at home will enter very cheerfully upon a contest which is to harm 'the American Eagle', or circumscribe the limits of republican institutions.[57]

A dismal view of O'Connell's speech was offered by Mr O'Brien, a prominent member of the Repeal Association in Boston. He speculated that Britain was enjoying the divisions within America concerning the war in Texas. However, he warned that if anybody believed that Irishmen would desert the American flag, they were 'egregiously deceived' as 'the Irishmen of America, whether naturalized or not, will fight to the last man in the defence of the American eagle'.[58] He dismissed O'Connell and the Repeal Association in Ireland for their 'lack of wisdom of this issue'.[59] O'Connell's offer to support Britain in a war against the United States revealed that he was willing to use Irish military support as a bargaining tool in the fight for repeal. The militaristic nature of O'Connell's words threw into question O'Connell's commitment to moral force, an issue that only a few months later he would use as a device to drive a wedge between Young Ireland and Old Ireland.[60]

O'Connell's speech was praised by Garrison in the columns of the *Liberator*, which congratulated him for not being bribed by American money but proving to be the 'incorruptible Liberator' of Ireland.[61] In a letter to Richard Webb in Ireland, Garrison admitted that public opinion – in particular, Irish-American public opinion – had been stirred up in favour of the annexation by England's opposition to it. He explained:

> Unhappily, at this juncture, in connection with slavery, the hatred of the Irish population amongst United States towards England is of a bitter and most implacable type, and it all goes in favour of the annexation of Texas, through motives of terror and revenge. It is a most deplorable circumstance that, religiously and politically, almost the entire body of Irishmen in this country are disposed to go with the accursed South

for any and every purpose, and to any extent. The patriotic and Christian appeals that have been made to them by Daniel O'Connell and Father Mathew, and others of their countrymen at home, on this subject, have to have the slightest perceptible effect on their minds. They are a mighty obstacle, therefore, in the way of negro emancipation on our soil.[62]

Pessimistically, he warned 'the greediness if the Slave Power will not be satisfied with the annexation of Texas. Its settled purpose is to conquer all Mexico, and on its fertile plains to establish slavery and the slave trade'.[63] O'Connell was undaunted by the criticisms, responding 'I do not shrink from it', adding 'I am the advocate of civil and religious liberty all over the globe'.[64] He further pointed out that he had first attended an anti-slavery meeting in England in 1825, he added that in 1839 he had not been allowed to speak in Exeter Hall.[65] As O'Connell recognized, his association with the anti-slavery movement had frequently been turbulent. Yet again O'Connell's interventions had angered people on both sides of the Atlantic, and even the American President had been the object of his scathing scorn.

Garrison

Whilst O'Connell was causing consternation in the United States with his sustained attacks on slavery, he was creating controversy by publicly attacking the leading American abolitionist, William Lloyd Garrison. In the months following the London Convention, O'Connell had been distancing himself from the leader of the AASS, possibly to appease those who regarded Garrison's politics as extreme. In 1841, he had criticized Garrison's radical views, especially in regard to religion, accusing the American leaders of being anti-Catholic – a charge frequently directed at abolitionists. Even American abolitionists, who did not support Garrison, were saddened by these criticisms. Gerrit Smith of the American Liberal Party rebuked O'Connell for his lapse of judgement, saying 'How greatly do I lament that ignorance of Wm Lloyd Garrison ... Whatever else Mr Garrison may or may not be, he is certainly a true-hearted abolitionist; and, in my judgment, a decided Christian'.[66] Further distancing was apparent in 1842. On 18 October, at a meeting of the Repeal Association, O'Connell attacked Garrison for his dislike of Sunday observation and of clerical interference. Although questioning O'Connell's motives for doing so, Garrison responded that:

> Never as a man, as an American citizen, and especially as the advocate of my enslaved countrymen, shall I cease to remember his with a grateful heart, and to appreciate in the most exalted sense, the testimonies he has borne, the labours he has performed, the personal aid he has afforded me and my anti-slavery coadjutors, the untiring zeal and moral intrepidity he has manifested, for the immediate and eternal overthrow of American slavery, 'the vilest that ever saw the light of the sun, and the sum of all villainies'.[67]

Throughout 1843, O'Connell continued to uphold the principles of abolition, while condemning its most prominent campaigner. At the meeting of the Repeal Association on 4 August 1843, during a speech attacking slaveholders, O'Connell disparaged Garrison, declaring him to be 'something of a maniac' for his religious views, in particular his sabbatarian ideas.[68] At this stage, O'Connell seemed to be moving closer to the more moderate American and Foreign Anti-Slavery Association, who had declared their support for repeal and had been sending donations for the campaign.[69] Members of the Hibernian Anti-Slavery Association, who had maintained good relationships with Garrison, were dismayed. Haughton gently reprimanded O'Connell for criticizing Garrison's religious views, saying:

> Do not think unkindly of this good man; he is possessed of every quality which must make you esteem him – gentleness, courage, disinterestedness, firmness ... Such men as O'Connell and Garrison should never speak of each other but in the language of kindness and respect. You are both laboring to make men happy, and however great may be your differences on religious matters (and it is probably I differ widely from both), may you have a glorious reward for your labours.[70]

The Irish Quaker abolitionist Richard Webb, who was not always an admirer of O'Connell, was scathing about his motives and his sincerity, believing him to be 'either a great bigot or a rank hypocrite ... he meanly throws a sop to Cerberus by denouncing Garrison as "a Mr Lloyd Garrison with whom he could have no intercourse" on account of his religious or rather irreligious opinions'.[71] Webb pointed out to the American Edmund Quincy:

> Even James Haughton – and I know no more sincere worshipper of O'Connell than he is ... even he confesses himself ashamed of him in his treatment of Garrison. He thinks there is a want of magnanimity and good manners, which he was not prepared to expect. I am not and never was surprised – for I looked for no better. O'Connell would spare no man and regard no man who stood in his way – no man is his friend any more than while he can make use of him. I am persuaded that while he has a great head he has a cold heart.[72]

Elizabeth Pease, a radical Quaker who was leaders of the Women's Abolition of Slavery Society in Darlington in England, although disliking O'Connell's actions, adopted a philosophical approach:

> Perhaps it is well for the United States that great men should now and again commit a flaw of this sort, to shew the United States that none are removed from the imperfections of human nature ...I was thinking more of O'Connell's mean behavior towards our beloved Garrison. I never knew an action, I think, so at variance with the rest of his character – in many or most respects, O'Connell is a great man, in its truest meaning – tho' not so great by immeasurable degrees (in my estimation at least) as he whom he affected to despise. I cannot think what sudden fit of aberration seized him ... This is a sad stain on his fame. O'Connell is nevertheless, a great man.[73]

Pease went on to praise O'Connell's campaign for a repeal of the Union as 'one of the grandest movements that was ever enacted in the theatre of the world'. She was a pacifist and she viewed the campaign as 'a splendid example of the superiority of a moral over a blood-stained revolution'.[74]

Garrison responded to O'Connell's comments in the columns of the *Liberator*. He praised O'Connell's unwavering support for abolition, but questioned his mixing condemnation of slavery with a personal attack on his religious views. He also made a counter-attack, alleging that O'Connell looked ridiculous when he performed the religious practice of crossing himself before he ate his dinner.[75] Haughton and Webb tried to make peace between the two leaders, informing O'Connell that Garrison had not been personally responsible for the offending article. O'Connell responded by praising Gerrit Smith and Lewis Tappan, American abolitionists who did not support Garrison and had split from the AASS.[76] Disappointed at the loss of such a notable ally, supporters of Garrison rationalized O'Connell's actions on the grounds that he did not want to lose the financial contributions for his repeal movement from the Southern states.[77] Supporters of Garrison were less restrained. Wendell Phillips, previously an admirer of O'Connell, concluded that O'Connell's lips had been 'clogged with gold', referring to the money sent to the Repeal Association from the slave-owning states, and that the Irishman was the 'great beggarman' for allowing his actions to be governed by financial considerations.[78] By 1843, therefore, O'Connell's fiery comments were not only angering slaveholders, they were also alienating a number of his fellow abolitionists. At the same time, while O'Connell was making his final push to bring about a repeal of the Union, he also became enmeshed in a further transatlantic controversy over slavery.

Cincinnati

The determination by the British government to prevent O'Connell's Clontarf meeting in October 1843 proved to be a watershed in the repeal movement. While O'Connell was facing prosecution, he not only maintained his commitment to abolition, he also made one of his most powerful and controversial pronouncements on the institution of slavery. According to one historian, the statement was 'his most closely argued and unequivocal address on slavery and Irish-American attitudes'.[79] The declaration made by O'Connell became known as 'the Cincinnati Letter' and, on the eve of the American Civil War, it was frequently used as a tool in the propaganda war by the North.

The controversy followed a few years of unrest in the city. Freed black people had fled from Ohio in 1829 following a number of attacks of their community and they had subsequebntly founded a colony in Upper Canada. Irishmen had been among their attackers.[80] During a riot in September 1841, a party of Irishmen had attacked a number of Negro boarding houses and fired on and attacked the inhabitants. The activities of the pro-slavery lobby, led by Caleb McNulty, an Irish-American politician and a supporter of the Democratic Party,[81] led the *Liberator* at the beginning of 1842 to describe the city as 'vile and despicable' and 'the most ferocious and the most infamous city in the republic'.[82] Richard Allen, the Dublin abolitionist, condemned the Irish who lived there and were involved in the rioting, describing them as belonging to 'that old, degraded, whiskey-drinking class', adding, 'one class of slavery upholds another'. He had been confident that the Irish Address of 1842 would have a beneficial impact, underestimating the antagonism that it would arouse.[83]

The large Irish community in Cincinnati made it inevitable that O'Connell's Repeal Association would find some support. In fact, Cincinnati became one of the most successful supporters of repeal in the United States. In 1842, the anti-abolitionist *Truth-Teller* praised the repeal movement in the city, describing them as an example to the rest of the United States.[84] They had raised hundreds of dollars to be sent to Ireland. As was the case with organizations elsewhere, they were uncomfortable with connecting repeal with abolition. Their distancing from the latter was evident from their invitation to Lewis Cass, a leading member of the anti-abolition Democratic Party who adopted a traditional stand on slavery, to speak at a large repeal meeting to be held in Cincinnati on 3 July 1843. He sent a message to say he supported them, but could not be there.[85] An estimated 9,000 to 10,000 people attended, which meant that it had to be held in the open.

Over summer, the Cincinnati repealers raised over $600, which they sent to Ireland.[86] However, in their correspondence they made it clear that many local members did not want the repeal question to be mixed with the abolition one. When O'Connell received the donation from Cincinnati, he accepted the money but his son John said they would need to consider their reply.[87] A response to Cincinnati was read by the Liberator at meeting of the Repeal Association on Wednesday, 11 October. O'Connell had first called for a vote of thanks to 'American friends. It was cheering to have the support of good men and patriots'. He then asked for his address 'to the Irishmen in Ohio' to be brought forward so that he could read it. It was unanimously approved. O'Connell told his audience that while he was dictating it, he was simultaneously modeling for a sculpture, which meant that he was 'standing for Hogan and denouncing slavery at one and the same time'.[88]

The Cincinnati Letter was long – almost ten pages when printed – and in it, O'Connell systematically refuted the assertions made by the Cincinnati repealers. O'Connell's language was characteristically forceful: in his response he synthesized many of the arguments he had made over the previous few years, but the total document was powerful testimony to his twenty years of fighting on behalf of the slave and, at the same time, was a compelling indictment of all who had done otherwise. He commenced by berating the Cincinnati committee for their 'detailed and anxious vindication of the most hideous crime that has ever stained humanity'.[89] He further suggested they could not be true Irishmen, declaring:

> How can the generous, the charitable, the humane, and the noble emotions of the Irish heart have become extinct amongst you? How can your nature be so totally changed as that you should become the apologists and advocates of the execrable system which makes man the property of his fellow man – destroys the foundation of all moral and social virtues – condemns to ignorance, immorality and irreligion, millions of our fellow creatures ...?
>
> It was not in Ireland that you learned this cruelty. Your mothers were gentle, kind, and humane. Their bosoms overflowed with the honey of human charity ... How then, can you be so depraved? How can your souls have become stained with a darkness blacker than the negro's skin?[90]

Throughout he demonstrated his abiding concern for the welfare of the slave – something that not all abolitionists shared:

> Your advocacy of Slavery is founded on a gross error. You take for granted that man can be the property of his fellow-man. You speak in terms of indignation of those who would deprive white men of their 'property', and thereby render themselves incapable of supporting their families in affluence. You forget the other side of the picture. You have neither sorrow nor sympathy for those who are iniquitously compelled to labour for the affluence of others; those who work without wages – who toil without recompense – who spend their lives in procuring for others the splendour and wealth in which they do not participate.
>
> You totally forget the sufferings of the wretched black man, who are deprived of their all without any compensation or recompense. If you, yourselves, all of you – or if any one of you were, without crime or offence committed by you, handed over into perpetual slavery; if you were compelled to work from sunrise to sunset without wages, supplied only with such coarse food and raiment as would keep you in work order; if, when your 'owner' fell into debt you were sold to pay his debts, not your own; if it were made a crime to teach you to read and write; if you were liable to be separated, in the distribution of assets, from your wives and your children; if you (above all) were to fall into the hands of a brutal master – and you condescended to admit that there are some brutal masters in America – if, among all these circumstances, some friendly spirits of a more generous order were desirous to give liberty to you and your families – with what ineffable disgust would not you laugh to scorn those who should traduce the generous spirits who would relieve you. And you now, pseudo Irishmen – shame upon you! – have traduced and vilified the Abolitionists of North America.[91]

O'Connell referred to the assertion made by the Cincinnati repealers that 'the two races, viz.; the black and white, cannot exist on equal terms', by dismissing it as 'an extraordinary statement', followed by examples of where they did live in harmony. He repeatedly, and controversially, made the point that black and white people were equal.[92]

O'Connell used the argument that slavery degraded everybody, and therefore abolition would not only benefit the slaves, but also their white masters. In contrast, Irish-American involvement in abolition would bring credit on them and on Ireland. He challenged the religious sincerity of those who opposed abolition because:

> slavery was a hateful crime; a crime which the Pope has so completely condemned, namely, the diabolical raising of slaves for sale and selling them to other states ... if you be Catholics, you should devote your time and your best exertions to working out the pious exertions of His Holiness.[93]

The Cincinnati letter won widespread support from abolitionists in Ireland and America. It was praised by Garrison and his supporters, who had been criticizing O'Connell only a few months earlier.[94] The Irish-born Unitarian minister, George Armstrong, demanded of the American abolitionist Samuel May Jr, who was then visiting Europe:

> Have you seen the *magnificent* Address of O'Connell to *certain Irish* defenders of slavery, – at Cincinnati? If not, enquire for it by all means: and do not go to America without it.[95]

The Dublin abolitionist, Richard Davis Webb, who had not always been an admirer of O'Connell, offered a lengthy and frank evaluation of this incident to his friend and fellow abolitionist in Boston, Edmund Quincy. He believed that O'Connell's response to the Cincinnati repealers was 'the best thing of the kind he ever wrote', continuing:

> You cannot fail to admire and publish as far and wide as you are able O'Connell's Anti Slavery Address. I wish I could think him what I do not – an honest and a great man. I think that in the interval between the interposition of government to stop the Clontarf meeting and the time of his arrest, he penned and published this great address as a diversion to his mind and from a desire in this crisis of his fate to restore himself to the confidence of a class whom I am sure in his heart he respects – though so lately he half disowned their acquaintance – I mean of course yourselves.

He concluded by requesting:

> Will you be sure to tell all people on all hands that it was Daniel O'Connell's personal request that his address would be sent to the Abolitionists of America. Mark how gently he hath spoken to you – see how plain it is he has James Haughton at his elbow.[96]

However, the response of the Cincinnati repealers was not totally welcomed in Ireland. The *Nation*, which was the mouthpiece of the Young Ireland group, was nervous that O'Connell was going too far in his criticism of American institutions.[97] Moreover, some repealers in America disliked O'Connell's public berating of their colleagues. At a meeting in Faneuil Hall in November 1843, John Tucker, vice-president of the Boston Repeal Association, said it 'was his duty to remind the audience that the Irish-Americans were ruled neither from Rome nor home'.[98]

Within Cincinnati, reaction to the address was mixed. A local periodical, *Facts for the People* mocked the repealers for suggesting that 'the whole power of the repeal movement rests upon the American people'. Furthermore, by aligning against O'Connell, 'you desert Irish Liberty, for American slavery'.[99] The Cincinnati repealers, who were at the centre of the controversy, chose not to respond to O'Connell. It was left to a breakaway group, the Friends of Liberty, Ireland and Repeal to pen an address, on 30 November. One of the signers of the letter was the local politician, the Honorable Salmon Chase. The letter started by praising O'Connell for all that he had done for Ireland, but went on to say:

> With shame and grief do we acknowledge the existence of this foul and dishonorable blot on our national character; but our shame becomes indignation, and our grief is turned into horror, when we see American citizens, whether native or naturalized, vindicating the continuance and extension of slavery in this country by an elaborate argument, and with unblushing impudence claiming for this organized crime a place among our national institutions.[100]

Chases's words fell on unreceptive ears. In the following months, many repeal societies in America showed that they did not agree with either O'Connell or with Chase. Twenty years later, on the eve of the American Civil War, O'Connell's and Chase's letters were republished in America and the reception was very different to what it had been when they were first written. In 1843 and 1844 however, O'Connell's attacks on slavery and his criticisms of Irish-America, alienated many of his supporters and resulted in him being criticized by nationalists in the United States, but also by Irish repealers who did not want him to engulf the repeal American associations in this issue. According to the historian, Maurice Bric, 'By 1845, influential sections of Irish America had come to regard O'Connell's opinions on slavery as a mixture of mischief, arrogance and intrusion'. Nonetheless, his interventions 'marked an important chapter in the reinvention of an Irish diaspora that, in at least in so far as the Atlantic world was concerned, was the sum of two halves, the New and Old countries'.[101]

Young and Old Ireland

It was not just within the abolition movement that O'Connell was divisive. Since his release from prison in 1844 O'Connell had been at odds with the Young Ireland group over a number of issues, including approaches to non-denominational education and slavery. In 1846, the tensions came to a head, although the resulting split was triggered by a disagreement over the use of physical force.

In 1841, members of the Repeal Association had worked with the Hibernian Anti-Slavery Society to collect signatures for the Irish Address. They could not have foreseen the extent of antagonism it would attract: antagonism that grew as O'Connell continued to lambast Irish-Americans who did not support abolition. The American response contributed to a growing wariness about continuing to involve Irish-Americans in such a contentious issue. This was increasingly the attitude of the Young Ireland group who had emerged within the Repeal Association in 1842. But even within Young Ireland there were different approaches. The idealist lawyer, Thomas Davis, disliked slavery but disapproved of O'Connell's approach; others, included John Mitchel, were influenced by the writings of Thomas Carlyle, and viewed the owning of slaves as free right; others were concerned that slavery was a distraction from the key objective of achieving a repeal of the Union.

In 1843, the repeal year, many Young Irelanders disapproved of O'Connell's continuing high-level, and high-profile, involvement with anti-slavery. They felt that O'Connell should concentrate on domestic affairs and that repeal and abolition should be kept separate.[102] The debate that ensued as a result of the Cincinnati Letter and O'Connell's uncompromising response to it appeared to increase divisions with the Irish repeal movement, as well as in the American one. The Young Ireland group was clearly uncomfortable with O'Connell's statements on this issue. In January 1844, as O'Connell and some of his fellow repealers faced imprisonment, the *Nation* carried an editorial that stated bluntly:

> Repeal must not be put in conflict with *any* party in the States. The men of the Southern states must not have their institutions interfered with, whether right or wrong ... We might as well refuse English contributions because of the horrors of mill slavery ... as well as quarrel with Americans because of their domestic institutions, however we may condemn and once for all protest against them. We received help on Catholic Emancipation from America in 1828 when they held slaves as now, and from England, then a slave-owner, and now a slave-trader.[103]

These differences were increasingly aired in the columns of the *Nation,* which had become the most influential and widely read paper in Ireland. The paper's popularity mirrored the growing influence of Young Ireland within the repeal movement. A number of articles in the *Nation* suggested that it was the English who had planted slavery in the States, and that while Ireland remained in a position of such miserable subjection, she could not afford to alienate her allies.[104]

Although the *Nation* disapproved of the interventions of O'Connell on abolition, they did give column space to those amongst their own party who had similar opinions. This included publishing a letter by James Haughton, which he had written to the Irish in America asking them to condemn slavery. In it, he had criticized the *Nation* for not condemning American slaveholders who were supporters of repeal.[105] However, an editorial pointed out that 'A gentleman so respectable and well-intentioned as Mr Haughton is entitled to be heard, and not the less because he differs from us'.[106]

The dislike of O'Connell's anti-slavery activities was not confined to Young Irelanders. In August 1845, the *Nation* reported that Richard Scott, a Dublin-based lawyer and leading Old Irelander, had criticized O'Connell's interventions in abolition issues on the grounds that it was divisive and it detracted from the main issue of achieving repeal.[107] The paper also pointed out that in the late 1820s, during the Catholic Emancipation campaign, O'Connell had accepted money from slaveholding states.[108] The differences did not go away, leading to a further editorial in the *Nation* in May that stated:

> They [repealers] deny that Ireland has a quixotic mission to redress all the wrongs of humanity, and they assert that our strength needs husbanding, and should not be directed to such remote quarrels; but all condemn slavery – each allows the purity of the other's motive – and all see that the difference is on a minor and external subject.[109]

The *Freeman's Journal,* an avid supporter of O'Connell on many political issues, was ambivalent regarding his support for abolition. While they were happy to publish his attacks on slavery in India, which they characterized as a further example of British injustice, they were less willing to give coverage to his attacks on American institutions.[110]

Richard Webb, who was frequently critical of O'Connell, admitted that making Irish-Americans into abolitionists was not an easy task. He confided to a friend in the United States:

> ... he will not make an abolitionist among them all. They are too ignorant, too bigoted, and their perceptions of human rights and of liberty is altogether too obscure and imperfect. Send from the United States a few thousand blacks for a year and I have little doubt that prejudice against colour and the pro-slavery spirit would prevail among the millions here as they amongst you.[111]

Regarding the Repeal Association, Richard Webb was sceptical about the level of genuine support for abolition:

> Amongst the active Repealers there is not a genuine anti-slavery man, as far as I know, but O'Connell. The rest are angry with him for what he has said and written against proslavery Americans. They cling to the ultimate idea of receiving help from Brother Jonathan.[112]

In the wake of Clontarf, the aged O'Connell no longer seemed able to unite his party and the political initiative was increasingly passing to Young Ireland. Moreover, following O'Connell's release from prison, his health had been deteriorating and the mantle of the slave question was being taken up by his son, John. John lacked his father's charisma, although he shared O'Connell's passion for abolition. A speech by John O'Connell to the Repeal Association in August 1845 prompted a letter of praise from the committee of the Hibernian Anti-Slavery Society for his condemnation of the annexation of Texas and his 'noble and uncompromising maintenance of the full and equal right of the coloured race with the whites to the inalienable blessing of liberty'.[113] John O'Connell responded to the HASS by condemning the northern states of the United States for their hypocrisy in promoting the degradation and segregation of 'the coloured man'.[114] He added, 'It would seem that some of the Americans, not being satisfied with making scoundrels of themselves by their nefarious practice of trafficking in human flesh, want to make a scoundrel of my father'.[115] At the meeting, Tom Steele described the Irish Repeal Association as 'the greatest anti-slavery society in the world.[116] However, Richard Scott of the Repeal Association criticized John O'Connell for devoting so much time to the slavery issue, arguing that it should be left to the Hibernian Anti-Slavery Society.[117] Scott's views represented those of many members of the Repeal Association, including those of Young Ireland. These divisions became more intense as O'Connell's health declined further and his son John took over more responsibilities. John failed to exert authority over some of the more radical members of the Repeal Association. At the end of 1845, O'Connell admitted to William Smith O'Brien, unofficial leader of Young Ireland, that O'Brien's popularity was challenging his own and that of his son.[118] The appearance of a mysterious blight on the potato crop in 1845 initially united the repeal movement as they sought ways to help the poor who had lost their staple food. It was into this political cauldron that the black former slave Frederick Douglass made his first visit to Ireland.

Douglass and Ireland

A feature of the cooperation between the transatlantic anti-slavery movements was the large amount of correspondence that flowed to and fro across the ocean. Abolitionist groups on both sides of the Atlantic also visited each other on lecture tours; Garrison, for example, travelled to the United Kingdom many times. A number of black speakers also made the journey. Those who visited Ireland included Equiano, Charles Lenox Remond, and Frederick Douglass. Both Remond and Douglass were, when they visited, members of Garrison's American Anti-Slavery Society.

When Frederick Douglass travelled to the United Kingdom in 1845, he was already well known in the American anti-slavery movement. Apart from his fame as an escaped slave, he was a noted writer. In 1845 his *Narrative* had been published. In August 1845 he sailed to Liverpool as the guest of British and Irish abolitionists. Because of his colour, he had been forced to travel steerage, but he later said that the voyage became a liberating, transformative one for him, symbolizing his journey to freedom.[119] Shortly after arriving in Britain, he travelled to Ireland where he lectured throughout the country, from Cork to Belfast. He caused excitement wherever he went and it re-energized his own support for abolition. He first stayed with Richard Webb in Dublin. Webb, a printer, brought out the Irish edition of Douglass's *Narrative*, which included a new Preface. Privately, Webb found Douglass to be haughty, impatient and suspicious.[120] Although Douglass (an ordained minister in African Methodist Episcopal Zion Church) addressed both Catholic and Protestant audiences, he felt more comfortable with Protestant ones. In general, he was, like a number of American abolitionists, anti-Catholic, although his Irish sojourn may have helped to modify his views.[121] While in Ireland, he spent time with Father Mathew, Douglass sharing the priest's passion for temperance. He also lectured alongside his hero, O'Connell. O'Connell's reputation had preceded him but Douglass's expectations were exceeded. In 1846, O'Connell was aged seventy-one and his health was deteriorating. Increasingly, he was leaving the day-to-day control of the repeal movement to his son John, but there were serious divisions within the movement, which became evident with the departure of the Young Ireland group in the summer of 1846.[122] Douglass, however, was impressed with the Liberator:

> His eloquence came down upon the vast assembly like a summer shower upon a dusty road. He could at will stir the multitude to a tempest of wrath or reduce it to the silence with which a mother leaves the cradle side of her sleeping babe. Such tenderness, such pathos, such world-embracing love – and, on the other hand, such indignation, such fiery and thunderous denunciation, such wit and humour, I never heard surpassed, if equaled at home and abroad. He held Ireland within the grasp of his strong hand and could lead it withersoever he would, for Ireland believed in him as she loved and believed in no leader since.[123]

Douglass's eloquence resulted in his being referred to as 'the black O'Connell', a considerable tribute to the self-taught twenty-seven-year-old.[124] Douglass, in turn, had great respect for the Irish Liberator. In the 1849 edition of the *Narrative*, Douglass quoted a speech by O'Connell about the brutalizing effects of slavery.[125]

In Belfast, Douglass was warmly welcomed with full attendances at his lectures.[126] There, anti-slavery was mostly linked with the Presbyterian and Methodist Churches, and the leadership was dominated by ministers. Douglass appealed to his audience to bring pressure to bear on their sister-churches in the United States, many of whom continued to endorse slavery. The missionary nature of the work of the Belfast society was evident with a motion being passed of the need to 'take an interest in the melancholy condition of 3,000,000 of slaves in southern states of American, deprived of access to the Scriptures'.[127] In January 1846, a public breakfast given in Douglass's honour was chaired by the local radical MP, William Sharman Crawford. At it, Douglass thanked the committee because, when he arrived in Belfast, they had taken him 'by the hand, and I will say they have not ceased to hold my hand since I arrived in the town'.[128] He repeatedly paid tribute to Irish and British abolitionists who had raised their voices on behalf of the slave because 'they had much to do in forming the moral feeling of America'.[129]

Douglass spent six months in Ireland, which he later described as some of the happiest days of his life. The historian Fionnghuala Sweeney has argued that in Ireland Douglass, emboldened by the respect which he encountered, found his own literary and political voice, rather than being a mouthpiece for New England abolitionists.[130] Unbeknown to him, his visit coincided with the onset of a period of suffering known as the Great Hunger. Douglass followed his visit to Ireland with one to Scotland and while there, he criticized the association between the Free Church of Scotland and their sister churches in the United States, both of whom supported slavery.[131] By doing so, he lost support in both Scotland and Ireland. According to Mary Ireland, a teacher in Belfast, 'those who usually take the lead in other good works, offended by the uncompromising tone of Mr Douglass in regard to the Free Church of Scotland, are either avowed enemies to the present movement or very hollow friends'.[132]

One outcome of Douglass's tour was the revival of the female Anti-Slavery Society in Belfast. One of the founding members had been Mary Ann McCracken, sister of Henry Joy, the executed United Irishman. Maria Webb, of the Quaker Webb family, was the Corresponding Secretary. According to Mary Ireland, 'I am convinced there is scarcely a lady in Belfast who would not be anxious to join in any means calculated to promote the enfranchisement of the deeply injured Africans'.[133] Apart from raising money, women also viewed their role as that of educators in the fight against slavery. This was especially evident within the Belfast ASS, which had been formed in the wake of Douglass's visit. Especially important was the influence they would have on future emigrants, because 'We are informed that Irish emigrants, with their minds proverbially open to be acted on by prejudice and adopting the current sentiments of American society, usually join the pro-slavery ranks after crossing the Atlantic'.[134] The role that could be played by women in countering this was explained by Maria Webb of the Belfast society:

> If the sons and daughters of Erin ere they leave their own sea-girt isle were intellectually prepared to sympathize with the enslaved and the injured coloured inhabitants of your land, what a different influence might the emigrants carry with them to the homes and circles they form in America. As the case now stands we fear that our country-men on reaching your shores more frequently join in proslavery prejudice and outcry, instead of seeking to promote anti-slavery efforts.[135]

To further this cause, women in Belfast were 'informing their minds by reading' so that they could take their anti-slavery message into the schools and educate people about slavery before they left Ireland. When Douglass finally left the United Kingdom in April 1847, he was 'the finished independent man, cut from the whole cloth and able to make his own decisions about the strategies and ideologies of the abolitionist movement'.[136]

Famine and Death

When Frederick Douglass had visited Ireland at the end of 1845, he had been shocked and touched by the level of poverty he had seen there, leading him to draw a comparison between the suffering of the Irish and that of slaves.[137] Writing to Garrison he said:

> Men and women, married and single, old and young, lie down together, in much the same degradation as the American slaves. I see much here to remind me of my former condition, and I confess I should be ashamed to lift up my voice against American slavery, but that I know the cause of humanity is one the world over.[138]

Douglass's time in Ireland coincided with the appearance of a new type of blight, which destroyed approximately 40 per cent of the potato crop in 1845 – the subsistence food of over half of the population. The reappearance of blight over the following six years led to a period known as the Great Hunger or Great Famine. The Famine not only resulted in the deaths of over 1,000,000 people, it also led to the emigration of approximately 2,000,000, many of whom chose North America as their final destination.[139] A number of emigrants travelled on ships that had been formerly used to transport slaves.[140] While the circumstances under which the Irish and the Negroes travelled were very different, the level of fatalities was similar – with an estimated 20 per cent average loss during the

'Middle Passage', that is the enforced journey from Africa to the Americas, and a similar number of fatalities for the Irish, either during their voyage or within a few years of arrival.[141] Ireland's famine coincided with a period of food shortages and political upheaval throughout Europe, which also led to a surge in emigration to North America. These emigrants, many of whom were poor and drawn from agricultural areas, settled in the eastern towns and cities of North America, where they changed the economic, social and religious composition of their host society. Many of the poor Irish who emigrated to North America were unskilled Catholics and their arrival consolidated the prejudices of the anti-immigrant Know-Nothing Party.

When the potato blight first appeared in Ireland, O'Connell, despite his advanced years, proved to be an energetic advocate for the poor, serving on the Mansion House Committee in Dublin and arguing there and in Parliament for more relief and the closing of the ports to keep food in Ireland. By 1846, he was also considering entering a fresh alliance with the Whig Party, believing they would be more responsive to the needs of the suffering Irish poor than the Tory Party.[142] For members of Young Ireland, who were becoming more radical as a consequence of the famine, this proposed alliance was an act of betrayal. In 1846, O'Connell's son John orchestrated an argument within the Repeal Association on the spurious issue of physical versus moral force. The Young Ireland group, led by John Mitchel, Thomas Francis Meagher and William Smith O'Brien, had refused to promise that they would never make use of violence, seeing it as an abstract argument. The outcome was that they seceded from the Association.[143] They were joined by James Haughton, O'Connell's long-term friend and fellow abolitionist. There were now two repeal movements in Ireland and the dream of O'Connell to build a mass movement to win legislative independence for Ireland was in shards. Increasingly, the Liberator withdrew from public life.

In January 1847, Young Ireland formed the Irish Confederation. Divisions instantly emerged. At the first meeting, Haughton, the veteran anti-slaver, spoke, and suggested that they should not accept donations from American slaveholders.[144] John Kenyon, a radical priest and friend of John Mitchel, responded by pointing out that the Scriptures had never forbidden slavery.[145] The issue did not go away. The various editorial comments made it clear that the editors of the *Nation* – Charles Gavan Duffy and John Mitchel – wished that it would. Following the split in the repeal association, the *Nation* increasingly argued that Irishmen should focus on their own problems and not get caught up in the disputes of others.[146]

In February 1847, the paper included an editorial comment responding to a letter it had received, which said:

> We have to say, once and for all, that we will have nothing to do with 'abolition' for the future, either *con* or *pro* ... Our enemies are nearer home than Carolina, and we must be permitted to deal with them first.[147]

These assertions were not fully welcomed by certain members of the Confederation, and drew an angry response from Haughton.[148] In April, Haughton chaired a weekly meeting of the Confederation and urged those present not to accept money from 'the woman whippers and cradle plunderers of Baltimore and Charleston' or 'the blood-stained dollars of the slave driver'.[149] The audience was antagonistic to him and 'hissed and hooted', shouting 'no slave lecturing here'.[150] Haughton responded by accusing the meeting of demonstrating the same illiberal attitudes to free speech as had the Repeal Association.[151] At the same meeting, an address was passed thanking the Vice President of the United States, George Mifflin Dallas, who had held a fundraising meeting on behalf of Ireland. Haughton also opposed this motion on the grounds that Dallas was himself a slave-owner.[152] He added it was 'his strong conviction that they would never gain their own liberty if they were unmindful of the injuries done in the name of liberty abroad'.[153] Three weeks later, it was announced that because of this dispute, Haughton had withdrawn from the Confederation.[154] Privately, Haughton was concerned that donations being sent from American to help relieve the famine poor would dampen anti-slavery feeling in Ireland. He confided to a friend, 'A grateful feeling towards America has, to a great extent, destroyed our hatred of slavery as it exists amongst you. You have bought off our condemnation of your wicked system'.[155] The Confederation itself split at the end of 1847, with John Mitchel departing, having come to the conclusion that a political revolution to win independence from Britain needed to be accompanied by a social revolution to change the structure of landholding in Ireland.[156]

By 1847, it was clear that O'Connell was no longer the force that he had once been. He was now aged seventy-two and he had spent the greater part of his life in the public eye, being adored and abhorred in equal measure. Throughout his life he had battled with many powerful opponents, including the Protestant Ascendancy, the Orange Order, successive British governments and American slaveholders, each with considerable success. His final significant battle had been with his former supporters in the Repeal Association, and it appeared to be the one that wounded him most of all.

News of O'Connell's decline had reached his admirers in the United States. In April 1847, his long-term supporter and fellow abolitionist warned Maria Weston Chapman in Boston:

> Our once great O'Connell is no longer great. We have no certain accounts of the state of his mind or body, but I apprehend his mind is broken down, and that this sad result is caused in great measure by the feeling he has lost the confidence of the country, in consequence of his late errors (errors to use the mildest term) as a politician. His fate is striking evidence of the folly of a disingenuous course of action.[157]

O'Connell died in May 1847 in Genoa; far from his beloved Ireland. He was en route to Rome, where he had hoped to meet the Pope. His final speech in the House of Commons had been on behalf of the famine poor in Ireland. In Britain, O'Connell's death was met with some indifference. Greville commented that his departure 'which not long ago would have excited the greatest interest and filled the world with political speculations, was heard almost with unconcern, so entirely had his importance vanished'.[158] A local English newspaper reported 'The most eventful circumstance of the past week is the intelligence that the great agitator of Ireland, the man who has exercised and wielded more power for evil than any man this century – DANIEL O'CONNELL – is no more'.[159]

O'Connell's death unified temporarily the various sections of the repeal movement, not just in Ireland, but further afield. But his unwavering commitment to abolition tempered the acclaim with which he was remembered. For some repealers in the United States, O'Connell's heroism in achieving Catholic Emancipation and seeking repeal of the Union was tempered by his support for abolition. The Repeal Society of Savannah printed a Eulogy to O'Connell following his death. Its brief references to O'Connell's anti-slavery activities were oblique, it stating that 'Universal liberty and freedom of conscience, were with him a passion, and hence receiving his information from a party among ourselves, inimical to Southern institutions, he was betrayed into harsh expression towards a government which he otherwise loved and admired'.[160]

American abolitionists mourned O'Connell's passing and were in no doubt about his contribution to their humanitarian cause. In the *National Era,* John Greenleaf Whittier wrote:

> He was an Abolitionist of the most unequivocal and ultra stamp. His public appeals to the sympathy of his hearers, on behalf of the slave, are unsurpassed in their mournful beauty and touching pathos; whilst his denunciations of West India cruelty and Democratic slave-driving, for fierce invective and terrible sarcasm, are wholly without parallel in the English tongue There were unquestionable defects in his character – but no one can deny him the merit of a sincere love of Freedom and an intense abhorrence of slavery and oppression, wherever and by whomsoever exercised. .... Wherever humanity writhes under the heel of tyranny, there were found the fiery heart and trumpet voice of Daniel O'Connell, sympathizing with the victim and rebuking the tyrant'.[161]

Frederick Douglass lamented the passing of the Liberator, saying:

> I felt that a great champion had fallen, and that the cause of the American slave, not less than the cause of his country, had met a great loss. All the more was this felt when I saw the kind of men who came to the front when the voice of O'Connell was no longer heard in Ireland.

Douglass described O'Connell's successors as 'men who loved liberty in their own country, but were utterly destitute of sympathy with the cause of liberty in countries other than their own'.[162]

A moving valediction was made by the American Whig politician William Seward. Seward, an admirer of O'Connell who had sympathized with the repeal movement, had added his protests when O'Connell had been arrested in 1843.[163] For Seward, O'Connell's achievement lay in his 'mission to teach mankind that Liberty was not estranged from Christianity'. He added that although O'Connell had left 'his mighty enterprise unfinished', the granting of Irish independence was 'not distant'.[164] When O'Connell died, the abolition movement lost one of its most devoted, flamboyant and uncompromising international champions, and the slaves lost a man who had truly shown himself to be their friend.

7 'THE MAN OF ALL MEN'

O'Connell died in Genoa in May 1847, at the height of the famine. The potato crop failed again in 1848 and, to lesser degrees, in 1849, 1850 and 1851. As a consequence, a country renowned for its poverty underwent a catastrophe of unprecedented impact in terms of population loss and social upheaval. Within the space of six years, Ireland lost over a quarter of its population; approximately 1,000,000 people died and a higher number emigrated. Precise mortality and emigration statistics were not kept by the government, meaning that many of those who died or left remained uncounted and anonymous. As a consequence, the country that O'Connell had loved and fought many political battles for was vastly changed. In the midst of the famine, Young Ireland attempted an insurrection in the unlikely location of Ballingarry in Country Tipperary. It was swiftly defeated with no fatalities.[1] This defeat meant that Irish independence appeared more elusive than ever. Recovery from the years of famine was slow, with falling birth rates and high emigration continuing for decades. Moreover, many of the brilliant minds that had been attracted to the Repeal Association and Young Ireland, were either dead, in exile, or had been transported. Those who remained, like Charles Gavan Duffy, despaired of Ireland's future, socially and politically. Mass emigration had shifted the power balance as the majority of those who left Ireland sought refuge in North America. In the United States, they faced the hostility of the nativists, especially from the Know-Nothing Party. A new Ireland was being created outside the island of Ireland that tended to be politically militant and favoured physical over moral force. The founding of the Fenians and the Irish Republican Brotherhood in 1858, concurrently in Ireland and the United States, was an indication of the role that Irish-Americans would play in the future of Irish independence.

Post-Famine

Despite the years of famine, abolitionists in Ireland continued to support their American colleagues, especially through the fundraising efforts of women's bazaars. For years, Irish women had sent goods to Garrison's Anti-Slavery Society in Boston, rather than to Lewis Tappan's rival American and Anti-Slavery

Society, based out of New York. In 1846, Hannah White of the Cork Anti-Slavery Society informed the Boston group:

> We feared that our contribution this year would be but a small one owing to the distress in this country, but it is as good as usual and proves that those who feel for *any* suffering are inclined to feel for all. We find that the persons to give to us are those who are the readiest to assist in benevolent schemes at home.[2]

The newly formed female group in Belfast also sent goods for the Boston bazaar, but apologized for the coarseness of the materials used as that was the best they could obtain made by free labour, 'unpolluted by slave labour'.[3]

Nonetheless, as the famine progressed it did have an impact on what groups in Ireland could send. In November 1848, Richard Webb, who acted as a central co-coordinator for sending goods to Boston, admitted that 'There are very few workers or donors'.[4] The greatest contributors in Dublin were the daughters of James Haughton, the wealthy merchant who had been a close friend of O'Connell. Webb considered the Haughton women to be 'a little bit aristocratic and exclusive'. He urged that the Boston committee give praise to their donations 'for they might be the better of a little blarney, while we can get on very well without it'.[5] That year, the women of the Cork societies sent an eclectic collection of goods that included forty-two pieces made from seaweed, which proved to be good sellers.[6] The ladies privately lamented that by giving their support to Boston – and effectively Garrison – they were unable to give support to Frederick Douglass and his group in Rochester.[7] In 1849, Webb admitted despondently, 'All that goes in the Dublin box is contributed by very few persons and the number of our helpers is not increased but diminished from year to year'.[8] In 1851, the Cork group reported to Boston that 'the famine years have exercised a very depressing influence, and tho' the country is now as well off as before 1846, still that amount of prosperity is not enough to allow us to send money to America'.[9]

As good harvests returned to Ireland, there was a revival of anti-slavery in Dublin, which resulted in two new societies being established, one for men and one for women. Many of the same people were involved: Richard Webb was the Secretary and James Haughton was the Vice President of the former.[10] By the mid-1850s though, anti-slavery in Ireland again seemed to be in the doldrums. The country was still recovering from the famine, and mass emigration showed no signs of abatement. Although Webb and Haughton remained active, and continued to raise money for America, they were not attracting younger members. Moreover, there was no O'Connell to rouse and inspire people.[11] Frederick Douglass, who had met all three men during his four-months' stay in Ireland, considered the remaining Irish abolitionist leadership to be petty and lacklustre.[12] It was not only Dublin that was having problems. In Belfast, the men's abolition society had dissolved as the two aged secretaries, who were 'veterans in the West Indian struggle', had decided to resign and nobody had come forth to replace them, while the Ladies' Association had merged into a sewing circle.[13] The latter, however, continued to send goods to the annual bazaar, although this effort was dwindling. By 1857, only four women contributed goods to the Boston bazaar, one of whom was the eighty-seven-year-old Mary Ann McCracken, who was praised for being 'as ardent now in the cause of American anti-slavery as she was formerly in that of the West Indian slave'.[14]

United States

As the 1840s drew to a close, American abolitionists were optimistic that their agitation was having a positive impact on federal politics. In 1847, some politicians and anti-slavery groups had formed the Free Soil Party, whose motto was 'Free Soil for Free Men'. In 1848, the former President, Martin Van Buren, was nominated to represent them in the Presidential election. As the November election approached, the votes of Irish-Americans were sought by making a direct appeal to the memory of O'Connell and of another dead patriot, Robert Emmet. The inclusion of the latter was because Emmet's nephew, also called Robert Emmet, was standing for election in New York on behalf of the Party. A four-page broadside was produced entitled 'Irishmen! Hear the Voices of O'Connell and Emmet!!' One of O'Connell's anti-slavery speeches was included, which had concluded with a plea to Irish-Americans:

> Once again, and for the last time, we call upon you to come out of your councils of the slave owners, and at all events, to free yourself from participating in their guilt. Irishmen, I call on you to join in crushing slavery, and in giving liberty to every man, of every caste, creed and color.[15]

O'Connell's plea was followed by a new request, 'the time has arrived when by your votes you can carry out the wishes of O'Connell – an election for President is close at hand', asking 'Who that reveres the memory of O'Connell, or loves the name of Emmet (and what Irishman does not?) Can hesitate how to vote?'[16] Although Van Buren was unsuccessful, losing decisively to Zachary Taylor, a number of Free Soil members were elected to the House of Representatives. In 1854, the party was absorbed into the Republican Party. Although short-lived, the Free Soil Party was influential and its founding had pleased abolitionists. Garrison viewed it as 'unmistakable proof of the progress we have made under God, in changing public sentiment'.[17]

In 1849, Father Mathew, the temperance crusader, visited the United States. In 1841 he had put his name, alongside that of O'Connell, to a petition or Address, urging Irish-Americans to join in the fight against slavery. Mathew had declared that the purpose of his mission was to thank Americans for their aid during the famine. Inevitably, he was brought into the ongoing abolitionist debate. When in Boston, Garrison invited him to attend an anti-slavery event. Mathew refused on the grounds that his mission was directed at temperance. He added that there was nothing in the scriptures against slavery.[18] His comments and attitude seemed in direct contradiction to the appeal made in the Address. As with everything to do with slavery, opinions on Mathew's attitude were polarized, with newspapers in the South, and those who disliked Garrison's militant approach, supporting the priest. Mathew, sometimes viewed as a religious maverick, received mixed support from the Catholic Church in the United States. However, Archbishop Hughes did not want him to visit New York, but when he did so, told him to behave.[19] Mathew's stance was not enough to convince all slaveholders of his neutrality. Although he was invited to attend the House of Representatives, there were objections to his sitting in the Senate, with Senator Clemens of Alabama describing the 1842 Address as a 'sin and a crime'.[20] However, Mathew was invited to dinner by President Tyler, who supported gradual abolition although he himself was a slaveholder.

In August 1849, Mathew was invited to a large meeting in Worcester to commemorate emancipation in the British West Indies. He did not respond to the invitation, leaving Samuel May to speculate 'he seems about to ignore all his anti-slavery and to fall into the wake of other British clergymen who have visited this country'.[21] Mathew was also criticized by Frederick Douglass, who had taken the pledge from him in 1845. Douglass believed that the priest was following the path of other British and Irish opponents of anti-slavery who, upon arriving in America had abandoned their principles.[22] Garrison regarded Mathew's actions as typical of that of the Catholic Church, writing 'Not a Catholic priest, not a Catholic journal, can be found in this great country, pleading for the liberation of the enslaved; on the contrary, they most heartily stigmatize the abolitionists and all their movements'.[23] An honorable exception was O'Connell, who was praised for standing up to the abolitionists in Cincinnati.[24] Despite losing the support of his former allies, Mathew believed he had done the right thing – if he had spoken against slavery he would not have been allowed to visit the South and make converts.[25]

As had become evident during the visit of Father Mathew, the death of O'Connell had not diminished his value as a champion of American abolitionists. Throughout the 1850s, his words were frequently invoked and his speeches quoted. Garrison, in particular, rarely spoke at an annual meeting of the Anti-Slavery Society without mentioning the Liberator.[26] All past differences were forgotten. In June 1849 'People of Color' in Columbiana County in Ohio held a mass meeting at which a number of resolutions were passed, condemning slavery, supporting temperance, criticizing colonization, wishing for the 'speedy dissolution of the American Union', and endorsing 'the lofty sentiment of Daniel O'Connell that "No reformation is worthy the shedding of one drop of human blood"'. The meeting and its resolutions were viewed as proof that 'these long injured men begin to feel their manhood'.[27]

In August 1849, the escaped slave William Wells Brown travelled to France as the American Peace Society's delegate to the International Peace Congress in Paris. While there, he visited Ireland and lectured in Dublin. The veteran James Haughton was in the chair. During his lecture he made lengthy reference to O'Connell – 'a man now departed, whose life was one continued and noble struggle for the religious and civil liberty of his native land'. Brown referred to the time that O'Connell had refused to shake hands with Stephenson [*sic*], the American Ambassador, for which he was loudly cheered.

In August 1849, the *National Era* included the life of O'Connell in a series of *Sketches of Modern Reformers*. It was written by Henry Brewster Stanton, abolitionist and social reformer. Although it started by saying that 'In many important respects he is the greatest of Irishmen', throughout it referred to his flaws and failures. It explained that the latter were 'partly due to the evil times in which he lived'. The article concluded that:

> Impartial history will record that his fury was usually poured out on the heads of meanness, fraud, injustice and oppression; that he was the friend, the champion, the brother, of depressed and outraged manhood, irrespective of clime, colour or creed; and that wherever humanity writhed under the hell of tyranny, there were found the glowing heart and trumpet voice of Daniel O'Connell, sympathizing with the victim and rebuking the tyrant.[28]

O'Connell was kept in the public eye in other ways. In 1851, Frederick Douglass produced his own sketch of O'Connell for his paper, which ran to many columns. The article was written in order to commemorate the fourth anniversary of receiving news of his death. The article (incorrectly) placed the year of his birth as 1776, 'a circumstance not unworthy of notice' that 'the birth of a man so strongly identified with the cause of civil liberty should have been placed in a year allowed by one of its most glorious achievements'.[29] The article was full of praise for O'Connell's skills and his various humanitarian stands, which were all the more remarkable as 'No Patriot, we believe, ever encountered more opposition in his struggles, or encountered more obloquy and contempt from his fellows ; nor is there an instance when reproach and insult have been more solidly changed to respect and praise'.[30] In May 1851, the *National Era* ran a series of articles entitled 'The Duty of Anti-Slavery Voters' criticizing immigrants who did not support abolition, pointing out:

> The English and the Irish poor tacitly assent to emancipation doctrines at home, where they mean nothing practical to themselves; but not an immigrant in a hundred

from either of these islands will acknowledge abolitionism here. They are Democrats and nothing else ... Daniel O'Connell might say what he pleased in their name at home, but here he lost all his power on this point, and Father Mathew altered his attitude to the subject marvelously when he came under the influence of our climate.[31]

Throughout the 1850s, the cause of pro-slavery seemed to be advancing, leading abolitionists to despair that successive national governments were in the thrall of slave-owners. In 1850, the American Congress passed the Fugitive Slave Law. Only four men voted against the measure. The law stated that in future any federal marshal who did not arrest an alleged runaway slave could be fined $1,000, and those suspected of being runaway slaves could be arrested. A captured slave was not entitled to a jury trial and nor could they testify on his or her own behalf. Anybody who assisted the runaway slave was liable to six months' imprisonment and a $1,000 fine. Incentive to capture runaway slaves was provided in the form of a bonus to be given to the capturing officer, whereas they could be fined for *not* capturing an escaped slave. Abolitionists on both sides of the Atlantic were appalled by this draconian measure, with even the moderate Arthur Tappan saying that the law should be disobeyed. An English abolitionist, Joseph Barker, who had been considering emigrating to the United States, now informed Garrison, 'if the northern people do not render this iniquitous law inoperative, and insist on its speedy abolition', he would change his plans.[32] The law did not stop the Underground Railroad, which was the system of aiding slaves fleeing from the South. A number of former slaves also sought refuge in Britain. One, who toured Britain and attracted much public attention was Josiah Henson. He was received at Windsor Castle by Queen Victoria, thus becoming the first freed slave to receive such an invitation. Henson was also the inspiration for Harriet Beecher Stowe's *Uncle Tom's Cabin*.[33]

Although American abolitionists were united in opposition against the Fugitive Slave Act, in other ways they were divided. In the early 1850s, Garrison lost some of his most ardent supporters in Britain. The anti-slavery societies in Edinburgh and Glasgow, offended by some anti-religious comments in the *Liberator*, decided to withdraw their support from the American Anti-Slavery Society. The move was led by the women abolitionists.[34] A split also occurred between two of the most famous American abolitionists, Douglass and Garrison. The division came to a head over the interpretation of the Constitution – Garrison believed it was a pro-slavery document whereas Douglass had come to see it as being anti-slavery. There had been other tensions. In 1851, Douglass had merged the *North Star* with Gerrit Smith's *Liberty Party Paper* to found the *Frederick Douglass' Paper*. This new paper was in direct competition with Garrison's own newspaper. George Thompson, who had visited the United States in 1851, disapproved of Douglass's change of heart. He observed 'Poor Douglass!

How changed he is', adding that his new paper was making 'herculean attempts to wash the Ethiop white'.[35]

Further divisions followed. In 1851, there was another split in the American Anti-Slavery Society, when Dr Cheever and Henry Ward Beecher seceded and set up the Church Anti-Slavery Society. The *New York Herald* described it as being a squabble between extremists, with the seceders seeking 'self-glorification'.[36] Webb admitted that the supporters in Ireland were 'terribly frightened by the talk there has been about heresy and new opinions in connection with Boston abolitionism'.[37] However, there were also differences in Ireland with Webb being considered too radical by many Quakers in the movement. Webb confided in Anne Weston, one of the founders of the Boston Female ASS that:

> I think there is a good deal of anti-slavery sentiment among "this people" but it is so much overladen by such things as emotions, notions or conditions, that it is not likely to bring forth much fruit.[38]

As a consequence of these splits, Garrison was increasingly isolated and by the mid-1850s, the AASS seemed to have lost its direction.

In 1853, Harriet Beecher Stowe, the author of *Uncle Tom's Cabin,* visited England. One of the first people she encountered in Liverpool was Sir George Stephen, a former colleague and admirer of O'Connell. The encounter prompted Stephen to write a history of the anti-slavery movement from his recollections, in the style of letters addressed to Beecher. In his final letter, dated 10 October 1854, Stephen questioned the lack of progress being made in achieving abolition in the United States:

> I presume there are 'a people' even in the Slave States, and a people not wholly blinded by selfish views. If I am wrong in this, republicanism is a fable; democracy a pure vision of wild imagination; federality a clumsy theory of political mechanics, to unite good and bad together a chimerical alliance. It cannot be: there must be a people with common sympathies and common consciousness of accountability to their common Creator. If not, there is no United States, and Washington lived and died in vain.[41]

In 1854, there was an attempt to rescind the Missouri Compromise of 1820, which regulated the spread of slavery. The implication was that slavery could then exist throughout the United States. Wendell Phillips was gloomy about these developments and believed the implication was that the slave trade might be permitted again by the American government. For him, 'the sky was never so dark'.[39] In 1855, the British and Foreign Anti-Slavery Society, which for years had been antagonistic to Garrison, made some overtures to the American Anti-Slavery Society regarding more cooperation. Followers of Garrison suspected that they were only doing so because the British group had been losing support for a number of years, whilst abolitionist feeling in the United States was again growing slowly, partly helped by the publication of *Uncle Tom's Cabin.*[40]

Regardless of the problems, British and Irish help remained important to American abolitionists. A resolution passed by Wendell Phillips in the Massachusetts Anti-Slavery Association in August 1851 said that the peace of Europe depended on the ending of slavery. Phillips thanked his British friends for 'moral support and the material aid'. He also thanked the British press. That year, half the Association's income had come from their 'English friends'. [42]

Kossuth and O'Connor

At the end of 1851, the Hungarian nationalist Lajos Kossuth travelled to the United States. Kossuth had been forced into exile as a consequence of the failure of the 1848 revolutions. Before travelling to the United States, he had spent time in England, where he had been warmly welcomed. His reception in America was expected to be equally positive as he was admired by radicals, abolitionists and members of the government for his stand against the Austrian Empire. Irish-Americans were more reserved, some disliking the fact that Kossuth had established friendly relationships with the British government, others influenced by Archbishop Hughes condemning Kossuth for being a 'red republican'. [43]

In a similar manner to Father Mathew, Kossuth disappointed American abolitionists, as he said that he was absolved from making any statement on slavery as he was there as the nation's guest. This alarmed members of the Dublin Anti-Slavery Society, who deemed that Kossuth had 'inflicted a serious injury on the anti-slavery cause by establishing a dangerous precedent for every other visitor to the United States'. [44] Kossuth was publicly criticized by Frederick Douglass for declaring his intention not to interfere in the internal affairs of America. At a meeting of the Massachusetts Anti-Slavery Society, Garrison lamented over Kossuth's behaviour and commenced to compare him to O'Connell. However, a Scottish man in the audience interrupted the eulogy by pointing out that O'Connell had opposed the Chartists and therefore was not a universal lover of liberty. This forced Garrison to admit that he knew nothing about this topic. [45] However, the American Anti-Slavery Society maintained its criticism of Kossuth in the form of a book, entitled *Letter to Louis Kossuth concerning Freedom and Slavery in the United States*. The Society was using the publication in order to 'convey to you [Kossuth] an expression of those feelings which your visit to the United States has awakened in our breasts'. [46] In it, they took extracts from Kossuth's speeches and juxtaposed them with the reality of his actions, 'to show how widely at variance with the truth are your encomiums'. [47] The latter part of the book included many of the speeches of O'Connell on slavery. O'Connell, it appeared, had become the benchmark of sincerity and commitment to the abolitionist cause.

Gerrit Smith of the American and Foreign Anti-Slavery Society, while praising Kossuth for being a good patriot, contrasted this with his unwillingness to
speak out for 'universal man'. As had become common, the reticence of Kossuth
was juxtaposed against the outspokenness of the dead O'Connell. Smith con-
curred, suggesting that:

> The man of all men, who should have come to America to plead for his oppressed
> countrymen, was Daniel O'Connell. O'Connell was a patriot. Never was there a
> more devoted one. He was, however, more than a patriot. He was a philanthropist.
> He was as true to the Negro, whom he had not seen, as to the Irishman, who he had
> seen. Kossuth can flatter the oppressor ... but O'Connell scorned the help offered by
> one set of oppressors against another.

The article went on to wish that the Irish in America could have 'the soul of
O'Connell', but:

> I confess that when I see the emigrants from Ireland – from the land of oppres-
> sion and the land of O'Connell – as ready as the emigrants from other countries,
> as ready as Native Americans, to fraternize with oppressors and with the revilers of
> O'Connell, to vote with them and for them – I confess when I see this, that I feel
> none the prouder for being the grandson of a woman who was born in Ireland.[48]

The praise given to O'Connell during the visits of Fr Mathew and Kossuth was
slightly disingenuous: in 1843 the Liberator had proposed to send his son, John,
together with Tom Steele, his right hand man in the Repeal Association, to collect repeal money in the United States. However, it had been made clear that
they would not become embroiled in the slave issue while there – a decision that
drew the criticism of Garrison at the time.[49]

Another visitor to the United States in 1852, a former associate of O'Connell,
proved to be controversial, but for different reasons. Cork-born Feargus
O'Connor had been elected to Parliament alongside O'Connell in the 1830s,
and had pledged to fight for a repeal of the Union. He fell out with O'Connell
when the latter refused to bring the matter before the House of Commons.
O'Connor then went on to lead the British Chartist movement, which campaigned for a reform of electoral practices, including the demand for universal
male suffrage. In April 1848, a mass meeting had been planned in London for
the presentation to Parliament of a Chartist petition. At the last minute, the
government banned the meeting and O'Connor called on the people to disperse
peacefully – mirroring O'Connell's activities in Clontarf in 1843. Following this,
O'Connor lost much support within the Chartist movement. In 1852, he visited
the United States. At this stage, he was suffering from some mental problems.
While talking about his love for Ireland, he spoke about his disagreement with
O'Connell over the timing of asking for repeal, adding his response had been to
say 'You villain, you have been robbing Ireland for the last ten years', and the next

day had added 'you ought to be hanged on the nearest tree'.[50] O'Connor's Irish-American audience was uncomfortable with this admission and had hissed at him. One member of the audience stood up and informed the speaker, 'We did not come here to hear any such talk. O'Connell is not here to defend himself'. When O'Connor completed his talk, he withdrew 'without much regret on the part of the audience'.[51]

In general, Irish-Americans remained distant from the abolition movement, and many were regarded as being actively opposed to abolition.[52] In 1853, Douglass made a speech in New York in which he distinguished between the Irish in Ireland and the Irish in America. He said of the latter, 'The cruel lie is told the Irish, that our adversity is essential to their prosperity. Sir, the Irish American will find out his mistake one day. He will find that in assuming our avocation, he has also assumed our degradation'.[53] Douglass's appeals were taken up by James Haughton who, in 1856, the year of a Presidential Election, addressed a public letter to the Irish in America, using some of the arguments employed by O'Connell over ten years earlier. Even in Ireland, his letter caused controversy with the *Freeman's Journal* describing his criticisms as being 'rather severe'. Haughton responded that he had hoped his letter would:

> produce an indignant denial from many Irishmen in the United States, accompanied by an honest and manly declaration that they always have been and ever will be true lovers of liberty, civil and religious, for all mankind ... That they have not done so in America is too true.[54]

One of the outcomes of the famine and the failed 1848 uprising was the large influx of poor Irish and supporters of Young Ireland into the United States. A number of supporters of the rebellion had fled to the States and in the early years of the 1850s they were joined by a number of the leaders who had been transported to Van Diemen's Land, or, in the case of John Mitchel, initially Bermuda and then Van Diemen's Land. There was considerable sympathy for the exiles in the United States. In February 1852, Seward made a speech before the Senate asking the President to intervene on their behalf with the British Government.[55] Four of the transported Young Ireland leaders, Thomas Francis Meagher, John Mitchel, Terence McManus and Patrick O'Donoghoe eventually had escaped to America.[56] While in Ireland, the Young Ireland leadership had opposed O'Connell's uncompromising attacks on slavery. Arriving in the US at the beginning of the 1850s it was inevitable that they should be asked for their political views.

In 1854, Charles Gavan Duffy, one of the few leaders of Young Ireland who remained in Ireland, included in the new *Nation* a letter written by Haughton, asking Young Ireland exiles in the United States to state their stand on slavery. Meagher, who had been transported to Van Diemen's Land for his part in the

1848, but had escaped to New York in 1852, made a public response. In a letter dated 23 March 1854, he said he did not 'recognize in Mr. Haughton, or any other person, to the public generally, any right or title to enquire from him an expression of an opinion regarding the question of African slavery in the United States'. He pointed out he had taken the oath of allegiance to the US, and it would take three years before he was a citizen and 'he postpones till then his declaration of opinion regarding African slavery in America, and every other question regarding the joint compact and constitution of the several states'.[57] Meagher, at this stage, did have some sympathy with the South, and their demand for cessation, although this changed with the outbreak of the Civil War when he pledged his support to the Union.[58]

John Mitchel, who had also escaped to New York, was less reticent when asked for his views. Arriving in New York in 1853, following his escape from Van Diemen's Land, he announced in the City Hall that he desired to own a 'plantation well-stocked with slaves'.[59] His first public lecture in the US was entitled 'The Duties of Adopted Citizens' in which he made it clear that citizens should give their full allegiance to the state that had adopted them.[60] His stance was very different from that of O'Connell a decade earlier who had urged the Irish in America to support abolition. While in the United States, Mitchel, who was former editor of the *Nation,* edited a series of newspapers in which he promoted slavery as an American institution. An article written in 1854 showed how his views of slavery had hardened, opining:

> We are not abolitionists: no more abolitionists than Moses or Socrates or Jesus Christ. We deny that it is a crime or a wrong, or even a peccadillo, to hold slaves, to buy slaves, to keep slaves to their work by flogging or other needful coercion.

Mitchel also reiterated his desire to own a slave plantation in Alabama.[61] Even more shockingly, he suggested that the slave trade should be resumed and the number of slaves increased.[62] His support for the slave states took a more concrete form when he and his family moved to Tennessee in 1855, where he openly championed slavery. Yet, Mitchel never used slave labour on his properties. His long-suffering wife, Jenny, realized that John's uncompromising stance on slavery would surprise their friends in Ireland, but explained that he supported the right of the Southern states to choose their own laws. He believed that the American South and the American North were fundamentally different and that the South, like Ireland, should have the right to self-determination. Mitchel, whose political outlook had been hardened by the experience of the famine, also believed that black slaves in America were often better treated that so-called free men in Ireland.[63]

Mitchel's comments were criticized by American abolitionists. At a meeting of the American Anti-Slavery Society in Boston in January 1854, Mitchel was denounced in a series of resolutions as, amongst other things, being a 'mock rebel' and a 'holiday patriot'. In contrast, at the same meeting they 'dropped a tear to the memory of the great and lamented O'Connell'.[64] Mitchel was also criticized by Douglass, who, in an article entitled, 'Going, going, gone', asked Mitchel not to get involved in the slavery debate. [65] But Mitchel would not be silenced. Mitchel was controversial in other ways; the commitment that he and Meagher continued to show to republican principles was denounced by the American Catholic Church, most vociferously by Hughes. Mitchel used his newspapers to defend republicanism against the attacks by the Church and its press, urging Irish people to remember the legacy of men such as Wolfe Tone and Robert Emmet. [66]

The year 1854 was not a good one for either abolitionists or Irish-Americans in Massachusetts, due to the appointment of a Know-Nothing legislature and governor. The party was a collection of people who were pro-slavery and wanted to silence the abolitionists.[67] In February 1854, Garrison lectured in New York on 'Northern Responsibility for Slavery'. His message was pessimistic: he stated that 'abolitionist' was 'the most unpopular appellation that any man can have applied to him'.[68] He quoted at length from O'Connell's speeches, including the one in which O'Connell advised that every American should be asked whether or not he is a slaveholder. If he answered that he was, 'turn from him as if he had the cholera or the plague – for there is a moral cholera and a political plague upon him.'[69] Garrison again made a plea for a dissolution of the Union, arguing that the South could not exist without the North, therefore it would precipitate the ending of slavery. In 1854 also, The Kansas–Nebraska Act created the territories of Kansas and Nebraska. It repealed the Missouri Compromise of 1820, which had drawn a line between the North and the South, in order to allow the settlers to vote on whether or not to permit slavery. The expansion of slavery into the North appalled abolitionists and resulted in creation of the Republican Party, which absorbed the Free Soil Party.

In 1855, English-born Julia Griffiths, a close friend of Douglass who had tutored his children, travelled to Britain and visited Ireland. Her letters to Douglass were published in his newspaper. In Dublin, she viewed an exhibition of goods that were going to be sent to the Rochester Anti-Slavery Bazaar. She also visited the tomb of O'Connell, which, she reported, was decorated with fresh flowers every week. In Belfast, she met the Ladies' Anti-Slavery Society. Everywhere she went she said that people remembered Douglass and wanted to help him.[70] While in Scotland she was asked her views about working with non-Christians in the cause of abolition. She answered by saying:

> I hold myself ready, at all times, to co-operate with Jews, Hindus, infidels, or heretics, for the abolition of slavery ... Daniel O'Connell and Lord Brougham could unite there. No two men ever did greater service to the cause of Freedom than they.[71]

O'Connell's memory was kept alive in other ways. In June 1856, Archbishop Hughes gave a public lecture in New York, on 'The Life and Times of Daniel O'Connell', as a way of raising funds for the completion of the Church of the Immaculate Conception. The admission fee was high – $1 – but the building was full.[72] For Hughes, what made O'Connell truly great and distinguished him from talented Irish politicians such as Edmund Burke was the fact that he was a 'Catholic Statesman' and therefore possessed 'the key of the heart of Ireland'. Most of the lecture related to O'Connell's religious views, but Hughes concluded by referring to his first meeting with O'Connell in London:

> And he [Hughes] was introduced to him with a determination to have a struggle with him on a certain question; that was, on the asperity, as he thought, with which Mr O'Connell spoke of a certain social institution in this country. He (the Archbishop) told him, after the ordinary introduction, 'You are not surprised Mr O'Connell, that while you have many friends in America, there are some that are much displeased with certain of your public remarks'.
>
> He asked 'What remarks?' It was replied that he (the Archbishop) though he was too severe upon an institution for which the present generation, or the present Government of America, was by no means responsible; he meant Slavery. He paused and said it would be strange indeed if he should not be the friend of the slave throughout the world, he who was born a slave himself (cheers).[73]

Hughes informed the audience, 'He silenced me, although he did not convince me'.[74] Hughes's lecture prompted Michael Hennessy, an immigrant from County Kilkenny, to write to the *New York Times* with his own recollection of O'Connell. He urged Irishmen who had found freedom in America to work to extend it to all.[75] Hughes, however, disagreed.[76] Despite continuing to admire O'Connell for his Irish campaigns, he continued to undermine his abolitionist messages. And in the years preceding the commencement of war, Hughes was still suggesting abolitionists should be placed in straitjackets.[77]

The 1856 election proved to be a bitter contest, with the Democrats upholding the Kansas-Nebraska Act, while the Republicans, under John Fremont, opposed it. Again, the words of the dead O'Connell were invoked to bolster the anti-slavery cause, and the electoral chances of Fremont. Given that Irish immigrants had traditionally supported the pro-slavery Democratic Party, a massive swing in opinion was required. In a pamphlet entitled 'The Pope's Bull and the Words of Daniel O'Connell', an appeal was made to 'Catholic Citizens', on the grounds that the Democratic Party not only supported slavery, but also opposed the Catholic Church.[78] Using the Pope's Letter of 1839 was an unusual tactic, but it was accompanied by what had become a commonplace reference to O'Connell's letter to the Cincinnati repealers. His importance was explained as being 'another name which Irish Catholics must always hear with love and veneration – the name of that illustrious patriot, the friend of Ireland and the friend of man, Daniel O'Connell. That distinguished man was profoundly grieved that any son of Ireland should be found an apologist for slavery in the United States'.[79] However, the document had not appealed to all sons of Ireland, but had appealed to Irish Catholics, whose numbers – and political importance – had increased as a consequence of the famine. At the same time, massive Catholic immigration, together with an evangelical revival in the 1850s, had contributed to a hardening of divisions between Irish Catholics and Irish Protestants. Increasingly, their history in the United States would be viewed separately.[80]

The Democratic candidate, James Buchanan, who was of Irish descent and had supported the campaign for repeal, won the Presidential election in 1856. Although he was pro-slavery he led a weak administration, which abolitionists hoped they could exploit.[81] The Dred Scott case in 1857, however, was a blow for the abolitionist cause. Scott, a slave, had moved with his master to the North where he had been allowed to live in relative freedom. Upon returning to Missouri, Scott had reverted to slave status. His situation was appealed at the highest level. One outcome was that the Supreme Court ruled that nobody of African ancestry could claim American citizenship, therefore Scott was not allowed to appeal on the grounds that no slave or descendant of a slave had a right of legal recourse.[82] This controversial decision appeared to rule out the possibility of either the federal government or the territorial governments ever legally prohibiting slavery in their territories.

As the 1850s drew to a close, the work of the abolitionists continued both in the United States and further afield, although progress had been mixed. At the twenty-sixth annual meeting of American Anti-Slavery Society in 1859, Garrison emphasized the need for the condemnation of Europe in bringing about an end to slavery.[83] To emphasize this, guest speakers continued to travel across the Atlantic. One of Garrison's most-devoted supporters, the Reverend Samuel Joseph May, visited Europe in 1858–9, although he made only a few public appearances. He was accompanied by Sarah Parker Remond, sister of the famous black abolitionist, Charles, who undertook an active schedule in Britain and Ireland.

Remond's visit was reported in great detail in Garrison's *Liberator* and her popularity helped to revive support for Garrison on both sides of the Atlantic.[84] In Ireland, she stayed with Richard Webb, who had hosted so many American visitors before. He was very impressed and wrote of her:

> She is really very clever – the most so of all the coloured people I ever met, except Douglass, and she is a very much more sensible and thoroughgoing person than he ... She has more common sense – and her devotion to the cause and its friends is thorough. We like her very much.[85]

Remond spoke in Dublin on a number of occasions, hosted by the local Ladies' Anti-Slavery Society. Her audience included clergymen and university professors, all of whom were 'spellbound'.[86] During a lecture on 11 March 1859, she appealed particularly to women on behalf of female slaves and said that the slaves depicted in *Uncle Tom's Cabin* were neither imagined nor fanciful. She condemned the Fugitive Slave Law, but she praised Garrison for all the work he had done. Although the Republican Party said they hostile to slavery, they 'had not laid the axe to the root of the tree'. James Haughton chaired meeting and Richard Webb attended.[87] When in Waterford she reiterated the importance of having the sympathy and opinion of European people in helping to end slavery. She pointed out that in the last thirty years great changes had come about in the northern states – in the past, abolitionists had been beaten up. One of the speakers noted that whereas in the past Irish emigrants had been reproached for supporting slavery, they were now helped by a strong anti-slavery feeling in Europe.[88] In 1860 the New York Anti-Slavery Society reprinted a number of speeches of O'Connell. In the Preface they stated:

> Among all the distinguished and eloquent advocates of negro emancipation, on either side of the Atlantic, perhaps no-one has ever surpassed in earnestness of zeal, or potency of speech, the late Daniel O'Connell, the Irish 'Liberator' ... There was something sublime in the attitude maintained by O'Connell upon the question of American slavery ... he loved uncompromising justice more than he did the transient reputation which general corruption bestows upon its apologist, and impartial liberty more than fame.

It pointed out that despite attempts by repeal associations in the United States to make him stop interfering in the slavery debate, he had refused to be silenced, answering 'though it should be a blow against Ireland, it is a blow in favour of human liberty, and I will strike that blow'. The Preface concluded with an appeal to Irishmen of American 'will you not give heed to these testimonies, and unite as one man in espousing the cause of those in bondage?'[89]

Traditionally, the established churches in America had opposed abolition, and some had been openly pro-slavery. In 1860, 238 Methodist ministers in America sent an appeal to their fellow brethren in Britain and Ireland to protest against slaveholding. They also said that the Methodist church in America was thinking of dividing into a Southern and Northern church, pointing out, 'it must be borne in mind that during the last few years a rapid change has taken place in the feelings of the Christian Churches of North America on the subject of professing Christians holding slaves, which has led to some of them purging themselves from this abomination'.[90] It was not only organized religion that was appearing to publicly reject slavery. In the Presidential election at the end of the 1860, American abolitionists supported the Republican Party and its candidate,

Abraham Lincoln. Lincoln had promised he would allow no further expansion of slavery. Samuel May was sceptical, predicting that if Lincoln was chosen:

> His administration will undoubtedly be an exceedingly cautious and conservative one. No abolitionist will be in the least surprised to see him go [to] great lengths in conciliating the South. It is greatly feared he will make unmanly and cowardly concessions to them. If, as many Southern fire-eaters threaten, a forcible resistance shall be made to his inauguration or administration, it is to be hoped that he will not hesitate to treat the ringleaders as the Laws require that traitors and public enemies should be treated; otherwise he will be despised, both North and South. [91]

Before Lincoln took office in March 1861, a number of Southern states announced that they were seceding from the Union. War appeared to be a distinct possibility. Conflict commenced on 12 April when Confederate forces attacked a military installation at Fort Sumter in South Carolina. The new President responded by calling for each state to create a volunteer force. Patriotism for the Union played an important part in Irish-Americans supporting the war. They were also urged to do so by two powerful influences, the Boston *Pilot* and Archbishop Hughes. The latter argued that the rebellion needed to be put down, but he still opposed any attempt to mix this issue up with the ending of slavery.[92] What had occurred was more than a rebellion and the ensuing war lasted for four years, in the course of which, 620,000 lives were lost. Approximately 200,000 Irishmen enlisted, 180,000 of whom fought for the North. [93] The war may not initially have been fought over slavery, but by the end of it, many Irish-Americans in the North who had supported the institution, including Hughes, came to oppose it.

War

As the United States moved to war, the writings of O'Connell were employed as part of the battle for hearts and minds that preceded it. In 1860, the American Anti-Slavery Society published a collection of some of O'Connell's speeches on slavery. The Preface opened by saying:

> Among all the distinguished and eloquent advocates of negro emancipation, on either side of the Atlantic, perhaps no one has ever surpassed in earnestness or zeal, or potency of speech, the late Daniel O'Connell, the 'Irish Liberator'. Especially was his soul filled with horror and disgust in view of the existence and rapid growth of slavery in America.[94]

The outbreak of war caused divisions amongst the supporters of Garrison. He had long supported the principle of secession, or disunion. When war broke out many of his supporters, in a reversal of their previous position, supported using arms in order to force the South to stay in the Union. James Haughton in Dublin was one of the Irish abolitionists who voiced his opposition to the war on the grounds that the South should be allowed to leave the Union as a way of avoiding conflict.[95] Richard Webb also expressed surprise that people who had promoted non-aggression for so long should now support the war and with 'such unqualified gratification'.[96] Any fear that the United Kingdom would enter the war was assuaged when, on 13 May 1861, Queen Victoria issued a Proclamation stating that Britain would remain neutral during the hostilities between the North and the South.[97] Abolitionists were extremely disappointed at the statement, especially as British sympathy appeared to be more for the Southern states.[98]

Although many American abolitionists did welcome the war, many accepted that the government remained ambivalent in its attitude towards slavery. Some suspected that Lincoln and many of his Generals did not fully support emancipation.[99] The American abolitionist, Samuel May, defended Lincoln, believing him to be 'an honest man and a friend to his country; who aims at the good of its entire people; and that his policy, if weak, is not designedly wicked'.[100] However, the fact that the Emancipation Proclamation was not issued until September 1862 seemed to support the view that ending slavery was not the primary aim of the war. Nonetheless, the Proclamation, which declared that on 1 January 1863, the slaves in all areas that were in rebellion against the federal government would be free, was generally welcomed.[101] That day was significant for a further reason. As the war had progressed, although the British government had continued to favour the South, the North had the support of many of the working classes. On 1 January 1863, workers in Manchester, at the centre of British cotton production, issued an address to Lincoln asking him to 'strike off the fetters of the slave'. It helped the President in his resolve to expand the war effort.[102] In contrast, Webb commented on the opinion of the Irish working classes, 'I really do not know and it is of not much consequence – for they have little political weight – and 19 out of 20 of them are such slaves to their priests'.[103] However, the war had an effect on the British working classes. The Lancashire 'Cotton Famine' was caused by a reduction in the import of raw cotton, which led to widespread unemployment.

The war led to divisions amongst Irish-Americans, including those who had formerly been colleagues of O'Connell. The former Young Irelander, Thomas Francis Meagher, supported the Union and helped to establish an Irish Brigade in New York. He rose to the rank of Brigadier General. In 1848, Meagher had not been given a chance to take up arms on behalf of Ireland, but, over thirteen years later, he fought bravely and fiercely on behalf of his adopted country. The most notorious supporter of the Southern States was John Mitchel. Since arriving in the United States in 1853, he had been vocal in his support for slavery, using the columns of his newspapers, the *Citizen* and the *Southern Citizen* to champion the institution. During the Civil War, he made the ultimate personal sacrifice; his three sons fought for the Confederacy – two lost their lives, the third lost an arm. Although Mitchel offered his own services, he was considered too old.[104] However, the Mitchels were not the only Irish to fight on behalf of the South as in the region of 20,000 Irishmen served in the Confederate Army. For many of these men, Mitchel was their hero.[105]

A disgraceful incident took place in the summer of 1863, when violent racist riots took place in New York. The riots were triggered by Congress passing a new law to enlist men into the army. The riots were directed at black people, a number of whom were killed. It was widely agreed that the violence had been instigated by Irish Catholics.[106] The main motive given was that the unskilled Irish immigrants were increasingly fearful of black competition for their jobs.[107] However, once the violence had commenced, other white groups joined in and were just as violent.[108] The riots suggested that when the war was over, building an inclusive society was not going to be easy.

Even as some Irish-Americans were behaving disgracefully in New York, the words of Daniel O'Connell continued to be used to inspire them and their compatriots. Twenty years earlier, O'Connell had entered into a public quarrel with repealers in Cincinnati, who had objected to his repeated attacks on slavery. O'Connell, despite the fact that he was about to be imprisoned, had penned a long and detailed refutation of the address, and by doing so, had created what some considered to be his finest statement on abolition. At the time, many abolition societies in the United States reprinted copies of what became known as 'the Cincinnati Letter'.[109] During the Civil War, the letter was again widely circulated. In 1863, the Cincinnati *Catholic Telegraph* reprinted O'Connell's original answer, which they suggested had been kept hidden by a well-known Democrat since it had first been sent. O'Connell's letter, and the original response by Salmon Chase, who since 1861 had been a member of President Lincoln's War Cabinet, was reprinted by various groups throughout 1863. The Introduction to one pamphlet professed:

> This bold, manly, and indignant protest of the great Irish Orator against the cruel injustice of American slavery, and his eloquent reassertion of the principles of the Declaration of Independence, are opportunely reproduced in the present crisis of our affairs. The glowing words of the Liberator will be read with renewed interest by all lovers of human freedom, and not without increased admiration for that magnanimous soul which, in its love of Liberty, overleaped all barriers of nationality, and embraced all tribes and races of mankind.[110]

Copies of the 1843 correspondence were also published in a number of American newspapers.[111] The extensive coverage given to O'Connell's Cincinnati Letter suggested that, twenty years after it had been written, its message remained as powerful and relevant as ever.

In the same year, a thirty-two-page pamphlet was published in Philadelphia for gratuitous distribution entitled *The Irish Patriot. Daniel O'Connel's* [sic] *Legacy to Irish Americans*. It opened with a copy of the 1842 Address from the Irish People, which was followed by extracts from his many speeches condemning American slavery, commencing with one given before the Cork Anti-Slavery Society in 1829, and ending with a speech given before the Repeal Association in Dublin in September 1844.[112] The pamphlet was a reminder of the consistency and longevity of O'Connell's attacks.

In 1863, *The Life of Lunsford Lane*, a former slave, was published. Reference was made to O'Connell's outspokenness in regard to the Cincinnati Letter, details of which had been also published in the *Boston Journal* in July of that year. The section was preceded by a reference to the 'great O'Connell', adding, 'Men of great souls seldom entertain prejudices against the innocent and unoffending'.[113] In October 1863, a poster was produced in New York, entitled, 'Dan' O'Connell on Democracy!' Its author signed himself 'A Democratic Workingman'. It had been written in response to the 'eloquent and earnest appeal' of the *Catholic Telegraph* of Cincinnati which had reprinted a speech by O'Connell to the Irishmen of America during his dispute with the Cincinnati Repeal Association in 1843. The poster, quoting from O'Connell, said that 'the great Commoner never spoke a truer word. Slavery is anti-democratic because it is a war on the interests and rights of the workingman'. It concluded by exhorting its readers, 'Irishmen! Hear what Daniel O'Connell says!'[114]

Lincoln's commitment to ending slavery was evident from the passing of the Thirteenth Amendment to the United States Constitution, which officially prohibited slavery and involuntary servitude. It was passed by the Senate on 8 April 1864, and was finally adopted on 6 December 1865. The message of the Amendment was unequivocal and meant there could be no turning back after the war. However, within the abolition movement there continued to be divisions. Wendell Phillips disapproved of choosing Lincoln as a candidate in the 1864 Presidential election, resulting in him parting company with Garrison's supporters.[115] On 8 November 1864, Abraham Lincoln, leader of the Republican Party, was re-elected President with a large majority. None of the Confederate states participated in the election. A few days later, a large meeting was held in New York to celebrate the 'bloodless victory'. Most of the speakers were generals or captains in the Union Army. When Captain Haggerty spoke, he explained that he had left Ireland because of 'the oppression under which it groaned' and that 'As an Irishman, he was true to Daniel O'Connell's idea of universal freedom' – a statement that drew cheers from the audience.[116]

On 1 April 1865, President Lincoln was assassinated. His death shocked and upset Northern abolitionists. Only a few days later, the Confederate General Lee surrendered, which effectively meant the end of the war. On 23 June 1865, a ceasefire was signed. Northern victory meant an end to the Confederacy and an end to slavery, But to get to this outcome, over 600,000 soldiers had died, as well as an unknown number of civilians, and the President had been assassinated. Slavery had ended in the United States, but it was a bittersweet victory as the human cost was so high. Furthermore, the war was over, but the challenge for those who had survived was to build an inclusive and egalitarian society.

8 'THE NEGRO'S FRIEND'

Following O'Connell's death, the repeal movement in Ireland had disintegrated. Within ten years, constitutional nationalism had been overtaken by the militant Fenian movement, with its reliance on physical force. In the late 1860s, Ireland was in the throes of a Fenian uprising that had little in common with O'Connell's pursuit of constitutional nationalism. Despite transatlantic involvement, the rebellion was unsuccessful and the nationalist pendulum again swung back to winning independence by peaceful methods. The Home Rule movement marked a return to peaceful, parliamentary methods as a means of winning limited independence for Ireland. Those who supported it admired O'Connell's methods and were willing to work with the British government to achieve an Irish Parliament.[1] However, by the late nineteenth century, 'advanced' nationalists on both sides of the Atlantic rejected the constitutional approach to gaining independence in favour of the taking up of arms. Moreover, O'Connell's pro-monarchy, pro-empire beliefs were increasingly out of line with the desire for an independent republic. The 1916 Rising and its aftermath left little room for constitutional politics of the type that O'Connell had advocated. The leaders of the Rising, including Patrick Pearse and James Connolly, did not look to O'Connell for their inspiration, preferring the more radical views of John Mitchel.[2] As nationalists turned their back on O'Connell in Ireland, the Catholic Church appropriated his memory and refashioned him in their own conservative image.[3] He was increasingly remembered as the champion of Catholic Emancipation in 1829, rather than for the repeal movement, his alliances with British radicals or for his campaigns of behalf of various oppressed peoples. Yet O'Connell's achievements had extended beyond winning Catholic Emancipation. For decades, he was the most prominent and influential, not to mention controversial, politician within the United Kingdom, if not throughout Europe. Moreover, during his lifetime, his fame and authority spread across the Atlantic, and extended long beyond his death.

In the United States, in the years following the Civil War, O'Connell was remembered primarily for his contribution to abolition.[4] One of the founders of Cornell University, Andrew Dickson White, in a lecture on the American freedom in 1866, referred to O'Connell as 'the great champion of the downtrodden slave', for which he received a cheer. He went on to repeat one of O'Connell's anecdotes about the stupidity of slavery.[5] O'Connell was also remembered by his fellow abolitionists. As a result of the Civil War, Garrison had decided to withdraw from the American Anti-Slavery Society, which he had helped found over thirty years earlier, on the grounds that his life work was done. Wendell Phillips took over as President. At the thirty-fourth annual meeting in 1867, Phillips informed his audience, 'The actual war has closed, but the war of opinion and politics has commenced'. He argued that vigilance was necessary to ensure 'the civil and political liberty of the coloured man'.[5] During the meeting, extended tribute was made to the 'statesman-like mind' of O'Connell.[6] In 1873, O'Connell's long-time friend and fellow abolitionist James Haughton died. William Lloyd Garrison wrote a tribute entitled 'Three Distinguished Irishmen', in which Haughton's life was linked with that of Richard Webb and O'Connell. The speech made by O'Connell in 1843, in which he had exhorted Irish-Americans to support abolition or he would 'recognize them as Irishmen no longer', was reprinted. Garrison explained that, in his estimation, 'I do not remember anything finer from the lips of any European or American patriot'.[7]

In 1875, the centenary of O'Connell's birth was celebrated in many parts of the world. In Ireland, a Committee was appointed to oversee the Dublin commemorations. The resulting Centenary Address was by John O'Hagan, a supporter of Young Ireland in his youth, and now a Lord. It opened: 'The commemoration which we make to-day is more than an honour to a man. It celebrates the redemption of a people'.[8] Throughout, O'Hagan reflected on O'Connell's achievements, but primarily eulogized him as a champion of Irish Catholics. Mention was made of his role in anti-slavery although, unlike in the American celebrations, it was brief:

> When the dispute about the abolition of slavery was coming to a close, and the Legislature prepared to make the enormous pecuniary sacrifice by which it was nobly purchased, O'Connell, though he resisted a compensation which he thought unrighteous, was foremost in commending the act of liberation to the acceptance of the country. He was entitled to speak on the subject with authority, for, as I have said, he had always been the negro's friend, even when to be so seemed inconsistent with the political interests of Ireland ... He denounced that evil institution in the Southern States as in the British colonies. He fought against it with fearless resolution: and the contributions, which would otherwise have been ample, were withheld. It was one of many occasions on which he proved himself to possess high moral courage and devotedness to duty.[9]

History was sanitized in the eulogy, as it was claimed that O'Connell had refused to accept money from America on the grounds that he would not compromise with slavery.[10] The reality had been more complex.

In the United States, the centenary commemorations were overwhelmingly a tribute to O'Connell's stance on the abolition question, and his role in ending slavery in the British empire and in the United States. Three of the greatest living American abolitionists paid homage to him; William Lloyd Garrison, John Greenleaf Whittier and Wendell Phillips. Their coming together on this occasion and their tributes to O'Connell suggested a unity that had not been present during O'Connell's lifetime. Although on this occasion they each praised O'Connell for his uncompromising principles, they had not always viewed him in this way. But even during the times that they had disapproved of his actions, they had still not wanted to lose the support of the foremost abolitionist in the world. The American eulogies were published, thus keeping alive the memory of an Irishman who had died almost forty years earlier, but a memory that emphasized – incorrectly – the unity of the abolition movement.

Tribute to O'Connell was also made by British abolitionists who had known and been inspired by him. In 1877, a memoir of James Haughton was published by his son. It was 'Dedicated to the Memory of Thomas Clarkson, Daniel O'Connell, and Joseph Sturge ...'[11] The British abolitionist, Sir George Stephen, left an account of the anti-slavery movement, which he addressed to the author, Harriet Beecher Stowe. In it, he singled O'Connell out for special mention. The length of the tribute, quoted below, was not accorded to any other campaigner and Stephen knew that it would surprise some:

> You must not be startled when I name O'Connell as the other to whom I must render justice. Never was a man so abused, never was a mortal so abhorred by a section of the community, as O'Connell. His moral character was unexceptional even in the judgement of his opponents; his political character was revered by his friends and reprobated by his enemies. I have nothing to do with either the one or the other, but I have occasionally seen him in his domestic character and there I have seen an abundance to love and admire. At present I only refer to him as an abolitionist, and as such he well merited the esteem and veneration of all our party. He did us great service by his speeches; so did many others; he was accessible at all hours, and under all circumstances, to the lowest as well as the highest, on abolition matters; so was every member in 1833; but Mr O'Connell did what no other man could do. He lent the whole of his powerful influence to keep the Irish public, as well as the Irish members, steady to the cause; he brought all his political weight to bear upon it. Ireland needed no agitation on abolition; from Cape Clear to the Giant's Causeway, Ireland was an abolitionist in heart and in action, irrespective of party feeling, whether in politics or religion; and much, nay, most of this, was due to O'Connell. He did it disinterestedly; he made no bargain for reciprocal support; he was content to fight his own battles with his own forces. I believe that, as a general rule, the Parliamentary abolitionists seldom divided with him; but he always voted for them, and led on his followers, and compelled them to attend. This justice is due to O'Connell, and he well deserves it at our hands On your side of the water you may think it strange that I should deem it necessary to insist on this; but in England it

was long the daily object, in some of our most influential papers, to crush him with obloquy, and annihilate him in a storm of public indignation. It is too much our way in a bad cause ... Mr O'Connell is scarcely forgiven yet, and therefore, as a brother abolitionist, I speak of him with the gratitude and the honour that he well deserves'[12]

Some accolades to O'Connell were more unusual. When Wendell Phillips died in 1884 it was revealed that he possessed a cane that had been owned by O'Connell. [13]

A number of Irish-Americans also paid tribute to the Liberator for his contribution to ending slavery. At a meeting of the Irish-American Republican Association in 1880, Irish-born General Dennis Burke, a veteran of the Civil War, praised the Republican Party for liberating 4,000,000 human beings. He went on to aver, 'Irishmen had an instinctive love for liberty, and the first man who raised his voice against negro slavery was Daniel O'Connell'.[14] At this stage, the traditional relationship between Irish-Americans and the Democratic Party appeared to be broken, with large numbers deserting it.[15] Only forty years earlier, however, the reverse of this situation had been true, as O'Connell's failure to persuade Irish-Americans to support abolition had demonstrated.

O'Connell's involvement with American abolition had a long pedigree. As early as 1829, O'Connell had publicly denounced slavery in the United States. His attacks were uncompromising and ferocious, criticizing not only slaveholders but also those who stood by and allowed the institution to exist. According to the historian Bruce Nelson, O'Connell's 'sustained diatribe against the "White Republic" was as sweeping and audacious as it was politically risky'.[16] O'Connell liked to claim that Irish Catholics – who had been slaves for so long themselves and had never been associated with the slave trade – were uniquely placed to promote abolition. When they failed to do so, he accused them of being, amongst other things, 'pseudo-Irishmen'.[17]

Why had Irish immigrants in the United States taken so long to adopt the cause of anti-slavery? Various reasons have been put forward – economic rivalry, they wanted to be accepted in the home of their adoption, their own low status as Irishmen, and the militancy and the anti-religionist stance of many abolitionists. Irish immigrants who arrived in the United States, even before the famine, were the first non-Protestant group to arrive in large numbers. Their ethnicity and class marked them as being unlike other immigrants, while their Catholicism, which gave them their unity and their identity, also marked them as being different to their hosts. In addition, according to Gilbert Osofsky, Garrison's attempts to reach out to poor Irish immigrants were hampered by 'the generally prevalent unwillingness to recognize the difficulties inherent in class and cultural distinctions among America's peoples'.[18] The Irish had internalised a view of themselves as second-class citizens. In America, if they were to be released from this inferiority, they had to become American. Irish immigrants therefore developed a double consciousness; in the United States they were both Irish and American, and O'Connell's demands pulled them in opposing directions.

The mass arrival of Irish Catholics coincided with the emergence of Know-Nothing-ism. The leading abolitionists deprecated nativism, but this was not enough to bind the two groups in the struggle against slavery. As historian Neil O'Connell has pointed out, 'The advocacy by some of the abolitionists of such radical tenets as feminism, Unitarianism, temperance, free love, and communism was not very appealing to the conservative and more simple Irish-Catholic Americans'.[19] Moreover, if Irish immigrants showed any indication of forgetting their Catholic roots, Bishops England and Hughes were on hand to remind them.

In Ireland, O'Connell had relied on clerical leadership and support for his Emancipation and repeal campaigns. Within the United States, the hierarchy of the Catholic Church showed itself antagonistic to abolition and urged both their flock and O'Connell not to become involved with it. One of the most powerful opponents of abolition was the outspoken, Tyrone-born John Hughes, who became the first Irish Archbishop of New York. In many ways though, he personified the dilemmas facing all Irish-American immigrants. Hughes had been opposed to slavery in his early days in the United States, but in the 1830s as the debate became more public and polarized, he revised his opinion. As the war commenced, he again changed, giving his support to the Union. According to the historian Kevin Kenny, 'Sympathetic to the cause of abolition as a young man, Hughes had been hardened by the realities of American life, and especially by the treatment of Irish immigrants, defending his own 'tribe' in a society whose promise of universal liberty and equality he now regarded as little more than a pious lie'.[20]

Within the space of a few decades there had been a massive sea-change in attitudes towards slavery within the United States, and Irish-Americans had played an important part in this change. In 1842, O'Connell's Address had received a lukewarm reception, with some overt animosity. After 1861, thousands of Irishmen had signed up for the Union army to join in the military crusade against slavery. In the fifteen years that followed O'Connell's death, public sentiment towards slavery in the United States had undergone a change in attitude, with opinion for and against becoming more polarized. O'Connell had clearly underestimated the difficulties faced by Irish settlers in the United States: yet the value and relevance of his speeches were clear to abolitionists who continued to quote and reprint them long after his death. They inspired a new generation of abolitionists, while demonstrating his unparalleled contribution to the movement.

O'Connell's involvement in anti-slavery was remarkable in other ways. In an arena in which emotional, passionate speeches were usual, O'Connell added a further dimension to the debate. The eloquence and fervour of O'Connell's language – both written and spoken – thrilled his supporters and infuriated his opponents. The Quaker poet and ardent abolitionist, John Greenleaf Whittier, described a speech made in 1843 as 'the blow of a giant, as well-directed and terrible in its execution as Bruce's battle-axe at Bannockburn'.[21] Frederick Douglass, a noted orator himself, marvelled at O'Connell's ability to move seamlessly from one topic to another, 'from grave to gay, from lively to severe'.[22] Until the involvement of O'Connell, anti-slavery had been an overwhelmingly Protestant evangelical movement, with elements of anti-Catholicism. O'Connell had been first introduced to abolition by an English Quaker, James Cropper. O'Connell, a devout Catholic, and more devout as he got older, encouraged his fellow Catholics to become abolitionists. Moreover, he stood up to the Catholic Church hierarchy in his defence of abolition. He frequently sought an even higher authority, invoking the law of God, rather than any man-made law, when denouncing slaveholding.[23] Furthermore, throughout his career his politics proved to be ecumenical, international and egalitarian, as his promotion of the rights of the Dissenters and Jews demonstrated.

On the issue of slavery, O'Connell remained a divisive and inflammatory figure, with some abolitionists even having an abhorrence of him and his radical politics. Although O'Connell did not have to face the physical assaults made on American abolitionists, throughout his life he was berated in the press and in Parliament, frequently in *ad hominem* attacks. Even after his election to Westminster, he remained a controversial figure in both Irish and British politics. Yet, he rose above these criticisms to make his presence felt as a parliamentarian. In 1843, while the repeal movement was in disarray following the banning of the Clontarf meeting, O'Connell made what many regarded as his greatest statement opposing slavery. The Irish abolitionist, Richard Davis Webb, who had sometimes doubted the purity of O'Connell's motives, like Stephen, acknowledged the difficulties that O'Connell had to overcome:

> The Irish Tory papers are full of the gall of all hatred, hostility, and bitterness against him. They would be delighted to hear he was hanging or to be present at the hanging. The Irish Orangemen and nine-tenths of all Irish Protestants ... hate him much more fervently than they hate the devil – whatever they may say in their prayers. O'Connell is the darling, the idol of ragged Ireland, of the Catholic millions of all who live in Cabins – on the bogs – on the mountain-sides – in the poor houses ... Right or wrong they are with him ... I can't help feeling something towards O'Connell now as a true American feels towards Washington. Though Daniel has none of George's magnanimity ... Yet I would be sorry to see him suffer or crestfallen ... Though I don't approve of him it would go to my heart to see him baffled or pinioned in his old days.[24]

Biographers of O'Connell have traditionally highlighted his pragmatism and his contradictions.[25] He was full of paradoxes; a fluent speaker of Irish, who advocated the use of English; a supporter of peaceful methods who had killed a man in a duel and sent his fourteen-year-old son to fight with Simon Bolivar; and a supporter of the British empire who forcefully spoke out against the brutality of colonization. O'Connell undoubtedly had many flaws. He could be egotistical, opinionated, self-serving and dynastic, and his political decisions were often pragmatic and opportunistic. Nonetheless, regardless of entrenched opposition by sections of the press, Parliament, the Protestant Ascendancy, the British public and slaveholders everywhere, together with intermittent opposition from his fellow repealers and abolitionists, he remained a consistent champion of human rights. And he never wavered from his support for abolition. He held true to his belief that no man had the right to own another man. Overall, O'Connell's contribution to ending slavery was extraordinary in its range, depth and longevity. Furthermore, seen through the eyes of fellow abolitionists and former slaves, O'Connell made a remarkable and unique contribution to this humanitarian cause.

O'Connell had frequently stated that, if treated properly, black people were the equals of white people. His demands for full human and civil rights went beyond what many of his fellow abolitionists, who opposed the institution of slavery on moral grounds, desired. Nor, like many of his fellow abolitionists, did he view abolition through an evangelical, redemptive prism. By seeing slaves as human beings, he brought a humanity to the debate that gave the slaves a dignity that not all abolitionists ascribed to them. For him, full emancipation and equality, not repatriation to Africa or piecemeal and partial liberation, were crucial to the success of abolition. However, the Civil War may have led to emancipation, but it did not bring an end to prejudice in the United States. In 1875, the centenary of O'Connell's birth, the US Congress passed a civil rights law. It was later overturned by the Supreme Court which led Douglass to make an impassioned speech in Lincoln Hall. In it, he lambasted Irish Americans for their role in perpetuating segregation, saying:

> Perhaps no class of our fellow citizens has carried this prejudice against colour to a point more extreme and dangerous than have our Catholic Irish fellow-citizens, and yet no people on the face of the earth have been more relentlessly persecuted and oppressed on account of race and religion than have the same Irish people ... Fellow citizens! We want no Black Ireland in America.[26]

It took a further hundred years, and another struggle, for civil rights to be granted and then, only as a result of an organized movement that mobilized public opinion.[27] It was not until 2008 that the United States elected its first black President, Barack Obama. The *New York Times* described his victory as 'sweeping away the last racial barrier in American politics'.[28] Obama was unusual in terms of the diversity of his background although, in common with many previous Presidents, he had Irish roots; in his case, in Moneygall in County Offaly.

O'Connell often referred to himself as a friend of the slave throughout the world. Others agreed. William Lloyd Garrison, upon first meeting O'Connell in 1833, testified, 'To that fearless and eloquent champion of liberty, that first of Irish patriots, Daniel O'Connell Esq., the coloured population of this country and their advocates are under heavy obligations for his masterly vindication of their cause, his terrible castigation of American slavery, and his withering satire upon the colonization humbug'.[29] Regardless of fierce opposition, until his death O'Connell truly proved himself to be a friend of the slave, and, in answer to the question, 'Am I not a man and a brother?', his resounding and consistent response had always been 'yes'.

NOTES

Introduction: Black, White and Green

1. Daniel O'Connell cited in the *Liberator*, 29 December 1832.
2. M. R. O'Connell, 'O'Connell, Young Ireland, and Negro Slavery: An Exercise in Romantic Nationalism', *Thought*, 64:253 (June 1989), pp. 131–6, on p. 131.
3. D. O'Connell to James Haughton, 4 February 1845, S. Haughton, *Memoir of James Haughton: with Extracts from his Private and Published Letters* (Dublin, 1877), p. 72.
4. M. F. Cusack, *The Speeches and Public Letters of the Liberator; with Preface and Historical Notes* (Dublin: McGlashan, 1875), p. xi.
5. O'Connell's response to the Address, *A Full and Corrected Report of the Proceedings at the Public Meeting held in Hope Street Baptist Chapel to present the Emancipation Society's Address to Daniel O'Connell Esq., MP, 23 September 1835* (Glasgow: D. Prentice and Co., 1835), p. 5.
6. J. G. Whittier, 'Sketch of Daniel O'Connell', first published in *Pennsylvania Freeman*, 25 April 1839, republished in Whittier, *Daniel O'Connell* (Boston, MA, 1839), vol. 11, p. 329.
7. Ibid., p. 7.
8. O'Connell, *A Full and Correct Report of the Proceedings*, p. 4.
9. M. O'Connell (ed.), *The Correspondence of Daniel O'Connell*, 8 vols (Dublin: Irish Manuscripts Commission, 1977).
10. J. R. Oldfield, *Popular Politics and British Anti-Slavery: The Mobilisation of Public Opinion against the Slave Trade, 1787–1807* (Abingdon: Routledge, 2008); J. McCarthy, *Modern England* (London: G. P. Putnam, 1898), the section on the 1833 Emancipation Bill, (part three) ignores O'Connell's pivotal role. Recent researchers who have looked at O'Connell in terms of his contribution to anti-slavery include, Maurice Bric, Angela Murphy, Gilbert Osofsky, John Quinn, Douglas Riach and Nini Rodgers. See also C. Kinealy (ed.), *Lives of Victorian Political Figures: Daniel O'Connell* (London: Pickering and Chatto, 2007), pp. 63–116.
11. M. J. Bric, 'Daniel O'Connell and the Debate on Anti-Slavery, 1820–50', in T. Dunne and L. M. Geary (eds), *History and the Public Sphere: Essays in Honour of John A. Murphy* (Cork: Cork University Press, 2005), pp. 69–83, on p. 82.
12. G. Osofsky, 'Abolitionists, Irish Immigrants, and the Dilemmas of Romantic Nationalism', *American Historical Review* (October 1975), pp. 889–912, on p. 890.

13. V. Gosse, '"As a Nation, the English are our Friends": The Emergence of African American Politics in the British Atlantic World, 1772–1861', *American Historical Review* (October 2008), pp. 1003–28, on pp. 1003–4.

14. The American abolitionist, James Birney, referred to O'Connell as 'a British statesman', D. I. Dumond (ed.), *Letters of James Gillespie Birney 1831–1857*, 2 vols (Mass: Peter Sith, 1966), vol. 2, p. 1185.

15. G. Stephen, *Anti-Slavery Recollections in a Series of Letters Addressed to Mrs Beecher Stowe at her Request*, 2nd edn (London: Frank Cass, 1971), pp. 83–4.

16. N. Rodgers, 'Two Quakers and a Unitarian: The Reaction of Three Irish Women Writers to the Problem of Slavery 1789–1807', *Proceedings of the Royal Irish Academy* 100C:4 (2000), pp. 137–57, on p. 149.

17. J. Mullalla, *A Compilation on the Slave Trade, Respectfully Addressed to the People of Ireland* (Dublin: William McKenzie, 1792), p. 26.

18. C. Kinealy, *A Disunited Kingdom? England, Ireland, Scotland and Wales, 1800–1949* (Cambridge: Cambridge University Press, 1999); T. McDonough (ed.), *Was Ireland a Colony?* (Dublin: Irish Academic Press, 2005).

19. R. N. Lebow, *White Britain and Black Ireland* (Philadelphia, PA: Institute for the Study of Human Issues, 1976).

20. N. J. O'Connell, 'Irish Emancipation – Black Abolition: A Broken Partnership', in R. Holtman (ed.), *Consortium on Revolutionary Europe* (Alabama: Proceedings of the Consortium on Revolutionary Europe, 1980), p. 58.

21. Quoted in L. P. Curtis Jr, *Anglo-Saxons and Celts* (Bridgeport, CT: University of Bridgeport, 1968), p. 84.

22. J. Jeremie, *Four Essays on Colonial Slavery* (London: J. Hatchard and Son, 1832), p. 73.

23. H. Brotz, *African American Political Thought 1850–1920* (New Jersey: Transaction Publishers, 1992), p. 240.

24. D. O'Connell, *Memoir of Ireland, Native and Saxon, 1172–1660* (New York: Casserly and Sons, 1843), vol. 1, pp. 1–3.

25. C. Kinealy, *A Death-Dealing Famine: The Great Hunger in Ireland* (London: Pluto Press, 1997), pp. 69–70.

26. Ibid., pp. 125–9.

27. J. Mitchel, *Jail Journal, or, Five Years in British Prisons* (Glasgow: Cameron & Ferguson, 1876).

28. Meeting of Cork Anti-Slavery Society, 3 September 1829, *Anti-Slavery Monthly Reporter*, 5:3 (October 1829), p. 95.

29. Stephen, *Anti-Slavery Recollections*, p. 54.

30. For example, George Thompson visited in 1834, and lectured in the Boston area. He and his wife were ejected from a hotel in New York because of their beliefs, *Manchester Times and Gazette*, 15 November 1834.

31. J. A. Collins to R. D. Webb, 1 January 1842, C. Taylor, *British and American Abolitionists* (Edinburgh: Edinburgh University Press, 1974), p. 160.

32. Quoted in B. Quarles, *Black Abolitionists* (New York: Oxford University Press, 1969), p. 132.

33. *Liberator*, 16 October 1840.

34. Garrison to George Benson, 22 March 1842, Taylor, *British and American Abolitionists*, p. 170.

35. For the history and historiography of Irish emigrants to the United States see J. J. Lee, chapter 1 in J. Lee and M. R. Casey, *Making the Irish American: History and Heritage of the Irish in the United States* (New York: New York University Press, 2006), pp. 1–62.

36. *National Era*, 15 June 1851.

37. *Boston Pilot*, 25 June 1842.

38. J. A. Collins to Richard Webb, 1 January 1842, Taylor, *British and American Abolitionists*, p. 161.

39. J. A. Collins to Richard Allen, 30 March 1842, Taylor, *British and American Abolitionists*, p. 174.

40. T. W. Allen, *The Invention of the White Race: Racial Oppression and Social Control* (London: Verso, 1994), p. 22.

41. Ibid., p. 23.

42. N. Ignatiev, *How the Irish Became White* (New York: Routledge, 1995), particularly chapter 1, where the author frames his argument.

43. P. O'Neill, 'Frederick Douglass and the Irish', *Foilsiú: Ireland and Race*, 5:1 (Spring 2006), pp. 57–81, on p. 58.

44. Ibid., p. 79.

45. Quoted in Quarles, *Black Abolitionists*, p. 133.

46. B. Rolston, 'Ireland of the Welcomes? Racism and Anti-Racism in Nineteenth Century Ireland', *Patterns of Prejudice*, 38:4 (2004), pp. 355–70.

47. W. G. Sharrow, 'John Hughes and a Catholic Response to Slavery in Antebellum America' in *The Journal of Negro History*, 57:3 (July 1972), pp. 254–69, on p. 263.

48. *Morning Herald*, 20 October 1838.

49. D. C. Riach, 'Daniel O'Connell and American Anti-slavery', *Irish Historical Studies*, 20:77 (March 1977), p. 22.

50. A. Peckover, *Life of Joseph Sturge* (London: Swan Sonnenschein and Co., 1890), p. 45.

51. For example, Anon., *Daniel O'Connell upon American Slavery: with other Irish Testimonies* (New York: American Anti-Slavery Society, 1860).

52. Meeting of Cork Anti-Slavery Society, 3 September 1829, *Anti-Slavery Monthly Reporter*, 5:3 (October 1829), p. 93.

53. N. Rodgers, *Ireland, Slavery and Anti-Slavery* (London: Palgrave Macmillan, 2007), p. 277.

1 'The Colour of Servitude'

1. Oldfield, *Popular Politics*, p. 33.

2. Stephen, *Anti-Slavery Recollections*, p. 179.

3. Oldfield, *Popular Politics*, p. 42.

4. T. Clarkson, *An Essay on the Slavery and Commerce of the Human Species, particularly the African* (London, 1785).

5. J. Walvin, *Black Ivory: A History of Black Slavery* (London: Harper Collins, 1992), p. 53.

6. Oldfield, *Popular Politics*, p. 2.

7. Ibid., p. 156.

8. Ibid., p. 41.

9. Ibid., pp. 2–3, 45–6.

10. 'Anti-Slavery Pioneers', *New Internationalist*, 398 (March 2007), p. 1.

11. N. Rodgers, 'The Irish and the Atlantic Slave Trade', *History Ireland*, 15:3 (May 2007), pp. 17–23, on p. 17.

12. Public Record Office of Northern Ireland (PRONI), *Ulster and Slavery* (Belfast: PRONI), p. 12. At: http://www.proni.gov.uk/ulsterandslavery-3.pdf, accessed 4 May 2010.

13. D. H. Akenson, *If the Irish Ran the World: Montserrat, 1630–1730* (Liverpool: Liverpool University Press, 1997).

14. Rodgers, 'The Irish and the Atlantic Slave Trade', p. 22.

15. Rodgers, *Ireland, Slavery and Anti-Slavery*, ch. 1.

16. B. Rolston, '"A Lying Old Scoundrel": Waddell Cunningham and Belfast's Role in the Slave Trade', *History Ireland*, 11:1 (Spring 2003), pp. 24–7.

17. PRONI, *Ulster and Slavery*, p. 11.

18. Ibid.

19. Rogers, 'Two Quakers and a Unitarian', p. 138.

20. Ibid.

21. C. Midgley, *Women against Slavery: The British Campaigns, 1780–1870* (London: Routledge, 1992), p. 34.

22. W. A. Hart, 'Africans in Eighteenth-Century Ireland', *Irish Historical Studies*, 33:29 (May 2002), p. 24.

23. Ibid., p. 27.

24. M. R. O'Connell (ed.), *The Correspondence of Daniel O'Connell*, 8 vols (Dublin: Irish Manuscript Commission, 1977), vol. 3, p. 91.

25. PRONI, *Ulster and Slavery*, p. 11.

26. N. Rodgers, *Equiano and Anti-Slavery in Eighteenth-Century Belfast* (Belfast: Linen Hall Library, 2000), p. 16.

27. Mullalla, *A Compilation on the Slave Trade*, p. 18.

28. Ibid., p. 24.

29. Ibid., p. 26.

30. Ibid., p. 27.

31. Rodgers, 'Two Quakers and a Unitarian', p. 143.

32. 'Sketch of Daniel O'Connell', in *Frederick Douglass Paper*, 21 August 1851.

33. Speech by O'Connell before Catholic Board, 14 January 1814, J. O'Connell (ed.), *Selected Speeches of Daniel O'Connell, Edited with Historical Sections* (Dublin: J. Duffy, 1865), pp. 28–30.

34. J. O'Connell, *Life and Speeches of Daniel O'Connell* (New York: McGee 1875), p. 19.

35. Ibid., p. 125.

36. Rodgers, 'Two Quakers and a Unitarian', p. 151.

37. Bric, 'Daniel O'Connell and the Debate on Anti-Slavery', p. 69.

38. Rodgers, *Ireland, Slavery and Anti-Slavery*, p. 260.

39. Foreign Slave Trade Act 1806 (46 Geo III c 52).

40. An Act for the Abolition of the Slave Trade (47° Georgii III, Session 1, cap. XXXVI).

41. The Abolition of the Slave Trade, 1807, US Constitution, at: http://abolition.nypl.org/essays/us_constitution/5/, accessed 4 March 2009.

42. F. F. Wayland, *Andrew Stevenson: Democrat and Diplomat, 1785–1857* (Philadelphia, PA: University of Pennsylvania Press, 1949), pp. 122–3.

43. D. Murray, *Odious Commerce: Britain, Spain and the Abolition of the Cuban Slave Trade* (Cambridge: Cambridge University Press, 1980), p. 112.

44. Rodgers, *Ireland, Slavery and Anti-Slavery*, p. 266.

45. D. B. Davis, *From Homicide to Slavery: Studies in American Culture* (New York: Oxford University Press, 1986), p. 267.

46. W. Wilberforce, *An Appeal to the Religion, Justice, and Humanity of the Inhabitants of the British Empire in behalf of the Negro Slaves in the West Indies* (London: J. Hatchard and Son, 1823).

47. Ibid., p. 2.

48. *Westminster Review*, (London: Baldwin, Craddock and Joy, First Quarter, 1824), p. 337.

49. Stephen, *Anti-Slavery Recollections*, p. 65.

50. Ibid., pp. 60–1.

51. Peckover, *Joseph Surge*, p. 16.

52. C. Sussman, 'Women and the Politics of Sugar, 1792', *Representations* (Autumn 1994), pp. 48–69, on p. 48.

53. I. Gross, 'The Abolition of Negro Slavery and British Parliamentary Politics 1832–3', *Historical Journal*, 23:1 (1980), pp. 63–5, on p. 63.

54. Stephen, *Anti-Slavery Recollections*, p. 242.

55. Mary O'Connell to O'Connell, 7 April 1824, Maurice O'Connell (ed.), *Correspondence*, vol. 3, p. 24.

56. K. Charlton, 'The State of Ireland in the 1820s. James Cropper's Plan', *Irish Historical Studies*, 17:67 (March 1971), p. 322.

57. Ibid., p. 328.

58. D. B. Davis, 'James Cropper and the British Anti-Slavery Movement, 1823–33', *The Journal of Negro History*, 46:3 (April 1961), p. 154.

59. Davis, *From Homicide to Slavery*, p. 262.

60. Ibid., p. 226.

61. Davis, 'James Cropper', p. 159; Cropper, J., *Present State of Ireland, with a Plan for Improving the Condition of the People* (Liverpool: George Smith, 1825).

62. P. N. Geoghegan, *King Dan: The Rise of Daniel O'Connell 1775–1829* (Dublin: Gill and Macmillan, 2008), p. 30.

63. Charlton, 'James Cropper's Plan', p. 338.

64. Bric, 'Daniel O'Connell and the Debate on Anti-Slavery', p. 71.

65. Davis, 'James Cropper', p. 160.

66. Anti-Slavery Society, *Second Report of the Committee of the Society for the Mitigation and Gradual Abolition of Slavery Throughout the British Dominions: Read at the General Meeting of the Society held on the 30th day of April, 1825* (London, 1825), p. 1.

67. Ibid., pp. 61–2.

68. Ibid., p. 66.

69. Daniel O'Connell to Mary O'Connell, 30 April 1825, MS Daniel O'Connell Papers, National Library of Ireland, MS 33, 565, ff. 24.

70. Ibid.

71. Ibid.

72. Anti-Slavery Society, *Second Report*, pp. 45–6.

73. Stephen, *Anti-Slavery Recollections*, p. 79.

74. Ibid.

75. Ibid., p. 83.

76. Geoghegan, *King Dan*, pp. 319–20.

77. O'Connell to the Knight of Kerry, 31 December 1826, O'Connell (ed.), *Correspondence*, vol. 3, p. 283.

78. Ibid., Thomas Steele to O'Connell, 12 November 1826, p. 423.

79. C. Greville and H. Reeve, *The Greville Memoirs: a Journal of the Reigns of King George IV, King William IV, and Queen Victoria* (London: Longmans, Green, and Co., 1896), vol. 1, pp. 216–19, 254–8.
80. P. J. Jupp, 'Irish Parliamentary Elections and the Influence of the Catholic Vote', *Historical Journal*, 10:2 (1967), pp. 183–96, on p. 193.
81. *The Times*, 2 April 1829.
82. The Catholic Relief Act, 1829 (10 Geo IV c.7).
83. O'Connell to his wife, Mary, 6 March 1829, O'Connell (ed.), *Correspondence,* vol. 4, p. 20.
84. Ibid., O'Connell to the O'Conor Don, 6 March 1829, p. 22.
85. Ibid.
86. 'Speech at the Bar of the House of Commons, to Maintain his Right to Sit as Member for Clare', in O'Connell, *Life and Speeches*, pp. 152–65.
87. O'Connell to Edward Dwyer, 11 March 1829, M. O'Connell, *Correspondence,* vol.4 p. 26.
88. O'Connell, *Life and Speeches,* pp. 6–7.
89. Bric, 'Daniel O'Connell and the Debate on Anti-Slavery', p. 70.
90. Greville and Reeve, *The Greville Memoirs*, 28 December 1828, vol. 1, pp. 224–5.

2 'Agitate, Agitate, Agitate'

1. Bric, 'Daniel O'Connell and the Debate on Anti-Slavery', p. 73.
2. Meeting of Cork Anti-Slavery Society, 3 September 1829, *Anti-Slavery Monthly Reporter*, 5:3 (October 1829), p. 96.
3. Gross, 'The Abolition of Negro Slavery', pp. 63–4.
4. Stephen, *Anti-Slavery Recollections*, pp. 215–6.
5. This story is repeated by, amongst others, O'Connell, 'Irish Emancipation', p. 58.
6. This story was retold by Wendell Phillips and others, W. Phillips, *A Lecture delivered at the Academy of Music, New York, 12 May 1868*, in W. Phillips, *Lectures and Speeches* (New York and London: Street and Smith, 1902), pp. 188–9.
7. Meeting of Cork Anti-Slavery Society, 3 September 1829, *Anti-Slavery Monthly Reporter*, 5:3 (October 1829), p. 93.
8. Quarles, *Black Abolitionists,* p. 9.
9. Ibid., p. 11.
10. Stephen, *Anti-Slavery Recollections*, p. 241.
11. Ibid., pp. 156–8.
12. H. Richard, *Memoirs of Joseph Sturge* (London: S. W. Partridge, 1864), p. 94.
13. Stephen, *Anti-Slavery Recollections*, pp. 130–1.
14. Rodgers, *Ireland, Slavery and Anti-Slavery*, p. 269.
15. Stephen, *Anti-Slavery Reflections*, pp. 148–9.
16. Ibid.
17. R. J. Blackett, 'And there shall be no more Sea', in R. J. Blackett, *William Lloyd Garrison and the American Abolitionist Movement*, p. 6. At: www.bu.edu/historic/conference08/Blackett.pdf, accessed 10 March 2010.
18. *Liberator,* 28 January 1832.
19. Ibid., 10 March 1832.
20. Quarles, *Black Abolitionists*, p. 14.
21. Ibid., p. 20.

22. From 'A North Ender', 7 October 1833, *Liberator,* 12 October 1833.

23. Ibid.

24. D. Kennedy and T. A. Bailey, *The American Spirit: United States History As Seen by Contemporaries*, 2nd edn (Boston, MA: Wadsworth, 2006), pp. 394–95.

25. Blackett, 'And there shall be no more Sea', p. 9.

26. Garrison on Exeter Hall Meeting, 9 November 1833, T. Nelson (ed.), *Documents of Upheaval: Selections from William Lloyd Garrison's 'The Liberator', 1831–65* (New York: Hill and Wang, 1966), p. 77.

27. Stephen, *Anti-Slavery Recollections*, p. 120.

28. Ibid., p. 198.

29. *Fraser's Magazine*, 1 (1830), p. 610.

30. *The Times*, 17 May 1830.

31. Bric, 'Daniel O'Connell and the Debate on Anti-Slavery', p. 73.

32. Meeting of Anti-Slavery Society, Freemason's Hall, 18 May 1830, in *Anti-Slavery Reporter*, 13:3 (June 1830), p. 259.

33. *The Times*, 17 May 1830.

34. *Fraser's Magazine*, 1 (1830), p. 613.

35. O'Connell to P. V. Fitzpatrick, 6 March 1833, O'Connell (ed.), *Correspondence*, vol. 5, p. 14.

36. *The Times*, 25 April 1831.

37. Ibid., 14 May 1832.

38. Stephen, *Anti-Slavery Reflections*, p. 183.

39. Peckover, *Joseph Sturge*, p. 20.

40. Gross, 'The Abolition of Negro Slavery', pp. 64–5.

41. *Report of the Debate in the House of Commons on 15 April 1831 on Mr Fowell Buxton's Motion to Consider and Adopt the Best Means for Effecting the Abolition of Colonial Slavery* (London: Mirror of Parliament, 1831).

42. C. Buxton, *Memoirs of Sir Thomas Fowell Buxton, Baronet: With Selections from his Correspondence* (London: John Murray, 1872), p. 225.

43. Ibid., p. 326.

44. O'Connell to V. Fitzpatrick, 31 August 1830, O'Connell (ed.), *Correspondence*, vol. 5 p. 220.

45. Peckover, *Joseph Sturge*, p. 19.

46. Ibid., p. 190.

47. *Address to the people of Great Britain and Ireland unanimously adopted at a general meeting of the London Anti-Slavery Committee, held on 23 April 1831, Signed on behalf of London Committee by Buxton, Gurney, Wilberforce, W. Smith, Macaulay, D. Wilson, R. Watson, S. Lushington, T. Clarkson,* Wilson Anti-Slavery Collection, Box 13, No.46.

48. Ibid.

49. Rodgers, 'Two Quakers and a Unitarian', p. 152.

50. *The Times,* 9 March 1831.

51. O'Connell to his wife, Mary, 10 March 1831, O'Connell (ed.), *Correspondence,* vol. 4, p. 289.

52. *An Act to Amend the Representation of the People in England and Wales*. Also referred to as Representation of the People Act 1832 (2 & 3 Wm. IV, c. 45).

53. O'Connell on Tithes in Ireland, 15 January 1838, Cusack (ed.) *The Speeches and Public Letters of the Liberator*, p. 525.

54. Rodgers, *Ireland, Slavery and Anti-Slavery*, p. 269.

55. Sir D. Le Marchant, *Memoir of John Charles, Viscount Althorp, Third Earl Spencer* (London: Richard Bentley, 1876), p. 448.
56. Stephen, *Anti-Slavery Recollections*, pp. 196–7.
57. Rodgers, *Ireland, Slavery and Anti-Slavery*, pp. 265–70.
58. Stephen, *Anti-Slavery Recollections*, p. 177.
59. O'Connell to Fitzpatrick, 10 May 1833, O'Connell (ed.), *Correspondence*, vol. 5, p. 29.
60. Gross, 'The Abolition of Negro Slavery', pp. 66–7.
61. Ibid., p. 71.
62. Peckover, *Joseph Sturge*, p. 21.
63. Hibernian Anti-Slavery Society, *Address of the Hibernian Anti-Slavery Society to the People of Ireland* (Dublin, 1837), 18 September 1837, p. 1.
64. Stephen, *Anti-Slavery Recollections*, p. 195.
65. Ibid., p. 199.
66. Ibid., pp. 203–5.
67. O'Connell, House of Commons, *Hansard*, 19 (24 July 1833), c. 1212.
68. Gross, 'The Abolition of Negro Slavery', p. 75.
69. O'Connell, House of Commons, *Hansard*, 19 (24 July 1833), cc. 1213–4.
70. Gross, 'The Abolition of Negro Slavery', p. 77.
71. Peckover, *Joseph Sturge*, p. 22.
72. Stephen, *Anti-Slavery Recollections*, p. 210.
73. O'Connell to Fitzpatrick, 29 May 1833, O'Connell (ed.), *Correspondence*, vol. 5, p. 34.
74. Gross, 'The Abolition of Negro Slavery', pp. 82–5.
75. Ibid., pp. 82–3.
76. Ibid., p. 89.
77. Stephen, *Anti-Slavery Recollections*, p. 207.
78. Ibid., p. 208.
79. Ibid., p. 209.
80. *Anti-Slavery Reporter*, 5:111 (October 1829), p. 82.
81. Bric, 'Daniel O'Connell and the Debate on Anti-Slavery', p. 71.
82. Ibid.
83. Midgley, *Women against Slavery*, pp. 54–5.
84. C. E. H. Orpen, *Principles of the Dublin Negro's Friend Society* (Dublin: August, 1829), p. 1.
85. Ibid.
86. Ibid.
87. Ibid., p. 2.
88. Ibid., pp. 2–3.
89. Ibid., p. 4.
90. Negro's Friend Society, *Appeal of the Negro's Friend Society to the People of Ireland on behalf of the Slaves of the British Colonies* (Dublin: R. D. Webb, n.d.), p. 2.
91. Ibid., p. 3.
92. Ibid., p. 4.
93. Ibid., p. 12.
94. Ibid., p. 15.
95. Ibid., p. 11.
96. Hibernian Negro's Friend Society, *The Principles, Plans and Objects of the 'Hibernian Negro's Friend Society', Contrasting with those of the Previously Existing Anti-Slavery Societies; being a Circular Addressed to all the Friends of the Negro, and Advocates for the*

Abolition and Extinction of Slavery; In the Form of a Letter, to Thomas Pringle, Esq. Secretary of the London Anti-Slavery Society, 8 January 1831 (Dublin, 1831), p. 12.

97. Ibid., p. 5.
98. *Liberator*, 11 February 1832.
99. Hibernian Negro's Friend Society, *The Principles, Plans and Objects of the 'Hibernian Negro's Friend Society'*, pp. 1–2.
100. Ibid., p. 3.
101. Ibid., p. 9.
102. Ibid., p. 10.
103. *Anti-Slavery Reporter*, 5:3 (October 1829), pp. 93–5.
104. *Anti-Slavery Reporter*, 111:19 (September 1830), p. 391.
105. Ibid., pp. 392–3.
106. Ibid., p. 392.
107. *Anti-Slavery Reporter*, 60:2 (May 1830), p. 215.
108. Ibid., p. 217.
109. Ibid.
110. Ibid., p. 219.
111. Ibid.
112. Secretary of the Hibernian Negro's Friend Society, 26 February 1831, O'Connell (ed.), *Correspondence*, vol. 4, p. 280.
113. Midgley, *Women against Slavery*, p. 59.
114. Cusack (ed.), *The Speeches and Public Letters of the Liberator*, p. 296.
115. Greville and Reeve, *The Greville Memoirs,* vol. 3, pp. 10–18.
116. O'Connell on Irish Reform Bill, 22 March 1831, Cusack, *The Speeches and Public Letters of the Liberator*, p. 109.
117. Ibid.
118. Ibid., O'Connell on Party Processions, 25 May 1832, p. 228.
119. Ibid., O'Connell on Tithes, 13 July 1832, p. 233.
120. O'Connell to Richard Barrett, 5 October 1831, O'Connell (ed.), *Correspondence*, vol. 4, p. 354.
121. O'Connell Speech, 30 April 1830, Cusack, *The Speeches and Public Letters of the Liberator*, p. 43; ibid., 17 May 1830, p. 59.
122. Ibid., O'Connell, 'A Petition for a Repeal of the Union', 22 March 1830, p. 32.
123. O'Connell to Michael Staunton, 11 October 1830, O'Connell (ed.), *Correspondence*, vol. 4, pp. 213–4.
124. *The Times*, 26 October 1830.
125. Le Marchant, *Memoir of John Charles*, p. 479.
126. Ibid.
127. Leslie Grove Jones to O'Connell 17 January 1831, O'Connell (ed.), *Correspondence*, vol. 4, p. 255.
128. Ibid., Mary O'Connell to O'Connell, 1 December 1830, p. 240.
129. Ibid., p. 252.
130. Ibid., p. 257.
131. Lord Althorp to Lord Spencer, 14 January 1831, Le Marchant, *Memoir of John Charles*, p. 288.
132. Thomas Wallace to O'Connell, 19 January 1831, O'Connell (ed.), *Correspondence*, vol. 4, p. 257.
133. Althorp to Spencer, 22 January 1831, Le Marchant, *Memoir of John Charles*, p. 288.

134. O'Connell (ed.), *Correspondence*, vol. 4, p. 258.

135. O'Connell on Repeal of the Union, 4 March 1831, Cusack, *The Speeches and Public Letters of the Liberator*, p. 106.

136. *The Times*, 7 March 1831.

137. Le Marchant, *Memoir of John Charles*. 2 July 1831, p. 326.

138. O'Connell (ed.), *Correspondence*, vol. 4, p. 355.

139. Ibid., O'Connell to Fitzpatrick, 6 June 1833, p. 38.

140. Ibid., p. 43.

141. O'Connell to Fitzpatrick, 19 June 1833, O'Connell (ed.), *Correspondence*, vol. 5, p. 45.

142. Ibid., O'Connell to Fitzpatrick, 26 July 1833, pp. 55–6.

143. O'Connell, House of Commons, *Hansard*, 20 (30 July 1833), c. 131.

144. O'Connell to Fitzpatrick, 26 July 1833, O'Connell (ed.), *Correspondence*, vol. 5, pp. 50–1.

145. O'Connell to Fitzpatrick, 5 August 1833, ibid., p. 57.

146. Cusack, *The Speeches and Public Letters of the Liberator*, vol. 1, p. ix.

147. O'Connell to Fitzpatrick, 8 March 1833, O'Connell (ed.), *Correspondence*, vol. 3, p. 15.

148. O'Connell on Coercion Laws for Ireland, 18 July 1833, Cusack, *The Speeches and Public Letters of the Liberator*, p. 297.

149. W. L. Garrison, *Abolitionist* (Boston, MA: New England Anti-Slavery Society), p. 28.

150. Quarles, *Black Abolitionists*, pp. 18–19.

151. *Liberator*, 1 January 1831.

152. Quarles, *Black Abolitionists*, p. 21.

153. Ibid., p. 16.

154. Blackett, 'And there shall be no more Sea', p. 12.

155. Quarles, *Black Abolitionists*, pp. 14–15.

156. Blackett, 'And there shall be no more Sea', p. 13.

3 'Slavery under another Name'

1. London Anti-Slavery Society, *An Address to the Public of Great Britain and Ireland on the Occasion of the Approaching Termination of Colonial Slavery on the First Day of August Next* (London, 1834), Wilson Anti-Slavery Collection, Box 13, No.47.

2. Garrison to Samuel J. May, 4 December 1832, Taylor, *British and American Abolitionists*, p. 21.

3. Stephen, *Anti-Slavery Recollections*, p. 213.

4. House of Commons Parliamentary Debates, *Hansard (22 July 1833), cc. 1056–69*.

5. Quarles, *Black Abolitionists*, p. 131.

6. *The Times*, 4 August 1834.

7. Ibid., 16 May 1835.

8. Ibid., 16 May 1835.

9. Ibid.

10. *A Full and Corrected Report of the Proceedings at the Public Meeting held in Hope Street Baptist Chapel to present the Emancipation Society's Address to Daniel O'Connell Esq., MP, 23 September 1835* (Glasgow: D. Prentice and Co., 1835), p. 3.

11. Ibid.

12. Ibid., p. 5.

13. Ibid., p. 6.

14. Glasgow Anti-Slavery Society, *Second Annual Report of Glasgow Anti-Slavery Society* (Glasgow: Aird and Russell, 1836), p. 16.
15. Ibid., 13–14.
16. Ibid., p. 7.
17. Ibid., p. 8.
18. Glasgow ASS, *Second Annual Report of Glasgow*, p. 16.
19. Peckover, *Joseph Sturge*, p. 29.
20. Richard, *Memoirs of Joseph Sturge*, pp. 114–7.
21. Ibid., p. 161.
22. Haughton, *Memoir*, p. 6.
23. *Liberator*, 7 January 1842.
24. J. P. Byrne, P. Coleman and J. King (eds), *Ireland and the Americas: Culture, Politics, and History*, 3 vols (California: ABC-CLIO, 2008), vol. 2, p. 914.
25. Riach, 'Daniel O'Connell and American Anti-Slavery', p. 9.
26. Bric, 'Daniel O'Connell and the Debate on Anti-Slavery', p. 74.
27. Hibernian Anti-Slavery Society, *Address of the Hibernian Anti-Slavery Society to the People of Ireland*, 18 September 1837 (Dublin, 1837), pp. 1–2.
28. Ibid.
29. Ibid., p. 1.
30. Ibid., p. 2.
31. *The Times*, 25 November 1837.
32. Ibid.
33. *Freeman's Journal*, 24 March 1838.
34. Ibid., 24 March 1838.
35. *Belfast News-Letter*, 27 April 1838.
36. Ibid.
37. C. E. Alma, *Second Appeal from the Dublin Ladies' Association to the Females of Ireland*, 26 October 1837 (Cork: George Ridings, 1837), p. 1.
38. Ibid.
39. Ibid., p. 2.
40. *Freeman's Journal*, 26 April 1838.
41. Ibid.
42. Ibid.
43. Bric, 'Daniel O'Connell and the Debate on Anti-Slavery', p. 74.
44. Richard, *Memoirs of Joseph Sturge*, p. 167.
45. Ibid., p. 168.
46. *Freeman's Journal*, 3 April 1838.
47. Richard, *Memoirs of Joseph Sturge*, p. 169.
48. Riach, 'Daniel O'Connell and American Anti-Slavery', pp. 4–5.
49. Richard, *Memoirs of Joseph Sturge*, p. 172.
50. *Leeds Mercury*, 15 June 1839.
51. James Haughton to William Haughton, 23 May 1838, Haughton, *Memoir*, p. 32.
52. Bric, 'Daniel O'Connell and the Debate on Anti-Slavery', p. 74.
53. O'Connell to Sturge, 7 July 1838, quoted in Richard, *Memoirs of Joseph Sturge*, pp. 175–6.
54. Address of Anti-Slavery Society, at:http://www.anti-slaverysociety.addr.com/society. htm, accessed 5 March 2010.
55. Inaugural meeting of British and Foreign Anti-Slavery Society, Rhodes House, Oxford, 1838.

56. Elizabeth Pease to Maria Weston Chapman, 11 July 1839, Taylor, *British and American Abolitionists*, p. 72.

57. Commons Debates, Hansard, 22 (23 April 1834), c. 1169.

58. Sir H. Taylor, on behalf of the King, to Lord Spencer, 23 April 1834, in Le Marchant, *Memoir of John Charles*, p. 568.

59. *The Times*, 23 November 1837.

60. O'Connell to Fitzpatrick, 4 September 1835, O'Connell (ed.), *Correspondence*, vol. 5, p. 329.

61. Ibid., O'Connell to P. V. Fitzpatrick, 4 September 1835, p. 329.

62. Ibid.

63. Ibid., p. 330.

64. Ibid.

65. Ibid., O'Connell to Fitzpatrick, 11 September 1835, p. 331.

66. *Annual Register,* 1835, quoted in O'Connell (ed.), *Correspondence,* p. 332.

67. Greville and Reeve, *The Greville Memoirs*, 4 December 1835, vol. 3, pp. 263–4.

68. *The Times*, 27 January 1836.

69. Ibid., 17 August 1836.

70. Ibid., 26 May 1836.

71. B. Disraeli, *The Runnymede Letters* (London: John McCrone, 1836).

72. *The Times*, 23 November 1837.

73. *Northern Star*, 24 March 1838.

74. Haughton, *Memoir*, p. 29.

75. Journals of Queen Victoria (Windsor Castle), vols 16–18, 21 February 1838; vol. 20, 11 June 1838 and 5 August 1838.

76. *Colored American,* 22 September 1838.

77. Speech of O'Connell made in London, 1833, J. Williams, *Narrative of James Williams, an American Slave, who was for Several Years a Driver on a Cotton Plantation in Alabama* (New York: the American Anti-Slavery Society and Boston: Isaac Knapp, 1838).

78. E. M. Davis to Elizabeth Pease, 12 November 1839, Taylor, *British and American Abolitionists*, p. 87.

79. John Binns to O'Connell, 2 February 1838, O'Connell (ed.), *Correspondence*, vol. 6, p. 6.

80. *Pilot* in *Morning Herald,* 18 October 1838.

81. *Ulster Times*, 20 November 1838.

82. Richard, *Memoirs of Joseph Sturge,* pp. 175–6.

83. H. Temperley, 'The O'Connell-Stevenson Contretemps: A Reflection of the Anglo-American Slavery Issue', *Journal of Negro History*, 47:4 (October 1962), pp. 217–33, p. 220.

84. *Spectator,* 4 August 1838; *Liberator*, 28 September 1838. An American who was present denied that O'Connell had provided an accurate account of his speech, see Temperley, 'The O'Connell-Stevenson Contretemps', p. 221.

85. *Portsmouth Journal of Literature and Politics,* 5 January 1839.

86. Quoted in Wayland, *Andrew Stevenson*, p. 115.

87. Ibid., pp. 122–3.

88. *Leeds Mercury*, 24 August 1839.

89. Temperley, 'The O'Connell-Stevenson Contretemps', p. 222.

90. F. F. Wayland, 'Slavebreeding in America: The Stevenson-O'Connell Imbroglio of 1838', in *the Virginia Magazine of History and Biography*, 50:1 (January 1942), pp. 47–54.

91. Temperley, 'The O'Connell-Stevenson Contretemps', p. 224.

92. *The Times, Morning Chronicle,* 15 September 1838.
93. *Morning Chronicle,* 15 September 1838.
94. Temperley, 'The O'Connell-Stevenson Contretemps', p. 225.
95. Ibid., Lewis Cass to Stevenson, p. 50.
96. *New-Bedford Mercury,* 5 October 1838.
97. D. O'Connell, *The Testimony of Daniel O'Connell, the Liberator of Ireland, against the Infamous System of American Slavery* (Reprinted as a poster by Scatherd and Adams, 1838).
98. Ibid.
99. Proceedings of Glasgow Emancipation Society, p. 4.
100. Quoted in *Richmond Enquirer,* 16 October 1838.
101. *New York Herald,* 12 October 1838.
102. *Richmond Enquirer,* 16 October 1838.
103. Ibid.
104. Ibid.
105. *Richmond Enquirer,* 18 December 1838.
106. J. Hamilton, 15 August 1838, *Richmond Enquirer,* reprinted in *Liberator,* 10 October 1838.
107. Ibid.
108. *Charlottesville Advocate*, quoted in the *Emancipator,* 11 October 1838.
109. *New Bedford Mercury,* 5 October 1838.
110. Quoted in the *Emancipator,* 4 October 1838.
111. *Emancipator,* 22 November 1838.
112. *Liberator,* 9 November 1838.
113. Fox to Palmerston, 11 June 1839, quoted in Wayland, 'Slavebreeding in America', pp. 49–50.
114. *Liberator,* 9 November 1838.
115. *New York Evangelist* quoted in the *Liberator,* 19 October 1838.
116. *Morning Chronicle,* 26 December 1838.
117. *Washington Globe,* 4 December 1838.
118. *Morning Chronicle,* 28 December 1838.
119. Ibid., 26 December 1838.
120. *Examiner,* 6 January 1839.
121. Wayland, 'Slavebreeding in America', p. 53.
122. Speech by Clay, Senator for Kentucky, 7 February 1839, *Congressional Globe,* p. 355.
123. Quoted in J. G. Whittier, 'Daniel O'Connell', *The Complete Writings of John Greenleaf Whittier* (Mass: Riverside Press 1992), vol. 2, pp. 321–2.
124. Bric, 'Daniel O'Connell, and the Debate on Anti-Slavery', p. 77.
125. Whittier, *Daniel O'Connell,* p. 321.
126. Ibid., p. 328.
127. *Emancipator,* 11 April 1839.
128. *Morning Herald* (NY), 19 October 1838.
129. Ibid., 20 October 1838.
130. Ibid.
131. Temperley, 'The O'Connell-Stevenson Contretemps', p. 233.
132. Garrison to Harriet Martineau, Taylor, *British and American Abolitionists,* pp. 22–3.
133. Inaugural Speech of Martin Van Buren, 4 March 1837. At:http://www.bartleby.com/124/pres25.html, accessed 4 November 2008.

134. Ibid.
135. Hibernian Anti-Slavery Society, *Address of the Hibernian Anti-Slavery Society to the People of Ireland* (Dublin, 1837), 18 September 1837, p. 2.
136. Bric, 'Daniel O'Connell and the Debate on Anti-Slavery', pp. 70–1.
137. Elizabeth Pease to William Lloyd Garrison, n.d., Taylor, *British and American Abolitionists*, p. 103.
138. E. M. Oldham, 'Irish Support of the Abolitionist Movement', *Boston Public Library Quarterly* (October 1958), pp. 175–87, p. 177.
139. Ibid., p. 179.
140. 'Apostolic Letter condemning the Slave Trade', written by Pope Gregory XVI and read during the 4th Provincial Council of Baltimore, 3 December 1839, reprinted in London, *The Times,* 31 December 1839.
141. Wayland, 'Slavebreeding in America', pp. 120–4.
142. J. F. Quinn, '"Three Cheers for the Abolitionist Pope!": American Reaction to Gregory XVI's Condemnation of the Slave Trade, 1840–60', *Catholic Historical Review*, 90:1 (2004), pp. 67–93, on pp. 68–70.
143. N. Rodgers, 'Richard Robert Madden: an Irish Anti-Slavery Activist in the Americas, in O. Walsh (ed.) *Ireland Abroad: Politics and Professions in the Nineteenth Century* (Dublin: Fours Courts Press, 2003), pp. 119–31.
144. Quinn, 'Three Cheers', pp. 72–4.
145. C. Kerrigan, 'Irish Temperance and US Anti-Slavery: Father Mathew and the Abolitionists', *History Workshop*, 31 (Spring 1991), pp. 108–9.
146. 'Slavery', Appendix to J. F. Maguire, *The Irish in America* (New York: D. and J. Sadlier, 1872), pp. 634–5.

4 'Murderers of Liberty'

1. Richard, *Memoirs of Joseph Sturge*, p. 206.
2. Ibid., pp. 207–8.
3. Ibid., p. 203.
4. Ibid., pp. 192–3.
5. Petition to House of Commons by inhabitants of Sheffield, n.d. [1840] in Wilson Anti-Slavery Collection, R. 107337.19.80.
6. Richard, *Memoirs of Joseph Sturge*, pp. 192–3.
7. British and Foreign Anti-Slavery Society, *Slavery and the Slave Trade in British India: with Notices of the Existence ...* (London: Thomas Ward, 1841), pp. 1–2.
8. W. Adam, *The Law and Custom of Slavery in British India: in a Series of Letters to Thomas Fowell Buxton, esq.* (Boston, MA: Weeks, Jordan and Company, 1840).
9. Ibid., p. 11. Reprinted by British and Foreign Anti-Slavery Society (London: Thomas Ward, 1841).
10. Joseph Pease to O'Connell, 10 March 1841, O'Connell (ed.), *Correspondence*, vol. 7, pp. 27–9.
11. Elizabeth Pease to Maria Weston Chapman, n.d., Taylor, *British and American Abolitionists*, p. 111.
12. James Haughton to O'Connell, 11 January 1840, Royal Irish Academy, Madden Collection, MS. 24 O 10, folio 11.
13. Ibid., Richard Madden to O'Connell, n.d., [1840], MS. 24 0 11/49, folio 60.
14. Rodgers, *Ireland, Slavery and Anti-Slavery*, p. 272.

15. O'Connell to Sturge, 27 March 1844, Richard, *Memoirs of Joseph Sturge,* pp. 279–80.
16. Ibid.
17. R. D. Webb to Elizabeth Pease, 26 May 1844, Taylor, *British and American Abolitionists,* pp. 220–1.
18. The Sugar Duties Act 1846 (9 & 10 Vict.).
19. Rodgers, *Ireland, Slavery and Anti-Slavery,* p. 272.
20. Richard, *Memoirs of Joseph Sturge,* p. 209.
21. *Leeds Mercury,* 15 June 1839.
22. *Belfast News-Letter,* 5 June 1840.
23. C. Buxton, *Memoirs of Sir Thomas Fowell Buxton,* p. 439.
24. The debate was reprinted in a number of British and Irish newspapers, see *Freeman's Journal,* 8 June 1840.
25. *Leicester Chronicle,* 13 June 1840.
26. 'Honest us' to the *Morning Chronicle, reprinted in Freeman's Journal,* 8 June 1840.
27. *Freeman's Journal,* 4 June 1840.
28. *Bristol Mercury,* 13 June 1840.
29. *Leicester Chronicle,* 13 June 1840.
30. Ibid.
31. Ibid.
32. Ibid.
33. *Bristol Mercury,* 13 June 1840.
34. J. Mott, *Three Months in Great Britain* (Philadelphia, PA: J. Miller, 1841), pp. 16–17.
35. Blackett, 'And there shall be no more Sea', p. 18.
36. *Morning Chronicle,* 21 May 1841.
37. Mott, *Three Months in Great Britain,* p. 14.
38. Irish and British delegates came from Aberdeen, Alton, Belfast, Boston, Bradbury, Bradford, Bristol, Bath, Birmingham, Brighton, Brompton, Barnard Castle, Bridgewater, Buzzard, Chatham, Circencester, Colchester, Carlisle, Chelmsford, Cork, Durham, Darlington, Devizes, Dublin, Doncaster, Derby, Edinburgh, Exeter, Farnham, Fenwick, Glasgow, Glastonbury, Gloucester, Hitchen, Hereford, Horncastle, Herts and South Bedfordshire, Ipswich, Kendal, Kingsbridge, Kettering, Leeds, Leighton, Liverpool, Leicester, Lewes, Louth, Leominster, Margate, Manchester, Maidstone, Newcastle-upon-Tyne, Nottingham, Norfolk, Norwich, Oxford, Pontefract, Paisley, Rochester, Ross, Staines, Salisbury, Swansea, Staffordshire, Sheffield, Strood, Stroud, Southampton, St Ives, Stockton, Spilsby, Tewkesbury, Taunton, Truro, Worcester, Witham, Woodbrook, Wisbeach, Wellinborough and York. *Leeds Mercury,* 13 June 1840.
39. Richard, *Memoirs of Joseph Sturge,* p. 215.
40. A. D. Hallowell, *James and Lucretia Mott: Life and Letters by their Grand-Daughter* (Boston, MA: Miflin and Co., 1884), p. 149.
41. F. B. Tolles, *Slavery and the Women Question: Lucretia Mott's Diary, 1840* (Pennsylvania, PA: Friends Historical Association, 1952), p. 13.
42. Taylor, *British and American Abolitionists,* p. 132.
43. Haughton, *Memoir,* p. 47.
44. Bric, 'Daniel O'Connell and the Debate on Anti-Slavery', p. 74.
45. *Freeman's Journal and Daily Commercial Advertiser,* 17 June 1840.
46. *Belfast News-Letter,* 19 June 1840.
47. *Morning Chronicle,* 18 June 1840.
48. *Belfast News-Letter,* 19 June 1840.

49. Richard, *Memoirs of Joseph Sturge*, pp. 216–7.
50. Mott, *Three Months in Great Britain*, p. 24.
51. Ibid., p. 18.
52. *Belfast News-Letter*, 19 June 1840.
53. Mott, *Three Months in Great Britain*, p. 18.
54. *Freeman's Journal*, 17 June 1840.
55. Ibid.
56. *The Times*, 13 June 1840.
57. Tolles, *Slavery and the Women Question*, p. 31.
58. *Colored American*, 5 October 1839.
59. *Morning Chronicle*, 13 June 1840.
60. Richard, *Memoirs of Joseph Sturge*, p. 214.
61. Bric, 'Daniel O'Connell and the Debate on Anti-Slavery', p. 76.
62. Lucretia Mott to Daniel O'Connell, 17 June 1840, Mott, *Three Weeks in Great Britain*, pp. 19–20.
63. Ibid., O'Connell to Lucretia Mott, 20 June 1840, p. 20.
64. Ibid.
65. Ibid.
66. Bric, 'Daniel O'Connell and the Debate on Anti-Slavery', p. 75.
67. Hallowell, *James and Lucretia,* p. 155.
68. Obituary of Elizabeth Cady Stanton, *New York Times,* 27 October 1902.
69. Hallowell, *James and Lucretia*, p. 156.
70. L. S. Hogan, 'A Time for Silence: William Lloyd Garrison and the 'Woman Question' at the 1840 World Anti-Slavery Convention', *Gender Issues*, 25:2 (June 2008), pp. 63–79.
71. *Freeman's Journal*, 17 June 1840.
72. *Leeds Mercury*, 20 June 1840.
73. *Freeman's Journal*, 18 June 1840.
74. Ibid., 20 June 1840.
75. Ibid.
76. Ibid.
77. *Leeds Mercury*, 20 June 1840.
78. R. R. Madden, *A Twelvemonth's Residence in the West Indies, during the Transition from Slavery to Apprenticeship; with Incidental Notice of the State of Society, Prospects, an Natural Resources of Jamaica and other Islands*, 2 vols (Philadelphia, PA: Carey, Lea and Blanchard, 1835).
79. *Morning Chronicle*, 18 June 1840.
80. Ibid., 20 June 1840.
81. Richard, *Memoirs of Joseph Sturge*, p. 216.
82. *Independent*, 7 July 2010.
83. B. R. Haydon, *The Autobiography and Memoirs of Benjamin Robert Haydon,* ed. T. Taylor (New York: Harcourt Brace and Co., 1859), pp. 684–5.
84. The portrait is now in the National Portrait Gallery in London.
85. Haydon, *The Autobiography and Memoirs,* p. 565.
86. Ibid., p. 566.
87. Ibid., p. 693.
88. *Belfast News-Letter*, 30 June 1840.
89. Dumond (ed.), *Birney Letters*, vol. 2, p. 682.

90. William Garrison to Helen Garrison, 29 June 1840, Taylor, *British and American Abolitionists*, p. 92.
91. Ibid., Elizabeth Pease to Maria Weston Chapman, n.d., p. 111.
92. C. Hall, 'The Lords of Humankind Re-visited', *Bulletin of the School of Oriental and African Studies*, 66:3 (2003), pp. 472–85.
93. *Colored American*, 18 July 1840.
94. William Garrison to Helen Garrison, London, 29 June 1840, Taylor, *British and American Abolitionists*, p. 91.
95. Ibid., 29 June 1841, p. 93.
96. J. A. Collins to Henry Grafton Chapman, 2 January 1841, Taylor, *British and American Abolitionists*, p. 138.
97. Blackett, 'And there shall be no more Sea', pp. 15–16.
98. Bric, 'Daniel O'Connell and the Debate on Anti-Slavery', p. 77.
99. Hallowell, *James and Lucretia*, pp. 168–9.
100. *Freeman's Journal*, 28 October 1840.
101. D. Hempton and M. Hill, *Evangelical Protestantism in Ulster Society 1740–1890* (London: Routledge, 1992), p. 123.
102. *Belfast News-Letter*, 3 November 1840.
103. Mary Ireland to Mrs Chapman, Boston, 19 June 1846, Oldham, 'Irish Support', p. 180.
104. Blackett, 'And there shall be no more Sea', pp. 17–18.
105. C. L. Remond, 'Slavery and the Irish', *Liberator*, 19 November 1841.
106. Ibid.
107. Ibid.
108. Ibid.
109. Remond to Mrs Chapman, quoted in Ellen M. Oldham, 'Irish Support of the Abolitionist Movement', *Boston Public Library Quarterly* (October 1958), p. 176.
110. Registration of Voters (Ireland), House of Commons Debates, *Hansard*, 54 (18 May 1840), c. 188.
111. D. O'Connell, *Report of the Committee Appointed at a Public Meeting held in Dublin, Thursday, March 19, 1840 [microform]: to Consider the Effect of Lord Stanley's Irish registration Bill* (Dublin, 1840).
112. *Belfast News-Letter*, 29 May 1840.
113. House of Commons, 11 June, reported in the *Newcastle Courant*, 19 June 1840.
114. Benjamin to Sarah Disraeli, 12 June 1840, M. G. Wiebe, J. A. Wilson Gunn (eds), *Benjamin Disraeli Letters: 1838–1841* (Toronto: University of Toronto, 1997), p. 275.
115. G. O. Trevelyan, *The Life and Letters of Lord Macaulay*, 2 vols (London: Longmans, Green and Co., 1876), vol. 2, p. 78.
116. House of Commons, 11 June, reported in the *Newcastle Courant*, 19 June 1840.
117. Ibid., House of Commons, Friday, 12 June 1840.
118. *Belfast News-Letter*, 4 August 1840.
119. Dumond (ed.), *Letters of James Gillespie Birney*, vol. 1, p. 683.
120. Rodgers, *Ireland, Slavery and Anti-Slavery*, p. 272.
121. Richard Cobden to Sturge, n.d., Richard, *Memoirs of Joseph Sturge*, p. 278.
122. C. L. Brightwell, *Memorials of the Life of Amelia Opie*, 2nd edn (Norwich: Fletcher and Alexander, 1854), pp. 345–6.
123. Ibid., p. 347.
124. Sturge to O'Connell, 31 January 1842, O'Connell (ed.), *Correspondence*, vol. 7, p. 132.
125. *Freeman's Journal*, 5 November 1840.

126. Ibid.

127. *Freeman's Journal*, 11 May 1842.

128. Haughton to O'Connell, 1 October 1842, O'Connell (ed.), *Correspondence*, vol. 7, p. 176.

129. Gerrit Smith to O'Connell, 2 July 1842, O'Connell (ed.), *Correspondence*, vol. 7. pp. 166–7.

130. *Truth Teller*, 29 January 1842.

131. J. Hughes, *The Emancipation of Irish Catholics: The First Great Sermon Delivered by Archbishop Hughes and Inscribed to Daniel O'Connell, the Liberator of Ireland* (New York: Metropolitan Record, 1864).

132. *Truth Teller*, 13 November 1841.

133. Sharrow, 'John Hughes and a Catholic Response to Slavery', p. 267.

134. Ibid., p. 264.

135. Kerrigan, 'Irish Temperance', p. 108.

136. Sharrow, 'John Hughes and a Catholic Response to Slavery', p. 255.

137. Remond, 'Slavery and the Irish'.

138. Taylor, *British and American Abolitionists*, p. 7.

139. Ibid., Garrison to George Benson, 22 March 1842, p. 170.

140. W. C. McDaniel, 'American Abolitionists, Irish Repeal, and the Origins of Garrisonian Disunionism', *Journal of the Early Republic*, 28:2 (Summer 2008), pp. 1–21, p. 1.

5 'Foreign Interference in the Domestic Concerns'

1. Haughton, *Memoir*, p. 59.

2. Kerrigan, 'Irish Temperance', p. 105.

3. *Liberator*, 29 April 1842.

4. *Address from the People of Ireland to Their Countrymen and Countrywomen in America* (Dublin: 1841).

5. Dumond (ed.), *Birney Letters*, p. 683.

6. *Liberator*, 4 February 1842.

7. J. A. Collins to R. Webb, 1 January 1842, Taylor, *British and American Abolitionists*, p. 160.

8. Boston College, 'A Brief History of the Boston *Pilot*', *at:* http://infowanted.bc.edu/history/briefhistory/ accessed 4 June 2009.

9. Collins to Webb, Taylor, *British and American Abolitionists*, p. 161.

10. Ibid., Garrison to George Benson, 22 March 1842, p. 171.

11. *New York Herald*, quoted in the *Liberator,* 11 February 1842.

12. Bric, 'Daniel O'Connell and the Debate on Anti-Slavery', p. 79.

13. *Liberator,* 4 February 1842.

14. *New York Herald*, 11 February 1842.

15. Ibid., 11 February 1842.

16. Garrison to Richard Webb, 27 February 1842, Taylor, *British and American Abolitionists*, p. 169.

17. *New York Herald*, 11 February 1842.

18. *Liberator*, 18 February 1842.

19. *Boston Pilot*, 25 June 1842.

20. *Liberator*, 18 February 1842.

21. *Boston Catholic Diary,* in the *Liberator,* 4 March 1842.

22. Ibid., 4 March 1842.
23. Quoted in the *Truth Teller,* 12 March 1842.
24. Ibid.
25. Ibid.
26. Ibid.
27. Ibid.
28. Dumond (ed.), *Birney Letters*, p. 684.
29. James Birney to the editor of the *Free Press,* Dumond (ed.), *Birney Letters,* vol. 2, p. 681.
30. Bric, 'Daniel O'Connell and the Debate on Anti-Slavery', p. 81.
31. Dumond (ed.), *Birney Letters*, p. 683.
32. E. M. Davis to Elizabeth Pease, 15 February 1842, Taylor, *British and American Abolitionists,* p. 167.
33. *Truth Teller*, 16 April 1842.
34. Ibid.
35. Ibid., 16 June 1842.
36. J. Grahame, *Who is to Blame? or, Cursory Review of 'American Apology for American Accession to Negro Slavery'* (London: Smith, Elder and Co., 1842), pp. 13–14.
37. *Liberator*, 18 February 1842.
38. Ibid., 29 April 1842.
39. Collins to R. Webb, 2 April 1842, Taylor, *British and American Abolitionists*, p. 174–5.
40. James Cannings Fuller to O'Connell, 28 March 1842, O'Connell, *Correspondence,* pp. 144–5.
41. Bric, 'Daniel O'Connell and the Debate on Anti-Slavery', p. 80.
42. Quarles, *Black Abolitionists,* p. 133.
43. Rodgers, *Ireland, Slavery and Anti-Slavery,* p. 274.
44. Bric, 'Daniel O'Connell and the Debate on Anti-Slavery', p. 78.
45. Ibid.
46. Ibid., p. 79.
47. Ignatiev, *How the Irish became White,* p. 8.
48. D. Knobel, *Paddy and the Republic: Ethnicity and Nationality in the Antebellum America* (Connecticut: Middletown, 1986), p. 57.
49. *Truth Teller*, 29 January 1842.
50. J. A. Collins to R. Webb, 1 January 1842, Taylor, *British and American Abolitionists*, p. 161.
51. *Truth Teller*, 30 April 1842.
52. R. M. Johnson, 'White Sulpher', 8 April 1842, to editor of *Truth Teller,* 14 May 1842.
53. Ibid., 4 June 1842.
54. C. M. Brosnan, Albany Repeal Association, to T. M. Ray, Loyal National Repeal Association, Dublin, reprinted in *Truth Teller,* 26 April 1842.
55. Ibid.
56. Ibid.
57. Ibid.
58. Greville and Reeve, *The Greville Memoirs,* 1 September 1842, vol. 5, p. 28.
59. The first volume of *A Memoir on Ireland: Native and Saxon,* was published in February 1843.
60. Report from Dublin to Rev. Purcell, the Bishop of Ohio, 5 February 1842, O'Connell, *Correspondence,* vol. 5, pp. 88–90.

61. O'Connell to John Barclay Sheil, MD, 17 November 1842, O'Connell (ed.), *Correspondence*, vol. 7, p. 180.

62. C. Kinealy, *Repeal and Revolution: 1848 in Ireland* (Manchester: Manchester University Press, 2009), pp. 27–35.

63. O'Connell to Patrick Fitzpatrick, 7 January 1843, O'Connell (ed.), *Correspondence*, vol. 7, p. 183.

64. O. MacDonagh, *The Emancipist: Daniel O'Connell 1830–1847* (London: Weidenfeld and Nicolson, 1989), pp. 202–4; 256–7.

65. Lord de Grey to Peel, 6 May 1843, C. S. Parker, *Sir Robert Peel from his Private Papers* (London: John Murray, 1899), vol. 3, p. 46.

66. Peel to de Grey, 9 May 1843, ibid., pp. 47–8.

67. 'Dismissal of Lord ffrench (Ireland)', House of Lords Debates, *Hansard,* 69 (30 May 1843), c. 1065.

68. Arms Bill (Ireland), 1843, 6 & 7 Vict. c.74.

69. Greville and Reeve, *The Greville Memoirs*, 15 June 1843, vol. 5, p. 99.

70. General Anti-Slavery Convention, *Proceedings of the General Anti-Slavery Convention* (London: General Anti-Slavery Convention, 1843), p. 1.

71. Richard, *Memoirs of Joseph Sturge,* p. 349.

72. *Anti-Slavery Convention*, pp. 27, 177.

73. Ibid., p. 93.

74. Ibid., p. 127.

75. *The Times,* 25 August 1843.

76. O'Connell to Richard Dowden, 5 September 1843, O'Connell (ed.), *Correspondence*, vol. 7, p. 223.

77. Greville and Reeve, *The Greville Memoirs*, 16 October 1843, vol. 5, p. 136.

78. O'Connell to Ray, 17 December 1843, O'Connell (ed.), *Correspondence*, vol. 7, p. 231.

79. Ibid., Joseph Sturge to O'Connell, 23 March 1844, p. 248.

80. *Bradford and Wakefield Observer,* 23 May 1844.

81. Joseph Sturge to O'Connell, 23 March 1844, O'Connell (ed.), *Correspondence*, vol. 7, p. 248.

82. Ibid., O'Connell to Fitzpatrick, 9 December 1843, p. 227.

83. Ibid., W. Simpson to O'Connell, 19 March 1844, pp. 245–6.

84. Ibid., O'Connell to Fitzpatrick, 25 March 1844, p. 249.

85. R. D. Webb to Edmund Quincy, 17 August 1844, Taylor, *British and American Abolitionists,* p. 225.

86. Ibid., Elizabeth Pease to unknown correspondent, n.d. [1844], p. 232.

87. *Truth Teller*, 27 April 1844.

88. Peel to Lord Heytesbury, 26 August 1844, Parker, *Peel,* vol. 3, p. 127.

89. Religious Disabilities Act, 1846, 9 & 10 Vict. c. 59.

90. Quoted in 'The New Encyclopaedia, at: http://www.newworldencyclopedia.org/ entry/Daniel_O%27Connell, accessed 10 April 2010.

6 'American Sympathy and Irish Blackguardism'

1. D. O'Connell, *Speeches of Daniel O'Connell and Thomas Steele on the Subject of American Slavery delivered before the Loyal National Repeal Association of Ireland in reply to certain letters received from Repeal Associations in the United States* (Philadelphia, PA: Pennsylvania Freeman, 1843), p. 2.
2. O'Connell to Richard Bennett, 23 March 1843, O'Connell (ed.), *Correspondence*, vol. 7, pp. 191–2.
3. J. F. Quinn, 'The Rise and Fall of Repeal: Slavery and Irish Nationalism in Antebellum Philadelphia', *Pennsylvania Magazine of History and Biography*, 130:1 (January 2006), pp. 45–78, on pp. 53–4.
4. James Haughton to O'Connell 1 October 1842, Haughton, *Memoir*, pp. 59–60.
5. *Freeman's Journal*, 4 April 1843.
6. O'Connell to Haughton, 6 April 1843, O'Connell (ed.), *Correspondence*, vol. 7, pp. 199–200.
7. *Liberator*, 12 May 1843.
8. *Freeman's Journal*, 11 April 1843.
9. *Liberator*, 12 May 1843.
10. Ibid., 2 June 1843.
11. Quinn, 'Rise and Fall of Repeal', p. 64.
12. Bric, 'Daniel O'Connell and the Debate on Anti-Slavery', p. 80.
13. *Nation*, 13 May 1843.
14. *New York Freeman's Journal* (hereafter *NY Freeman's*), 15 July 1843.
15. *Richmond Enquirer* reprinted in *NY Freeman's*, 15 July 1843.
16. Ibid.
17. *NY Freeman's*, 12 August 1843.
18. Ibid., 5 August 1843.
19. *Baltimore Saturday Visitor*, reprinted in *NY Freeman's*, 5 August 1843.
20. *NY Freeman's*, 5 August 1843.
21. Ibid., 5 August 1843.
22. *Brooklyn Eagle*, 10 June 1843.
23. *NY Freeman's*, 22 July 1843.
24. *Broome Republic*, reprinted in *NY Freeman's*, 22 July 1843.
25. *NY Freeman's*, 15 July 1843.
26. Ibid.
27. Ibid.
28. Ibid.
29. Quinn, 'Rise and Fall of Repeal', pp. 67–8.
30. James Haughton to O'Connell, 5 August 1843, O'Connell (ed.), *Correspondence*, vol. 7, p. 217.
31. Gerrit Smith to O'Connell, 28 July 1843, O'Connell (ed.), *Correspondence*, vol. 7, p. 214.
32. Ibid., p. 216.
33. Haughton to O'Connell, Haughton, *Memoir*, 13 August 1843, p. 65.
34. 'American Sympathy and Irish Blackguardism', Library of Congress, Washington, Call number: PC/US – 1843.C619, no. 29.
35. Ibid., 'O'Connell's Call and Pat's Reply', Call Number: PC/US - 1843.R661, no. 89.
36. K. Laird, 'Were Illustrators of the Golden Age Racists?', at: http://hubpages.com/hub/The-Problem-We-All-Live-With---Were-Illustrators-in-the-Golden-Age-Racists accessed 4 July 2010.

37. O'Connell to Haughton, 4 February 1845, Haughton, *Memoir*, p. 72.
38. A. Barr, *Black Texans: A History of African Americans in Texas, 1528–1995*, 2nd edn (Oklahoma: University of Oklahoma Press, 1996), pp. 14–17.
39. Resolution of Hibernian ASS, *The Times*, 9 January 1841.
40. Letter of HASS, 17 December 1840, in *The Times*, 9 January 1941.
41. Foreign Office to HASS, 24 December 1840, in *The Times*, 9 January 1841.
42. Joseph Sturge to O'Connell, 17 February 1841, O'Connell (ed.), *Correspondence*, vol. 7, pp. 22–3.
43. *Freeman's Journal*, 18 May 1844.
44. *Nation*, 29 March 1845.
45. *Liberator*, 2 May 1845.
46. Ibid.
47. Ibid.
48. Ibid.
49. *Nation*, 5 April 1845.
50. Ibid.
51. *Liberator*, 13 June 1845.
52. Ibid.
53. Ibid.
54. *Brooklyn Eagle*, 28 May 1845.
55. Ibid., 12 May 1845.
56. *Liberator*, 26 September 1845.
57. *Brooklyn Eagle*, 24 April 1845.
58. *Liberator*, 12 September 1845.
59. Ibid.
60. Kinealy, *Repeal and Revolution*, pp. 70–7.
61. *Liberator*, 2 May 1845.
62. Garrison to R. D. Webb, 1 March 1845, Taylor, *British and American Abolitionists*, pp. 234–5.
63. Ibid., p. 234.
64. *Liberator*, 24 October 1845.
65. Ibid.
66. Gerrit Smith to O'Connell, 2 July 1841, O'Connell, *Correspondence*, vol. 7, p. 167.
67. *Liberator*, 14 April 1843.
68. *Freeman's Journal*, 7 August 1843.
69. Lewis Tappan to O'Connell, 15 August 1843, O'Connell (ed.), *Correspondence*, vol. 7, p. 219.
70. James Haughton to O'Connell, 5 August 1843, Haughton, *Memoir*, pp. 60–1.
71. Quoted in Blackett, 'And there shall be no more Sea', p. 22.
72. Richard Webb to Edmund Quincy, 2 February 1844, Taylor, *British and American Abolitionists*, pp. 213–14.
73. Ibid., Elizabeth Pease to Anne Warren Weston, 27 January 1844, p. 211.
74. Ibid.
75. Blackett, 'And there shall be no more Sea', p. 22.
76. Riach, 'Daniel O'Connell and American Anti-Slavery', p. 13.
77. *Freeman's Journal*, 14 April 1842.

78. Quoted in Riach, 'Daniel O'Connell and American Anti-Slavery', pp. 12–15.

79. Bric, 'Daniel O'Connell and the Debate on Anti-Slavery', p. 80.

80. Richard Blackett, 'And there shall be no more Sea', p. 5.

81. J. K. Garrett, *Fort Worth: A Frontier Triumph* (Texas: Texas Christian University Press, 1999), p. 162.

82. *Liberator*, 21 January 1842.

83. Ibid., 7 January 1842.

84. *Truth Teller,* 5 February 1842.

85. *NY Freeman*, 22 July 1843.

86. Ibid., 5 August 1843.

87. *Nation*, 2 September 1843.

88. *Freeman's Journal*, 12 October 1843.

89. *Address by the Liberator before the Loyal National Repeal Association on 11 October 1843 in reply to an Address from the Cincinnati Irish Repeal Association* (Boston, MA: New England Anti Slavery Tract, No. 2, 1843), p. 1.

90. Ibid., pp. 1–2.

91. Ibid., pp. 2–3.

92. Ibid., p. 5.

93. Ibid., p. 8.

94. *National Anti-Slavery Standard*, 18 November 1843.

95. George Armstrong to Samuel May Jr., 30 October 1843, Taylor, *British and American Abolitionists*, p. 149.

96. Ibid., R. D. Webb to Edmund Quincy, 16 October 1843, pp. 200–1.

97. *Nation*, 13 January 1844.

98. Bric, 'Daniel O'Connell and the Debate on Anti-Slavery', p. 81.

99. *Facts for the People*, 1:7 (July 1843).

100. S. P. Chase to O'Connell, 30 November 1843, *Liberty or Slavery*, p. 10.

101. Bric, 'Daniel O'Connell and the Debate on Anti-Slavery', pp. 81–2.

102. Ibid., p. 81.

103. *Nation*, 13 January 1844.

104. Ibid., 12 April 1845.

105. Ibid., 23 March 1844.

106. Ibid.

107. Ibid., 9 August 1845.

108. Ibid.

109. Ibid., 31 May 1845.

110. Riach, 'Daniel O'Connell and American Anti-Slavery', p. 9.

111. Richard Webb to Edmund Quincy, 2 February 1844, Taylor, *British and American Abolitionists*, p. 215.

112. Ibid.

113. *Liberator*, 26 September 1845.

114. Ibid.

115. Ibid.

116. Ibid.

117. *Nation,* 9 August 1845.

118. O'Connell to O'Brien, 22 December 1845, O'Connell (ed.), *Correspondence*, vol. 7, p. 351.

119. O'Neill, 'Frederick Douglass and the Irish', pp. 58–9.

120. Richard Webb to unidentified correspondent, 3 August 1849, Taylor, *British and American Abolitionists*, p. 339.

121. O'Neill, 'Frederick Douglass and the Irish', p. 76.

122. Kinealy, *Repeal and Revolution*, p. 74.

123. Douglass, *The Life and Times*, p. 682.

124. C. W. Chesnutt, *Frederick Douglass* (Boston, MA: Small, Maynard & Company, 1899), p. 50.

125. F. Douglass, *Narrative of the life of Frederick Douglass, an American Slave* (Boston, MA: Anti-Slavery Office, 1849), p. vii.

126. *Belfast News-Letter,* 26 December 1845.

127. *Belfast Protestant Journal,* 11 July 1846.

128. *Belfast News-Letter,* 9 January 1846.

129. Ibid., 9 December 1845.

130. F. Sweeney, *Frederick Douglass and the Atlantic World* (Chicago, IL: University of Chicago Press, 2007), pp. 50–6.

131. F. Douglass, 'The Free Church of Scotland and American Slavery': An Address Delivered in Dundee, Scotland, on January 30, 1846, *Dublin Courier,* 3 February 1846. Chalmers, *Letter of the Rev. Dr Chalmers on American Slave-Holding with remarks by the Belfast Anti-Slavery Committee* (Belfast: J Mullen, 1846).

132. Mary Ireland to Mrs Chapman, Boston, 19 June 1846, quoted in Oldham, 'Irish Support', pp. 180–1.

133. Ibid., p. 180.

134. Ibid., Mary Ireland to Secretary of Boston Female Anti-Slavery Society, 2 November 1846, p. 182.

135. Ibid., Mary Ireland to Secretary of Mass. Female ASS, 17 June 1846, p. 182.

136. O'Neill, 'Frederick Douglass and the Irish', p. 59.

137. Douglass, *The Life and Times*, p. 184.

138. *Liberator,* 26 March 1846.

139. C. Kinealy, *This Great Calamity: The Irish Famine 1845–52*, 2nd edn (Dublin: Gill and Macmillan, 2006), pp. 297–341.

140. E. Laxton, *The Famine Ships: the Irish Exodus to America* (New York: Henry Holt, 1998), p. 7.

141. O'Neill, 'Frederick Douglass and the Irish', p. 62.

142. O'Connell to O'Brien, 22 December 1845, O'Connell (ed.), *Correspondence*, vol. 7, p. 353.

143. Kinealy, *Repeal and Revolution*, pp. 70–5.

144. *Nation,* 16 January 1847.

145. Ibid.

146. *Nation,* 6 February 1847.

147. Ibid.

148. Ibid., 20 February 1847.

149. *Mercury,* 13 April 1847.

150. Ibid.

151. *Nation,* 10 April 1847.

152. Ibid.

153. *Mercury,* 13 April 1847.

154. *Nation,* 1 May 1847.

155. Haughton to Rev. Samuel May, 30 August 1847, Taylor, *British and American Abolitionists*, pp. 319–20.
156. In February 1848, Mitchel founded the *United Irishman,* in which he expounded on these ideas. See Kinealy, *Repeal and Revolution,* pp. 133–5.
157. James Haughton to Maria Weston Chapman, 1 April 1847, Taylor, *British and American Abolitionists,* p. 311.
158. Greville and Reeve, *The Greville Memoirs,* 6 June 1847, vol. 5, p. 445.
159. *Essex Standard,* 28 May 1847.
160. Rev. J. J. O'Connell, *Eulogy on the Life and Character of the late Daniel O'Connell, Esq., M.P. delivered before the Repeal Society of Savannah in the Catholic Church of St John the Baptist* (Savannah: Edward J. Purse, 1847), p. 8.
161. *National Era,* 1 July 1847.
162. Douglass, *The Life and Times,* p. 684.
163. F. W. Seward, *Autobiography of William H. Seward from 1801 to 1834: With a memoir of his life, and selections from his letters from 1831 to 1840* (New York: Appleton and Co., 1877), p. 686.
164. *National Era,* 14 October 1847.

7 'The Man of All Men'

1. Kinealy, *Repeal and Revolution,* pp. 198–205.
2. Oldham, 'Irish Support', pp. 179–180.
3. Ibid., Maria Webb to Secretary of Boston Female ASS, 2 November 1846, p. 182.
4. Ibid., R. D. Webb to A. Weston, Boston, 14 November 1848, pp. 185–6.
5. Ibid.
6. Ibid., p. 176.
7. Ibid., p. 179.
8. Richard Webb to Anne Warren Weston, 5 July 1849, Taylor, *British and American Abolitionists,* p. 337.
9. Isabel Jennings to Mary Estlin, 24 March 1851, Oldham, 'Irish Support', p. 183.
10. Oldham, 'Irish Support', p. 186.
11. For example, on 20 December 1852, Haughton delivered a lecture before the Dublin Statistical Society on 'Should the Holders of Slave Property receive Compensation for the Abolition of Slavery? (Dublin: Hodges and Smith, 1853).
12. Douglass, *The Life and Times,* p. 238.
13. Oldham, 'Irish Support', pp. 183–4.
14. Ibid., Mary Ireland to the Committee of Boston bazaar, 13 November 1857, p. 185.
15. Free Soil Party, 'Irishmen! Hear the Voices of O'Connell and Emmet', 1848 (American Broadsides and Ephemera), p. 2, at: http://infoweb.newsbank.com.
16. Ibid., pp. 2,4.
17. William Lloyd Garrison to Samuel May, 2 December 1848, Taylor, *British and American Abolitionists,* p. 332.
18. Kerrigan, 'Irish Temperance', p. 106.
19. Sharrow, 'John Hughes and a Catholic Response to Slavery', p. 268.
20. Kerrigan, 'Irish Temperance', p. 113.
21. *North Star,* 10 August 1849.
22. Kerrigan, 'Irish Temperance', pp. 110–1.
23. Quoted in Kerrigan, 'Irish Temperance', p. 111.

24. Ibid.
25. Ibid., p. 116.
26. *New York Times,* 6 February 1852.
27. *North Star,* 6 July 1849.
28. Henry Staunton in the *National Era,* 9 August 1849.
29. *Frederick Douglass Paper,* 21 August 1851.
30. Ibid., 21 August 1851.
31. *National Era,* 15 May 1851.
32. Joseph Barker to Garrison, 24 October 1850, Taylor, *British and American Abolitionists,* pp. 350–1.
33. J. Henson, *Autobiography of Josiah Henson: An Inspiration for Harriet Beecher Stowe's Uncle Tom* (Mass: Addison Wesley, 1969), p. 153.
34. Glasgow Ladies Committee, May 1859, Taylor, *British and American Abolitionists,* pp. 342–4.; Ibid., Edinburgh Ladies' Emancipation Society, 16 July 1850.
35. Ibid., George Thompson to unknown correspondent, 15 August 1851, p. 381.
36. *New York Herald* quoted in *Liberator,* 27 May 1849.
37. Richard Webb, Dublin, to A. Weston, Boston, 4 April 1851, in Oldham 'Irish Support', p. 186.
38. Ibid. Webb to Miss Weston, 18 May 1851, p. 187.
39. Wendell Phillips to Elizabeth Pease Nicol, 7 August 1854, Taylor, *British and American Abolitionists,* p. 352.
40. Ibid., Samuel May to Richard Webb, 25 October 1854, pp. 412–13.
41. Stephen, *Anti-Slavery Recollections,* p. 250.
42. *Liberator,* 11 February 1859.
43. *Brooklyn Eagle,* 6 April 1852.
44. Meeting of Dublin Anti-Slavery Society, 7 January 1852, American Anti-Slavery Society, *Letter to Louis Kossuth Concerning Freedom and Slavery in the United States* (Boston, MA: R. F. Wallcut, 1852), p. 107.
45. *New York Daily Times,* 6 February 1852.
46. American ASS, *Letter to Louis Kossuth,* p. 3.
47. Ibid., p. 10.
48. Gerrit Smith, 25 May 1852, *Frederick Douglass Paper,* 3 June 1852.
49. *Freeman's Journal,* 11 April 1843.
50. *Brooklyn Eagle,* 12 May 1852.
51. Ibid.
52. *Frederick Douglass Paper,* 3 June 1852.
53. Douglass, *The Life and Times,* p. 441.
54. James Haughton to Editor of *Freeman's Journal,* 10 April 1856; Haughton, *Memoirs,* p. 317.
55. *New York Daily Times,* 14 February 1854.
56. Kinealy, *Repeal and Revolution,* pp. 234–75.
57. R. O'Connor, *Jenny Mitchel, Young Irelander: A Biography* (Arizona: O'Connor Trust, 1988), pp. 194–7.
58. P. R. Wylie, *The Irish General: Thomas Francis Meagher* (Oklahoma: University of Oklahoma Press, 2007), p. 18.
59. Harriet Jacobs's autobiography, quoted in O'Neill, 'Frederick Douglass and the Irish', p. 72.

60. J. Quinn, 'John Mitchel and the Rejection of the Nineteenth Century', *Eire-Ireland: a Journal of Irish Studies*, 38 (2003), pp. 90–108, on p. 98.
61. *Citizen*, 14 January 1854.
62. Ibid., 23 September 1854.
63. Jenny Mitchel to Mary Thompson, Letters of Jenny Mitchel, 1851–5, New York Public Library, Manuscripts and Archives Divisions, passim.
64. *New York Times*, 2 February 1854.
65. *Frederick Douglass Paper*, 22 December 1854.
66. *Citizen,* reprinted in *New York Daily Times*, 30 June 1854.
67. Osofsky, 'Abolitionists', p. 910.
68. *New York Daily Times,* 15 February 1854.
69. Ibid.
70. *Frederick Douglass Paper*, 23 November 1855.
71. Ibid., 26 October 1855.
72. *New York Daily Times*, 13 June 1856.
73. Ibid.
74. Ibid.
75. Ibid., 17 June 1856.
76. Sharrow, 'John Hughes and a Catholic Response to Slavery', p. 268.
77. Ibid., p. 261.
78. *The Pope's Bull and the Words of Daniel O'Connell* (New York: Joseph H. Ladd, 1852), p. 3.
79. Ibid., p. 6.
80. Lee, 'Interpreting Irish America', p. 23.
81. Taylor, *British and American Abolitionists*, p. 428.
82. Ibid., Dred Scott v. Sandford Case, p. 427.
83. *Liberator*, 25 May 1859.
84. Blackett, 'And there shall be no more Sea', p. 32.
85. Richard Webb to Samuel May, 3 May 1859, Taylor, *British and American Abolitionists*, p. 440.
86. Quarles, *Black Abolitionists*, p. 140.
87. *Liberator,* 22 April 1859.
88. Ibid.,13 May 1859.
89. D. O'Connell, *Daniel O'Connell upon American Slavery*, pp. 3–4.
90. J. Wilson, Secretary of Leeds Anti-Slavery Society, on behalf of Anti-Slavery Societies of GB and Ireland, *To the Superintendants of the 524 circuits of the Wesleyan Methodist Connection in Great Britain and Ireland* (London: British and Foreign Anti-Slavery Society, 1860), 15 February 1860.
91. Samuel May to R. D, Webb, 6 November 1860, Taylor, *British and American Abolitionists*, pp. 448–9.
92. Why the Irish Fought for the Civil War, Historynet at: http://www.historynet.com/americas-civil-war-why-the-irish-fought-for-the-union.htm, accessed 5 May 2010.
93. W. B. Rogers, 'The American Civil War', in Byrne, Coleman and King (eds), *Ireland and the Americas: Culture, Politics and History* (California: ABC-CLIO, 2008), vol. 1, pp. 47–51.
94. American Anti-Slavery Society, *Daniel O'Connell upon American Slavery, with other Irish Testimonies* (New York: AASS, 1860), p. 3.

95. Blackett, 'And there shall be no more Sea', p. 33.
96. Richard Webb to unidentified correspondent, 16 July 1861, Taylor, *British and American Abolitionists,* p. 455.
97. *The Times,* 22 May 1861.
98. Samuel May to Webb, 3 June 1861, Taylor, *British and American Abolitionists,* p. 454.
99. Ibid., Webb to Quincy, 31 January 1862, p. 476.
100. Ibid., May to Webb, 27 May 1861, p. 485.
101. Ibid., May to Webb, 23 September 1862, p. 486.
102. Address to President Lincoln by the Working-Men of Manchester, England, 1 January 1863, at: http://www.answers.com/topic/address-to-president-lincoln-by-the-working-men-of-manchester-england-31–december-1862, accessed 19 February 2010.
103. Webb to Quincy, 3 April 1863, Taylor, *British and American Abolitionists,* p. 502.
104. Kinealy, *Repeal and Revolution,* pp. 257–8.
105. D. T. Gleeson, '"To Live and Die [for] Dixie": Irish Civilians and the Confederate States of America', *Irish Studies Review,* 18:2 (May 2010), pp. 139–41.
106. Webb to May, 3 August 1862, Taylor, *British and American Abolitionists,* p. 510.
107. P. Man Jr, 'Labor Competition and the New York Draft Riots of 1863', *Journal of Negro History,* 36:4 (October 1951).
108. L. M. Harris, *In the Shadow of Slavery: African Americans in New York City, 1626–1863* (Chicago, IL: University Of Chicago Press, 2004), p. 283.
109. D. O'Connell, *Reading for Irishmen: an Old but Good Document: Daniel O'Connell and the Committee of the Irish Repeal Association of Cincinnati* (Cincinnati, OH: s.n., 1843); D. O'Connell, *The Committee to whom the Address from the Cincinnati Irish Repeal Association on the Subject of Negro Slavery* (Boston, MA: New England Anti-Slavery Tract Society, Tract 2, 1843).
110. D. O'Connell and S. P. Chase, *Liberty or Slavery? Letter of Daniel O'Connell on American Slavery* (Cincinnati, OH: Chronicle Print, 1863), p. 1.
111. For example, *Chicago Tribune,* 4 September 1863.
112. Anon., *The Irish Patriot: Daniel O'Connel's [sic] Legacy to Irish Americans* (Philadelphia, PA, 1863), pp. 5–6, 27–30.
113. W. G. Hawkins (ed.), *Lunsford Lane; or, Another Helper from North Carolina* (Boston, MA: Crosby & Nichols, 1863), p. 278.
114. A Democratic Workingman, *Daniel O'Connell on Democracy* (New York: Sinclair Tousey, 1863).
115. Quincy to Web, 16 October 1865, Taylor, *British and American Abolitionists,* p. 535.
116. *New York Times,* 12 November 1864.

8 'The Negro's Friend'

1. For example, William Gladstone, four times Prime Minister and architect of British support for Home Rule; W. E. Gladstone, 'Daniel O'Connell', *Nineteenth Century* (January 1889), pp. 149–68.
2. Arthur Griffith, founder of Sinn Féin, wrote the Introduction to the 1913 edition of Mitchel's *Jail Journal*. See also, Kinealy, *Repeal and Revolution,* p. 290.
3. D. McCartney, 'The Changing Image of O'Connell' in K. B. Nowlan and M. R. O'Connell (eds), *Daniel O'Connell: Portrait of a Radical* (New York: Fordham University Press, 1985), pp. 175–85.

4. J. Conness, *Speech of Hon. John Conness: delivered at Platt's Hall, San Francisco, on Tuesday Evening, October 18, 1864* (San Francisco, 1864).
5. D. White, *The American Freedman* (New York: American Freedman's Union Commission, 1866), p. 365.
6. *New York Times*, 8 May 1867.
7. Reprinted in *Dublin Morning Mail,* 9 April 1873.
8. J. O'Hagan, 'The O'Connell Centenary Address', in Lord O'Hagan, KP, *Occasional Papers and Addresses* (London: Kegan Paul, Trench & Co., 1884), p. 129.
9. Ibid., pp. 150–1.
10. Ibid.
11. Haughton, *Memoir*.
12. Stephen, *Anti-Slavery Recollections*, pp. 220–2.
13. *Christian Recorder*, 21 February 1884.
14. *New York Times*, 27 July 1880.
15. Ibid.
16. B. Nelson, '"Come Out of a Land, You Irishmen": Daniel O'Connell, American Slavery and the making of the Irish Race', *Eire-Ireland*, 42:1–2 (Spring/Summer 2007), pp. 58–81, on p. 65.
17. D. O'Connell, *Cincinnati Letter,* 11 October 1843.
18. Osofsky, 'Abolitionists', p. 890.
19. O'Connell, 'Irish Emancipation', p. 68.
20. Kenny quoted in O'Neill, 'Frederick Douglass and the Irish' in *Foilsiú: Ireland and Race*, 5:1 (Spring 2006), p. 74.
21. Whittier to Sturge, October 1843, Richard, *Memoirs of Joseph Sturge*, p. 362.
22. *Frederick Douglass Paper*, 21 August 1851.
23. The Cincinnati Letter provides a clear statement of his views on this subject.
24. R. D. Webb to Edmund Quincy, 16 October 1843, Taylor, *British and American Abolitionists*, pp. 200–1.
25. A. MacIntyre, *The Liberator: Daniel O'Connell and the Irish Party, 1830–47* (London: H. Hamilton, 1966).
26. Quoted in O'Neill, 'Frederick Douglass and the Irish', p. 73; Douglass, *The Life and Times*, p. 973.
27. The American Civil Rights Movement, in turn, inspired the formation of a civil rights movement in Northern Ireland, 'Black and Green, *An Phoblacht,* 20 August 1998.
28. *New York Times*, 4 November 2008.
29. Garrison, *William Lloyd Garrison 1805–79: The Story of His Life Told by his Children*, 2 vols (New York: The Century Co., 1885), vol. 1, pp. 388–9.

WORKS CITED

Manuscript Sources

British Library, London:
>Report of Anti-Slavery Convention, 1840.
>Report of Anti-Slavery Convention, 1843.
>John Rylands Library, Manchester.
>Wilson Anti-Slavery Collection.

Library of Congress, Washington:
>Lithographic Collection on Abolition.

Merseyside Maritime Museum, Liverpool
>Papers of James Cropper.

National Library of Ireland:
>Papers of William Smith O'Brien.
>Papers of Daniel O'Connell.

New York Public Library:
>Anti-Slavery Reporter. A Periodical (Boston, MA: 1833).
>Papers of Horace Greeley.
>Letters of Thomas Francis Meagher.
>Letters of Jenny Mitchel.

Rhodes House, Oxford University:
>Records of the British and Foreign Anti-Slavery Society.

Royal Irish Academy, Dublin:
>Minutes of Irish Confederation .
>Richard Madden Papers.

Windsor Castle:
>Journals of Queen Victoria.

Newspapers

An Phoblacht .

Belfast News-Letter.

Belfast Protestant Journal.

Bradford and Wakefield Observer.

Bristol Mercury.

British and Foreign Anti-Slavery Reporter.

Brooklyn Eagle.

Caledonian Mercury (Edinburgh).

Chicago Tribune.

Christian Recorder.

Citizen (New York).

Congressional Globe.

Colored American.

Connecticut Courant.

Dublin Evening Mail.

Dublin Morning Mail.

Emancipator and Republican (The Emancipator, New York*)*
    Essex Standard.
    Examiner (London).

Facts for the People (Ohio).

Floridian

Frederick Douglass Paper.

Freeman's Journal and Daily Commercial Advertiser (Dublin).

Leeds Mercury.

Leicester Chronicle.

Liberator (Boston).

Madisonian.

Manchester Times and Gazette.

Morning Chronicle.

Morning Herald (New York).

National Era.

New-Bedford Mercury .

New Internationalist .

New York Daily Times .

New York Freeman's Journal.

Newcastle Courant.

North Star.

Pennsylvanian Freeman.

Portsmouth Journal of Literature and Politics.

Richmond Enquirer.

Rhode Island Republican.

Salem Gazette.

Southern Citizen (Tennessee).

Spectator (London).

The Times (London).

Truth Teller (New York).

Ulster Times.

Washington Globe.

British Parliamentary Papers

Report from the Select Committee on Negro Apprenticeship in the Colonies; together with the Minutes of Evidence, House of Commons, 1836 (560).

US Congressional Records

Congressional Globe:
http://memory.loc.gov/cgi-bin/ampage?collId=llcg&fileName=006/llcg006.db&recNum=264

Primary Texts

Address to the people of Great Britain and Ireland unanimously adopted at a general meeting of the London Anti-Slavery Committee, held on 23 April 1831, Signed on behalf of the London Committee by T. Buxton, S. Gurney, W. Wilberforce, W. Smith, Z. Macaulay, D. Wilson, R. Watson, S. Lushington, T. Clarkson (Wilson Anti-Slavery Collection, John Rylands Library, Manchester).

'Address from the People of Ireland to Their Countrymen and Countrywomen in America' (Dublin: 1841).

Address by the Liberator before the Loyal National Repeal Association 11 October 1843 in reply to an Address from the Cincinnati Irish Repeal Association (Boston, New England Anti Slavery Tract, No. 2, 1843).

Address to President Lincoln by the Working-Men of Manchester, England, 1 January 1863, at:
http://www.answers.com/topic/address-to-president-lincoln-by-the-working-men-of-manchester-england-31–december-1862.

Alma, C. E., *Second Appeal from the Dublin Ladies' Association to the Females of Ireland, 26 October 1837* (Cork: George Ridings, 1837).

American Anti-Slavery Society, *Letter to Louis Kossuth concerning Freedom and Slavery in the United States* (Boston, MA: R.F. Wallcut, 1852).

American Anti-Slavery Society, *Daniel O'Connell upon American Slavery, with other Irish Testimonies* New York: AASS, 1860).

Anon., *Daniel O'Connell Upon American Slavery with Other Irish Testimonies* (New York: American Anti-Slavery Society, 1860).

Anon., *The Irish Patriot: Daniel O'Connell's Legacy to Irish Americans* (Philadelphia, 1863).

Anti-Slavery Monthly Reporter.

Anti-Slavery Society, *Second Report of the Committee of the Society for the Mitigation and Gradual Abolition of Slavery Throughout the British Dominions: Read at the General Meeting of the Society held on the 30th day of April, 1825* (London, 1825).

Brightwell, C. L., *Memorials of the Life of Amelia Opie*, 2nd edn (Norwich: Fletcher and Alexander, 1854).

British and Foreign Anti-Slavery Society, *Slavery and the Slave Trade in British India: with Notices of the Existence ...* (London: Thomas Ward, 1841).

Chalmers, T., *Letter of the Rev. Dr Chalmers on American Slave-Holding with remarks by the Belfast Anti-Slavery Committee* (Belfast: J Mullen, 1846).

Clarkson, T., *An Essay on the Slavery and Commerce of the Human Species, particularly the African* (London, 1785).

Conness, J., *Speech of Hon. John Conness : delivered at Platt's Hall, San Francisco, on Tuesday evening, October 18*, 1864 (San Francisco 1864).

Cusack, M. F. (ed) *The Speeches and Public Letters of the Liberator* (Dublin: McGlashan and Gill, 1975).

Cropper, J., *Present State of Ireland, with a Plan for Improving the Condition of the People* (Liverpool: George Smith, 1825).

A Democratic Workingman, *Daniel O'Connell on Democracy* (New York: Sinclair Tousey, 1863).

Disraeli, B., *Runnymede Letters* (London: John McCrone, 1836)

Douglass, F., *Narrative of the Life of Frederick Douglass, an American Slave* (Boston, MA: Boston Anti-Slavery Office, 1849).

—, *The Life and Times of Frederick Douglass written by himself*, ed. J. Lobb (London: Christian Age Office, 1882).

Free Soil Party, 'Irishmen! Hear the Voices of O'Connell and Emmet', 1848 (American Broadsides and Ephemera), at: http://infoweb.newsbank.com

General Anti-Slavery Convention, *Proceedings of the General Anti-Slavery Convention, 1843* (London: General Anti-Slavery Convention, 1843).

W. E. Gladstone, 'Daniel O'Connell', *Nineteenth Century* (January 1889), pp. 149–68.

Glasgow Argus, *Christianity Versus Slavery, or, A Report, published in the 'Glasgow Argus' newspaper, November 8, 1841, of a lecture delivered at an anti-slavery meeting in that city, by George Thompson Esq., An extract from a pamphlet, entitled 'Proceedings at the first public meeting of the Society for the Extinction of the Slave Trade and Colonization of Africa, held at Exeter Hall, his Royal Highness Prince Albert, President of the Society in the Chair, June 1 1840; three Papal briefs of Urban VIII, Benedict XIV, and of his present Holiness, Gregory XVI, December 3 1839, not alluded to in the above meeting, and now presented, with prefatory remarks, to the Catholics of Ireland, by Hugh Charles, Lord Clifford* (Dublin: W. Powell, 1841).

Glasgow Anti-Slavery Society, *Second Annual Report of Glasgow Anti-Slavery Society* (Glasgow: Aird and Russell, 1836).

Grahame, J., *Who is to Blame? or, Cursory Review of 'American Apology for American Accession to Negro Slavery'* (London: Smith, Elder and Co., 1842).

Greville, C., and H. Reeve, *The Greville Memoirs: a Journal of the Reigns of King George IV, King William IV, and Queen Victoria* (London: Longmans, Green, and Co., vol. 1, 1896)

James, G., *American Apology for American Accession to Negro Slavery* (Dublin: The Dublin Negro's Friend Society, August, 1829).

Fraser's Magazine for Town and Country.

Glasgow Emancipation Society, *A Full and Corrected Report of the Proceedings at the Public Meeting held in Hope Street Baptist Chapel to present the Emancipation Society's Address to Daniel O'Connell Esq., MP, 23 September 1835* (Glasgow: D. Prentice and Co., 1835).

Haughton, J., *'Should the Holders of Slave Property receive Compensation for the Abolition of Slavery?* (Dublin: Hodges and Smith, 1853).

Haydon, B. R., *The Autobiography and Memoirs of Benjamin Robert Haydon*, ed. T. Taylor (New York: Harcourt Brace and Co., 1859).

Hibernian Anti-Slavery Society, *Address of the Hibernian Anti-Slavery Society to the People of Ireland* (Dublin, 1837).

Hibernian Negro's Friend Society, *The Principles, Plans and Objects of the 'Hibernian Negro's Friend Society', Contrasting with those of the Previously Existing Anti-Slavery Societies; being a Circular Addressed to all the Friends of the Negro, and Advocates for the Abolition and Extinction of Slavery; In the Form of a Letter, to Thomas Pringle, Esq. Secretary of the London Anti-Slavery Society* (Dublin, 1831).

Hughes, J, *The Emancipation of Irish Catholics: The First Great Sermon Delivered by Archbishop Hughes and Inscribed to Daniel O'Connell, the Liberator of Ireland* (New York: Metropolitan Record, 1864).

Madden, R., *A Twelvemonth's Residence in the West Indies, during the Transition from Slavery to Apprenticeship; with Incidental Notice of the State of Society, Prospects, and Natural Resources of Jamaica and other Islands*, 2 vols (Philadelphia, PA: Carey, Lea and Blanchard, 1835).

Maguire, J. F., *The Irish in America* (New York: D. and J. Sadlier, 1872).

Mott, J., *Three Months in Great Britain* (Philadelphia, PA: J. Miller McKim, 1841).

Mitchel, J., *Jail Journal, or, Five Years in British Prisons* (Glasgow: Cameron & Ferguson, 1876).

Mullalla, J., *A Compilation on the Slave Trade, Respectfully Addressed to the People of Ireland* (Dublin: William McKenzie, 1792).

Negro's Friend Society, *Appeal of the Negro's friend Society to the people of Ireland on Behalf of the Slaves in the British Colonies* (Dublin: R D Webb, n.d.).

Nelson, T., (ed.), *Documents of Upheaval: Selections from William Lloyd Garrison's 'The Liberator', 1831–1865* (New York: Hill and Wang, n.d).

O'Connell, D., *A Full and Corrected Report of the Proceedings at the Public Meeting held in Hope Street Baptist Chapel to present the Emancipation Society's Address to Daniel O'Connell Esq., MP, 23 September 1835* (Glasgow: D. Prentice and Co., 1835).

—, *The Testimony of Daniel O'Connell, the Liberator of Ireland, against the infamous system of American Slavery* (Reprinted as a poster by Scatcherd and Adams Printers, 1838).

—, *Report of the Committee Appointed at a Public Meeting held in Dublin, Thursday, March 19, 1840, to Consider the Effect of Lord Stanley's Irish Registration Bill* (Dublin, 1840).

—, *Memoir of Ireland, Native and Saxon, vol. 1. 1172–1660* (New York: Casserly and Sons, 1843).

—, *Speeches of Daniel O'Connell and Thomas Steele on the Subject of American Slavery delivered before the Loyal National Repeal Association of Ireland in reply to certain letters received from Repeal Associations in the United States* (Philadelphia, PA: Pennsylvania Freeman, 1843).

—, *Address by the Liberator before the Loyal National Repeal Association on 11 October 1843 in reply to an Address from the Cincinnati Irish Repeal Association* (Boston, MA: New England Anti Slavery Tract, No. 2, 1843).

—, *Reading for Irishmen: an old but Good Document: Daniel O'Connell and the Committtee of the Irish Repeal Associaiton of Cincinnati* (Cincinnati, OH: s.n., 1843).

—, *The Committee to whom the address from the Cincinnati Irish Repeal Associaiton on the Subject of Negro Slavery* (Boston, MA: New England Anti-Slavery Tract Society, Tract 2, 1843).

O'Connell, D. and S. P. Chase, *Liberty or Slavery? Letter of Daniel O'Connell on American Slavery* (Cincinnati: Chronicle Print, 1863).

O'Connell Centenary Committee, *Daniel O'Connell: The Centenary Record* (Dublin, 1878).

O'Connell, Rev. J. J., *Eulogy on the Life and Character of the late Daniel O'Connell, Esq., M.P. Delivered before the Repeal Society of Savannah in the Catholic Church of St John the Baptist* (Savannah: Edward J. Purse, 1847).

O'Hagan, J., 'The O'Connell Centenary Address', in Lord O'Hagan, KP, *Occasional Papers and Addresses* (London: Kegan Paul, Trench & Co., 1884).

Orpen, C. E. H., *Principles of the Dublin Negro's Friend Society* (Dublin: August, 1829).

Richard, H., *Memoirs of Joseph Sturge* (London: S.W. Partridge, 1864).

Report of the Debate in the House of Commons on 15 April 1831 on Mr Fowell Buxton's motion to consider and adopt the best means for effecting the abolition of colonial slavery (London: Mirror of Parliament, 1831).

Society for the Mitigation and Gradual Abolition of Slavery Throughout the British Dominion. Second report of the committee of the Society for the Mitigation and Gradual Abolition of Slavery Throughout the British Dominions : read at the general meeting of the Society held on the 30th day of April, 1825 (London: Ellerton and Henderson, 1825).

The Pope's Bull and the Words of Daniel O'Connell (New York: Joseph H. Ladd, 1852).

White, A D., *The American Freedman* (New York: American Freedman's Union Commission, 1866).

Whittier, J. G., *Daniel O'Connell* (Boston, MA: 1839). Available: http://www.readbookonline.net/readOnLine/8399/

Williams, J., *Narrative of James Williams, an American Slave, who was for Several Years a Driver on a Cotton Plantation in Alabama* (Boston, MA: The American Anti-Slavery Society, NO. 143 Nassau Street, 1838).

Wilson, J., *To the Superintendants of the 524 circuits of the Wesleyan Methodist Connexion in Great Britain and Ireland* (London: British and Foreign Anti-Slavery Society, 1860).

Secondary Texts

Adam, W., *The Law and Custom of Slavery in British India: in a Series of Letters to Thomas Fowell Buxton, esq.* (Boston, MA: Weeks, Jordan and Company, 1840).

Akenson, D. H., *If the Irish Ran the World: Montserrat, 1630–1730* (Liverpool: Liverpool University Press, 1997).

Allen, T. W., *The Invention of the White Race: Racial Oppression and Social Control* (London: Verso, 1994).

Barr, A. *Black Texans: A history of African Americans in Texas, 1528–1995*, 2nd edn (Oklahoma: University of Oaklahoma Press, 1996).

Blackett, R., 'And There Shall Be No More Sea', in R. J. Blackett, *William Lloyd Garrison and the Transatlantic Abolitionist Movement*, at www.bu.edu/historic/conference08/Blackett.pdf accessed 10 March 2010.

Bric, M. J., 'Daniel O'Connell and the Debate on Anti-Slavery, 1820–50', in T. Dunne and L. M. Geary (eds), *History and the Public Sphere: Essays in Honour of John A. Murphy* (Cork: Cork University Press, 2005), pp. 69–83.

Brotz, H., *African American Political Thought 1850–1920* (New Jersey: Transaction Publishers, 1992).

Buxton, C., *Memoirs of Sir Thomas Fowell Buxton, Baronet* (London: J. Murray, 1848).

Chesnutt, C.W., *Frederick Douglass* (Boston, MA: Small, Maynard & Company, 1899).

Byrne J. P., P. Coleman and J. King (eds) *Ireland and the Americas: Culture, Politics and History*, 3 vols (California: ABC-CLIO, 2008).

Charlton, K, 'The State of Ireland in the 1820s. James Cropper's Plan', *Irish Historical Studies*, 17:67 (March 1971), pp. 320–39.

Curtis Jr, L. P., *Anglo-Saxons and Celts* (Bridgeport, CT: University of Bridgeport, 1968).

Cusack, M.F., *The Speeches and Public Letters of the Liberator with Preface and Historical Notes* (Dublin: McGlashan and Gill, 1875, 2 vols).

Davis, D. B., 'James Cropper and the British Anti-Slavery Movement, 1823–1833' in *The Journal of Negro History*, 46:3 (April 1961).

—, *From Homicide to Slavery: Studies in American Culture* (New York: Oxford University Press, 1986).

Dumond, D.I., (ed.), *Letters of James Gillespie Birney 1831–1857*, 2 vols (Mass: Peter Sith, 1966).

Dunne, T., L. M. Geary, *History and the Public Sphere: essays in honour of John A. Murphy* (Cork: Cork University Press, 2005).

Garrett, J. K., *Fort Worth: A Frontier Triumph* (Texas: Texas Christian Univeristy Press, 1999).

Garrison, W. G., *William Lloyd Garrison 1805–1879: The Story of His Life Told by his Children*, 2 vols (New York: The Century Co., 1885).

Geoghegan, P. N., *King Dan: The Rise of Daniel O'Connell 1775–1829* (Dublin: Gill and Macmillan, 2008).

Gleeson, D. T., '"To live and die [for] Dixie': Irish Civilians and the Confederate States of America', *Irish Studies Review*, 18:2 (May 2010), pp. 139–53.

Gosse, V., '"As a Nation, the English are our Friends": The Emergence of African American Politics in the British Atlantic World, 1772–1861', *American Historical Review* (October 2008), pp. 1003–28.

Gross, I., 'The Abolition of Negro Slavery and British Parliamentary Politics 1832–3', in *The Historical Journal*, 23:1 (1980), pp. 63–85.

Hallowell, A. D., *James and Lucretia Mott: Life and Letters by their Grand-Daughter* (Boston, MA: Mifflin and Co., 1884).

Hall, C., 'The Lords of Humankind Re-visited', *Bulletin of the School of Oriental and African Studies*, 66:3 (2003), pp. 472–85.

Hart, W. A., 'Africans in Eighteenth-Century Ireland' in *Irish Historical Studies*, 33:29 (May 2002), 19–32.

Harris L. M., *In the Shadow of Slavery: African Americans in New York City, 1626–1863* (Chicago, IL: University Of Chicago Press, 2004).

Haughton, S., *Memoir of James Haughton: with Extracts from his Private and Published Letters* (Dublin, 1877).

Hawkins, W. G. (ed), *Lunsford Lane; or, another helper from North Carolina* (Boston, MA: Crosby & Nichols, 1863).

Hempton, D and M. Hill, *Evangelical Protestantism in Ulster Society 1740–1890* (London: Routledge, 1992).

Henson, J., *Autobiography of Josiah Henson: An Inspiration for Harriet Beecher Stowe's Uncle Tom* (Mass: Addison Wesley, 1969).

Hogan, L. S., 'A Time for Silence: William Lloyd Garrison and the "Woman Question" at the 1840 World Anti-Slavery Convention', *Gender Issues*, 25:2 (June 2008), pp. 63–79.

Howitt, M., *Mary Howitt, An Autobiography* (London: Wm Isbister Ltd, 1889, 2 vols).

Ignatiev, N., *How the Irish Became White* (New York: Routledge, 1995).

Jeremie, J., *Four Essays on Colonial Slavery* (London: J. Hatchard and Son, 1832).

Jupp, P. J., 'Irish Parliamentary Elections and the Influence of the Catholic Vote', *Historical Journal*, 10:2 (1967), 183–96.

Kenneth, C., 'The State of Ireland in the 1820s. James Cropper's Plan', in *Irish Historical Studies* (vol. 17, 1970–71), 320–339.

Kennedy, D., and T. A. Bailey, *The American Spirit: United States History as Seen by Contemporaries*, 2nd edn (Boston, MA: Wadsworth, 2010)

Kerrigan, C., 'Irish Temperance and US Anti-Slavery: Father Mathew and the Abolitionists', *History Workshop*, 31 (Spring 1991), pp. 105–19.

Kennedy, D. and T. A. Bailey, T. Bailey, *The American Spirit: United States History As Seen by Contemporaries* (Boston, MA: Wadsworth, 2006).

Kinealy, C., *A Death-Dealing Famine. The Great Hunger in Ireland* (London: Pluto Press, 1997).

—, *A Disunited Kingdom? England, Ireland, Scotland and Wales, 1800–1949* (Cambridge: Cambridge University Press, 1999).

—, *This Great Calamity. The Irish Famine 1845–52*, 2nd edn (Dublin: Gill and Macmillan, 2006).

—, (ed.), *Lives of Victorian Political Figures. Daniel O'Connell* (London: Pickering and Chatto, 2007).

—, *Repeal and Revolution: 1848 in Ireland* (Manchester: Manchester University Press, 2009).

Knobel, D., *Paddy and the Republic: Ethnicity and Nationalty in the Antebellum America* (Connecticut: Weslyan, 1998).

Laird, K., 'Were Illustrators of the Golden Age Racists?', at: http://hubpages.com/hub/The-Problem-We-All-Live-With---Were-Illustrators-in-the-Golden-Age-Racists accessed 4 July 2010.

Laxton, E., *The Famine Ships: the Irish Exodus to America* (New York: Henry Holt, 1998).

Le Marchant, D., *Memoir of John Charles, Viscount Althorp, Third Earl Spencer* (London: Richard Bentley, 1876).

Lebow, R.N., *White Britian and Black Irealnd* (Philadelphia, PA: Institute for the Study of Human Issues, 1976).

Lee J. and M. R. Casey, *Making the Irish American: History and Heritage of the Irish in the United States* (New York: New York University Press, 2006),

McDaniel, W. C., 'Repealing Unions: American Abolitionists, Irish Repeal, and the Origins of Garrisonian Disunioism', *Journal of the Early Republic*, 28:2 (Summer 2008), pp. 1–20.

MacIntyre, A., *The Liberator: Daniel O'Connell and the Irish Party, 1830–47* (London: H. Hamilton, 1966).

MacDonagh, O., *The Emancipist: Daniel O'Connell 1830–1847* (London: Weidenfeld and Nicolson, 1989).

T. McDonough (ed.), *Was Ireland a Colony?* (Dublin: Irish Academic Press, 2005).

Man, Jr, A. P., 'Labor Competition and the New York Draft Riots of 1863', *Journal of Negro History*, 36:4 (October 1951).

McCarthy, J., *Modern England* (London: G. P. Putnam, 1898).

Midgley, C., *Women against Slavery: The British Campaigns, 1780–1870* (London: Routledge, 1992).

Murray, D., *Odious Commerce: Britain, Spain and the Abolition of the Cuban Slave Trade* (Cambridge: Cambridge University Press, 1980).

Nelson, B., '"Come Out of a Land, You Irishmen": Daniel O'Connell, American Slavery and the making of the Irish Race', *Eire-Ireland*, 42:1–2 (Spring/Summer 2007), pp. 58–81.

Nelson, T. (ed.), *Documents of Upheaval. Selections from William Lloyd Garrison's 'The Liberator', 1831–1865* (New York: Hill and Wang).

Nowlan K. B., and M. R. O'Connell (eds), *Daniel O'Connell: Portrait of a Radical* (New York: Fordham University Press, 1985).

O'Connell, J. (ed.), *Selected Speeches of Daniel O'Connell, Edited with Historical Sections* (Dublin: J. Duffy, 1865).

—, *Life and Speeches of Daniel O'Connell MP* (New York: J. A. McGee, 1875).

O'Connell, M. R. (ed.) *The Correspondence of Daniel O'Connell* (eight vols, Dublin: Irish Manuscript Commission, 1977).

O'Connell, M. R., *Daniel O'Connell: Portrait of a Radical* (New York: Fordham University Press, 1985).

—, 'O'Connell, Young Ireland, and Negro Slavery: An Exercise in Romantic Nationalism', *Thought*, 64:253 (June 1989), pp. 130–6.

O'Connell, N. J., 'Irish Emancipation – Black Abolition: A Broken Partnership', in Robert Holtman, *Consortium on Revolutionary Europe* (Alabama: Proceedings of the Consortium on Revolutionary Europe, 1980).

O'Connor, R., *Jenny Mitchel, Young Irelander: A Biography* (Arizona: O'Connor Trust, 1988).

Oldfield, J.R., *Popular Politics and British Anti-Slavery: The Mobilisation of Public Opinion against the Slave Trade, 1787–1807* (Abingdon: Routledge, 2008).

Oldham, E.M, 'Irish Support of the Abolitionist Movement', *Boston Public Library Quarterly* (October 1958), pp. 175–87.

O'Neill, P., 'Frederick Douglass and the Irish', *Foilsiú. Ireland and Race*, 5:1 (Spring 2006), pp. 57–81

Osofsky, G., 'Abolitionists, Irish Immigrants, and the Dilemnas of Romantic Nationalism', *American Historical Review* (October 1975), pp. 889–912.

Parker, C.S., *Sir Robert Peel from his Private Papers* (London: John Murray, 1899, 3 vols).

Peckover, A., *Life of Joseph Sturge* (London: Swan Sonnenschein and Co., 1890).

Phillips, W., *Lectures and Speeches* (New York and London: Street and Smith, 1902).

Quarles, B., *Black Abolitionists* (New York: Oxford University Press, 1969).

Quinn, J., 'John Mitchel and the Rejection of the Nineteenth Century' in *Eire-Ireland: a Journal of Irish Studies*, 38 (2003), pp. 90–108.

Quinn, J. F., '"Three Cheers for the Abolitionist Pope!": American Reaction to Gregory XVI's Condemnation of the Slave Trade, 1840–1860', *Catholic Historical Review*, 90:1 (2004), pp. 67–93.

—, 'The Rise and Fall of Repeal: Slavery and Irish Nationalism in Antebellum Philadelphia', *Pennsylvania Magazine of History and Biography*, 130:1 (January 2006), pp. 45–78.

Riach, D. C., 'Daniel O'Connell and American Anti-Slavery', *Irish Historical Studies*, 20:77 (March 1977), pp. 2–25.

Rodgers, N., *Equiano and Anti-Slavery in Eighteenth-Century Belfast* (Belfast: Linen Hall Library, 2000).

—, 'Richard Robert Madden: an Irish anti-slavery activist in the Americas, O. Walsh (ed.) *Ireland Abroad. Politics and Professions in the Nineteenth Century* (Dublin: Fours Courts Press, 2003).

—, *Ireland, Slavery and Anti-Slavery 1612–1865* (London: Palgrave Macmillan, 2007).

—, 'Two Quakers and a Unitarian: The Reaction of Three Irish Women Writers to the Problem of Slavery 1789–1807', *Proceedings of the Royal Irish Academy*, 100C:4 (2000), pp. 137–57.

—, 'The Irish and the Atlantic Slave Trade' in *History Ireland*, 15:3 (May 2007), pp. 17–23.

Rolston, B., '"A Lying Old Scoundral": Waddell Cunningham and Belfast's role in the slave trade', *History Ireland*, 11:1 (Spring 2003). pp. 24-7.

—, 'Ireland of the Welcomes? Racism and Anti-Racism in Nineteenth Century Ireland', *Patterns of Prejudice*, 38:4 (2004), pp. 355–70.

Saunders, R. F., Jr. and George A. Rogers, 'Bishop John England of Charleston: Catholic Spokesman and Southern Intellectual, 1820–1842', *Journal of the Early Republic* (vol.13, No. 3, Autumn 1993), pp. 301–322.

accessed 4 June 2009.

Seward, F. W., *Autobiography of William H. Seward from 1801 to 1834: With a memoir of his life, and selections from his letters from 1831 to 1840* (New York: Appleton and Co., 1877).

Sharrow, W. G., 'John Hughes and a Catholic Response to Slavery in Antebellum America', *The Journal of Negro History*, 57:3 (July 1972), pp. 254–69.

Stephen, G., *Anti-Slavery Recollection in a Series of Letters addressed to Mrs Beecher Stowe at her Request* (London: Frank Cass, 1971).

Sweeney, F., *Frederick Douglass and the Atlantic World* (Chicago, IL: University of Chicago Press, 2007).

Sussman, C., 'Women and the Politics of Sugar, 1792', *Representations* (Autumn 1994),

Taylor, C., *British and American Abolitionists* (Edinburgh: Edinburgh University Press, 1974).

Temperley, H., 'The O'Connell-Stevenson Contretemps: A Reflection of the Anglo-American Slavery Issue', *The Journal of Negro History*, 67:4 (October 1962), pp. 217–33.

Trevelyan, G. O., *The Life and Letters of Lord Macaulay*, 2 vols (London: Longmans, Green and Co., 1876).

Tolles F. B. (ed.), *Slavery and the Women Question: Lucretia Mott's Diary, 1840* (Pennsylvania, PA: Friends Historical AssociatIon, 1952).

Walvin, J., *Black Ivory: A History of Black Slavery* (London: Harper Collins, 1992).

Wayland, F.F., 'Slavebreeding in America: The Stevenson-O'Connell Imbroglio of 1838', in *the Virginia Magazine of History and Biography*, 50:1 (January 1942), pp. 47–54.

—, *Andrew Stevenson: Democrat and Diplomat, 1785–1857* (Philadelphia, PA: University of Pennsylvania Press, 1949).

Wiebe, M. G., and J. A. Wilson Gunn (eds), *Benjamin Disraeli Letters: 1838–1841* (Toronto: University of Toronto, 1997).

Whittier J. G., *The Complete Writings of John Greenleaf Whittier*, 6 vols (Mass: Riverside Press 1992).

Wylie, P. R., *The Irish General: Thomas Francis Meagher* (Oklahoma: University of Oklahoma Press, 2007).

Online Sources

Hansard:

http://hansard.millbanksystems.com/commons/

Samuel May Anti-Slavery Collection:

http://dlxs.library.cornell.edu/m/mayantislavery/
    Accessed 4 March 2009.

  Documenting the American South, Beginnings to 1920. http://docsouth.unc.edu

E. W. Clay and Henry R. Robinson, 'O'Connell's Call and Pat's Reply', Library of Congress
    Digitized Historical Collections: Cartoon Prints, American, 1766–1876. http://www.
    loc.gov/index.html

INDEX

CPSIA information can be obtained
at www.ICGtesting.com
Printed in the USA
LVHW081612301220
675431LV00004B/152